DIGITAL FICTION AND THE UNNATURAL

THEORY AND INTERPRETATION OF NARRATIVE
James Phelan, Katra Byram, and Faye Halpern, Series Editors

DIGITAL FICTION AND THE UNNATURAL

TRANSMEDIAL NARRATIVE THEORY, METHOD, AND ANALYSIS

Astrid Ensslin and Alice Bell

THE OHIO STATE UNIVERSITY PRESS
COLUMBUS

Copyright © 2021 by The Ohio State University.
All rights reserved.

Library of Congress Cataloging-in-Publication Data
Names: Ensslin, Astrid, author. | Bell, Alice, 1979– author.
Title: Digital fiction and the unnatural : transmedial narrative theory, method, and analysis / Astrid Ensslin, Alice Bell.
Other titles: Theory and interpretation of narrative series.
Description: Columbus : The Ohio State University Press, [2021] | Series: Theory and interpretation of narrative | Includes bibliographical references and index. | Summary: "Refines, critiques, and expands unnatural, cognitive, and transmedial narratology by looking at digital-born fictions ranging from hypertext and interactive fiction to 3D-narrative video games, app fiction, and virtual reality"—Provided by publisher.
Identifiers: LCCN 2020040044 | ISBN 9780814214565 (cloth) | ISBN 0814214568 (cloth) | ISBN 9780814281062 (ebook) | ISBN 0814281060 (ebook)
Subjects: LCSH: Hypertext fiction—History and criticism. | Fiction—Interactive multimedia.
Classification: LCC PN3448.H96 E57 2021 | DDC 808.3—dc23
LC record available at https://lccn.loc.gov/2020040044

Other identifiers: ISBN 9780814257852 (paper) | ISBN 0814257852 (paper)

Cover design by Susan Zucker
Text design by Juliet Williams
Type set in Adobe Minion Pro

CONTENTS

List of Illustrations	vii
Acknowledgments	ix
INTRODUCTION	1
1 Multilinearity and Narrative Contradiction	19
2 Interactional Metalepsis	49
3 Impossible Space and Time	83
4 "Extreme" Digital Narration	121
5 It's All About "You"	151
CONCLUSION	179
Bibliography	191
Index	205

ILLUSTRATIONS

FIGURE 1.1	Screenshot from *Zork* (Infocom, 1980)	27
FIGURE 2.1	Klimek's (2011, 25) scheme of simple forms of metaleptic transgressions in fictional texts	55
FIGURE 2.2	Screenshot from "The Schoolroom" in *Magister Ludi*, written and designed by Christy Dena and illustrated by Marigold Bartlett (2015)	60
FIGURE 2.3	Model of interactional metalepsis	62
FIGURE 2.4	Screenshot from *Karen,* by Blast Theory, developed in partnership with National Theatre Wales (2015)	73
FIGURE 2.5	Convergent interactional metalepsis	78
FIGURE 3.1	Surreal 3D navigable body space in *Inkubus*	97
FIGURE 3.2	Binary navigational choices in *Inkubus*	97
FIGURE 3.3	Enemy symbol to shoot, or throw light at, in *Inkubus*	98
FIGURE 3.4	Identity bubbles in *Inkubus*	98

FIGURE 4.1	Chinese box model of narrative communication in print fiction (adapted from Pfister 1977 and Jahn 2017). "S" stands for "sender" and "R" for "recipient."	132
FIGURE 4.2	Diegetic levels as suggested by *The Stanley Parable*'s Museum Ending	148
FIGURE 5.1	Functional types of textual "you"	153

ACKNOWLEDGMENTS

We would like to thank the authors of the following works for allowing us to include screenshots in this monograph: *Magister Ludi*, written and designed by Christy Dena and illustrated by Marigold Bartlett (2015); *Karen*, by Blast Theory, developed in partnership with National Theatre Wales (2015), co-commissioned by The Space and 539 Kickstarter backers, and developed with support from the Mixed Reality Lab at the University of Nottingham and in collaboration with Dr. Kelly Page; and *Inkubus*, by Andy Campbell and Christine Wilks (2014). We have attempted to contact copyright holders and obtain permission to reproduce the other material.

We would like to thank the series editors at The Ohio State University Press (Jim Phelan, Peter Rabinowitz, and Katra Byram) and the anonymous peer reviewer for invaluable feedback on this project. Further thanks go to Ana Jimenez-Moreno and her team at The Ohio State University Press for their patience and commitment to this project. We also gratefully recognize the financial support we received from the Faculty of Arts at the University of Alberta, through a generous Sheila Watson Fellowship.

We would also like to thank the following colleagues for reading and/or discussing our work on unnatural narrative and which helped develop our thinking and refine our approach: Jan Alber, Joe Bray, Sam Browse, Zara Dinnen, Anne Dippel, Sonia Fizek, Monika Fludernik, Joanna Gavins, Alison Gibbons, Per Krogh Hansen, Rüdiger Heinze, Stefan Iversen, Louise Brix

Jacobsen, Manfred Jahn, Brian McHale, Maria Mäkelä, Jessica Norledge, Brian Richardson, Lyle Skains, Henrik Skov Nielsen, Annika Waern, and Robyn Warhol.

Last, we would like to thank our families, Atik, Anton, Leo, Rob, and Romy, for supporting us while we worked on this book.

INTRODUCTION

In narratives across media, we as readers, viewers, listeners, and players regularly encounter moments of surprise, confusion, and bewilderment. These effects may be due to psychological, situative factors impeding our narrative comprehension, such as lack of concentration, technical glitches, or historical discrepancies between the time of text creation and reception. Yet, more often than not, they are part of authorial intent in texts that deliberately play with and subvert conventions of storytelling and narrative design. In novels, for example, we may be startled by a homodiegetic narrator suddenly addressing us as readers, thus seemingly pulling us into the ontological realm of the storyworld—a logical impossibility in its own right. A film director might plot a sequence of scenes in such a way as to suggest to viewers that multiple, mutually exclusive stories might have happened, thus disrupting our common habit of "narrativizing" (Fludernik 1996) or mentally construing a meaningful, nonambiguous story out of individual plot elements.[1] In videogames, we may be startled when a game world features a voiced-over narrator that tells a story—in the past tense—about what our reader/player(s) did in the very

---

1. Fludernik's (1996) concept of narrativization refers to a dynamic process of imposing narrativity upon a series of stimuli, such as a selection of textual chunks or a series of images. It is inspired by Culler's (1975) idea of naturalization, which relates to more general strategies employed by the reader to reconcile apparently inconsistent or otherwise confusing elements in a text.

situation that we as players, alias our reader/player, are facing momentarily, while simultaneously offering us a variety of options for how to deviate from the orally narrated storyline.

The ways in and degrees to which narratives across media might intentionally evoke feelings of surprise, bewilderment, or alienation are inextricably linked with the conventions that are associated with particular media and subsequently subverted or broken by such narratives. These conventions are highly genre- and medium-specific. While, for example, forms of second-person narration and reader address (or textual "you," in short; see Herman 1994) in prose fiction might—despite their increasing frequency throughout the medium's history—still perplex us as readers at least temporarily, in a videogame or interactive digital fiction we would be surprised if "you" was not ubiquitously employed to engage us ergodically in rule-based, narrative performance and enactment.[2]

Taking the medium-conscious, comparative framework of transmedial narratology (see Thon 2016; Ryan and Thon 2014) as both a starting point and a key goal for theoretical development, this book offers the first comprehensive and systematic examination of *unnatural narratives* as they occur in an emergent yet fast-evolving form of interactive, computer-based narrative: digital-born, literary, and ludic narrative media, or *digital fictions,* as we call them, which combine forms of written, oral, cinematographic, aural-acoustic, animated, ergodic-interactive, and ludonarrative storytelling. More specifically, digital fiction is "fiction written for and read on a computer screen that pursues its verbal, discursive and/or conceptual complexity through the digital medium, and would lose something of its aesthetic and semiotic function if it were removed from that medium" (Bell et al. 2010). It is a form of experimental fiction whose structure, form, and meaning are dictated by the computational context in which it is produced and received. It includes works of hypertext fiction, Flash fiction (as well as fiction produced using other digital, web-based multimedia software and programming languages, such as HTML5, QuickTime, and JavaScript), Interactive Fiction (IF), app-fictions for tablets and smartphones, and narrative videogames that experiment with and subvert conventions of ludonarrativity.[3] Semiotically, digital fictions

---

2. While we adopt a fairly broad concept of fictionality in this book, including forms of autobiography and memoir, we exclude traditionally journalistic genres such as (interactive) documentary and news reports. A more in-depth discussion of fictionality versus nonfictionality in digital narratives would exceed the confines of this project.

3. We use the terms *videogame, digital game,* and *game* as interchangeable, inclusive coverall terms, subsuming games across digital platforms such as consoles, home computers, and handheld and mobile devices. Our concept of narrative videogame is considerably broader than Ensslin's (2014a) literary game, which is restricted to games with foregrounded, and cre-

may be entirely text-based, involving written language only (such as in many hypertext and Interactive Fictions, as well as Twine games). Alternatively, they may combine literary creativity—in an inclusive sense that incorporates orality and writing—with other modes such as sound, image, animation, and/or film. In some cases, however, they may not feature much written or voiced-over text at all. Indeed, they may involve first- or third-person-avatar navigation through 3D worlds, and these embodied experiences increasingly involve Virtual Reality technologies like HTC Vive and Oculus Rift. Typically, yet not exclusively, digital fictions can be read, played, or experienced in multilinear ways, and reader/players often make choices about their journey through the text or storyworld by, for example, following links or responding to textual or visual prompts from the work. They are therefore involved in the construction of these multimodal narratives and must interact throughout the reading experience.

The second large terminological and theoretical apparatus we address in this book relates to unnatural narratives and unnatural narratology. The point of departure for the discipline of unnatural narratology is Fludernik's (1996) *Towards a Natural Narratology*, in which Fludernik defines "natural narrative" as "naturally occurring storytelling [and] . . . includes, mainly, spontaneous conversational storytelling" (13), which "cognitively correlate[s] with perceptual parameters of human experience" (9). By contrast, "non-natural narratives" are, according to Fludernik, "strategies or aspects of discourse that do not have a natural grounding in familiar cognitive parameters or in familiar real-life situations" (11). In Fludernik's dichotomy, the natural is based on human experience—or 'experientiality'—while the 'non-natural' lies beyond or subverts human experience. Needless to say, human experience is highly culture-specific, and notions of what is 'natural' and 'unnatural' therefore cannot be treated as anthropological universals but only within their specialized societal and cultural environments and paradigms. For example, in many Western cultures, children learn early the distinction between animate and inanimate units and are therefore led to believe that it would be 'unnatural' for rocks, landscapes, or meteorological phenomena to be alive and spirited. In many Indigenous cultures, conversely, all parts of the cosmos are considered animate and interrelated and thus 'naturally' spirited. The concepts of natural and unnatural narration assumed in this book are deeply anchored within a Western, Anglo-American tradition, and we are fully and acutely aware of the

---

atively implemented, verbal-literary features. Narrative games as understood in this study are computer-based games that foreground ludic narrativity, linking game rules and mechanics with elements of story and plot; character features, relationships, and development; and spatiotemporal setting.

infelicitous and problematic connotations commonly evoked by the existing nomenclature.

While most existing theories and analyses of unnatural narratives have been induced from and focus on print fictions, we assess the extent to which digital fiction also exhibits unnatural narrative structures. We examine the ways in which digital fiction helps us demonstrate and problematize some of the shortcomings of unnatural narratology, by investigating the extent to which unnatural narrative features we know from print have become highly conventional features of digital narratives, and how experimental digital fictions use idiosyncratic, or medium-specific techniques to defamiliarize reader/players. Where the unnatural devices deployed by some digital fictions cannot be accounted for in current theory, we propose new concepts, models, methods, theories, and strategies for analyzing them.

By the same token, we address Ryan's (2016) postulation of a "cognitive turn" (482) in unnatural narratology and take into account cognitive strategies used by readers to make sense of medium-specific unnatural narrative elements in digital fiction. According to Alber (2009), such an approach is needed "to clarify how some literary texts not only rely on but also aggressively challenge the mind's fundamental sense-making capabilities" (139). Moreover, as Alber, Nielsen and Richardson (2013) argue, "since we are always bound by our cognitive architecture, unnatural narratives can only be approached on the basis of cognitive frames and scripts" (7), and our cognitive frames and scripts are wired differently when we interact with digital, screen-based, interactive media than when we read a print narrative—no matter how defamiliarizing its composition may be (think of postmodern, nonlinear novels such as Mark Saporta's *Composition No. 1* and Nanni Balestrini's *Tristano*). Thus, this book contributes to and widens the scope of at least three contemporary narratologies: unnatural narratology, transmedial narratology, and cognitive narratology.

In this book we engage with existing theories of unnatural narratology (e.g., Alber 2016; Richardson 2006, 2015; Alber, Nielsen, and Richardson 2013; Alber and Heinze 2011) and investigate the extent to which core concepts such as antimimetic narration, multilinearity, impossible spatiality and temporality, metalepsis, and second-person as well as other extreme forms of narration can be applied to digital fiction. In our analyses we pay particular attention to (1) medium-specificity, that is, the distinct technological and phenomenological qualities exhibited by digital fiction, and the specific (unnatural) narrative forms afforded by them; (2) anti- as opposed to nonmimetic elements (Richardson 2011, 2016), that is, unconventional, "permanently defamiliarizing" (Iversen 2016, 459), logical-ontological impossibilities as opposed to simply nonrealistic features or easily naturalizable epistemological pitfalls for the reader; and, wherever appropriate, (3) considerations of discourse (syuzhet) vis-à-vis story (fabula) and the extent to which this theoretical distinction translates to interface versus story design. Among the core concerns of this book are the ways in which readers/players of digital fiction can naturalize (account for and comprehend through the deployment of specific reading strategies; Culler 1975) and narrativize (cognitively construe into a mentally represented, meaningful storyline; Fludernik 1996) unnatural narrative phenomena such as ontological hesitations between actual worlds and storyworlds, and create highly immersive, authentic, and convincing experiences from devices such as metalepses, doubly deictic references, and impossible spatiality and temporality.

Each chapter in this book makes theoretical contributions to unnatural and transmedial narratology either by refining existing theoretical apparatus for its application to digital narrative and/or by taking an inductive approach by using a wide range of primary texts as a starting point and forming analytical and theoretical concepts from our scholarly interactions with them.[4] Much, though not all, of our primary material has been garnered from the vast and fast-growing body of experimental digital writing and art/literary indie games available online and in digital collections, databases, and archives (e.g., the *Electronic Literature Collections 1–3*, the *Electronic Literature Directory*, and the *Electronic Literature as a Model of Creativity and Innovation in Practice [ELMCIP] Knowledge Database*).

To begin with, let us clarify some terminological questions. Within the relatively new discipline of unnatural narratology, theorists have defined *unnatural narrative* according to different parameters. Alber (2016) understands the unnatural as narratives that contain "physically, logically, and humanly impossible scenarios and events (regardless of whether we find them estranging or not)" (14). Importantly, Alber's account focuses on narrative structures and devices "rather than [on] readerly effects" (14). Yet, while Alber does not define unnatural narratives in terms of their effect on readers, a central element of Alber's approach is his emphasis on the cognitive techniques, or "reading

---

4. This book builds on earlier work we have done on digital fiction and unnatural narrative (Bell and Ensslin 2018; Bell 2013, 2016a; Bell and Alber 2012; Ensslin 2015; Thoss et al. 2018); ludostylistics, ludonarrativity, and literary gaming (Ensslin 2014a, 2014b); hypertext fiction and possible worlds theory (Bell 2010); unreliability (Ensslin 2012) and the textual *you* in digital fiction (Bell and Ensslin 2011; Ensslin and Bell 2012); cognitive approaches to analyzing hypertext fiction (Bell 2014a, 2014b); interactional metalepsis (Bell 2014a, 2016a, 2016b); extreme narration and impossible spatiotemporality in experimental videogames (Ensslin 2015), as well as the historical, narratological, aesthetic, critical, hermeneutic, and comparative theorization and analysis of digital fiction more generally (Ensslin 2005, 2007, 2010, 2017; Ensslin and Bell 2007; Ensslin and Skains 2017; Bell et al. 2014).

strategies" (2016, 47) that readers adopt when processing unnatural narratives. To reflect the conceptual and methodological differences between Alber's cognitively oriented method and more text-intrinsically inclined unnatural narratology, Richardson (2015) distinguishes between Alber's "extrinsic" approach, which seeks "to explain the cognitive function of unnatural narratives and determine their meaning" (19), and the "intrinsic" approach, which stresses the "primacy of the violation of mimetic conventions" (19) and thus focuses on the formal elements of the text in terms of their intentionally defamiliarizing effects on readers.

Leading the intrinsic side of the debate, Richardson (2011, 2015, 2016; cf. 2006) defines unnatural narratives by situating them against other forms of possible and impossible narratives. He distinguishes between narratives that "seek to reproduce in fiction typical characters and events from the actual world" (2011, 31)—what he calls "mimetic" narratives—and narratives that do not represent the actual world, which he defines as either "anti-mimetic" or "non-mimetic." As Alber et al. (2013) explain, "a non-mimetic text (such as a fairy tale) will follow non-realistic conventions; and an anti-mimetic narrative contains events that are clearly and strikingly impossible in the real world" (102). The difference between anti- and nonmimetic representations thus relates to the degree to which they "defamiliariz[e] . . . the basic elements of narrative" (Richardson 2011, 34), "contravene the presuppositions of nonfictional narratives, violate mimetic expectations and the practices of realism, and defy the conventions of existing, established genres" (Richardson 2015, 3). According to Richardson (2011), and in contradiction to Alber's nomenclature, nonmimetic texts, in which he includes fantasy, fairy tales, and science fiction, do not inherently qualify as "unnatural" because the "mimetic impulse remains constant" (31), whereas antimimetic texts do qualify because the antimimetic "points out its own constructedness, the artificiality of many of its techniques, and its inherent fictionality" (31). For something to qualify as unnatural for Richardson, the represented scenario has to be impossible in the real world and the techniques used have to be sufficiently unconventional for the reader to notice them.

In more recent work, Richardson (2016) offers the additional concept of *unnatural construction,* which he uses to "designate texts constructed to be processed in surprising and unexpected ways, particularly those that invert or defy conventional reading practices" (391). Offering Laurence Sterne's *Tristram Shandy*—which contains a completely black page to signify mourning—and B. S. Johnson's *The Unfortunates*—which exists as individual pamphlets that must be ordered by the reader—as archetypes of this kind of text, Richardson explains that unnatural constructions commonly feature events that "would qualify as unremarkable realism had they been presented in a conventional manner. What is unusual is their manner of presentation, which utterly transforms the experience of reading" (391). Unnatural constructions are thus cases in which texts utilize a material construction that makes what might otherwise be natural—such as the death of a fictional character or the nonchronological structure of a story—unnatural.

While Richardson sees his concept of unnatural construction as an "elastic term" (391) that can be applied to various degrees to a range of texts, he also recognizes that texts that deploy this strategy can "rapidly become conventionalized" (391). Nonetheless, the challenge imposed on the reader to "determine exactly how to process the book" vis-à-vis a lack of "instructions for using" it is "an integral component of the experience of processing unnatural narratives" (391). Richardson's category of unnatural construction is immediately relevant to the concerns of this book because, as we will show, digital fictions often utilize constructions—produced by technological affordances and augmented in their effects by either lacking or giving minimalistic user instructions—that inevitably make unnatural what might in digital and other media be fully conventionalized forms.

Nielsen's (2011) discussion of the unnatural also emphasizes the reception of particular narrative techniques for the categorization of particular texts. He distinguishes between *natural* and *unnatural* narratives and *conventional* and *unconventional* narratives. A *conventional unnatural* narrative contains narrative devices such as "use of omniscient narration, homogenized thought and speech representation etc" (85), which are impossible in the actual world but are found in "many traditional works of realism" (85) and are therefore "conventionalised over time" (85). This differs from *unconventional unnatural* narratives, which, in correspondence with Richardson's antimimetic narratives, include "experimental fiction [and] postmodernist narratives" (85), which also contain scenarios, events, or narrative styles that are impossible or unprecedented in the actual world but which have not yet been conventionalized. Of course, when relying on cultural shifts in terms of what is generally or widely perceived as conventional versus what is unconventional, there is always the question of who decides. Nielsen stresses that "there is no doubt that new forms and techniques become conventionalized over time" (85). Importantly, while unnatural narratology has paid attention to the relative reception of narrative techniques "over time" (e.g., Alber 2011; Richardson 2015), the field has not yet paid adequate attention to the way that narrative devices are received and therefore relatively *conventionalized* across media. Unnatural narratology, as Heinze (2013) argues, needs to "consider the conventions and rules of the particular medium" (37), and, as we show in this book, the media contexts and formats in which a narrative is produced, published, and interacted with are important for digital fiction because these formats are marked (i.e., they deviate from conventional print contexts) and shape reader/players' understanding of narrative meaning.

Importantly, the process of conventionalization differs from that of naturalization. Alber et al. (2010) state that they "discriminate between unnatural scenarios and events that have already been conventionalized . . . and events that still strike us as odd, strange, or unusual" (131). This aligns roughly with Iversen's (2016) idea of unnatural forms and techniques that are so strange and difficult to naturalize that they can be seen as "permanently defamiliarizing," in the sense that they "present[] the audience with unsolvable riddles that constantly resist recognition, with perpetual unrecognizability" (460). Hence, while in conventionalized unnatural narrative, the unnaturalness (such as omniscient narration) is accepted and unremarkable according to it being a convention of a particular genre or period in literary history, in unconventionalized unnatural narrative the unnaturalness is striking (think, for example, of Danielewski's *House of Leaves* [2000] and the way in which it displays both intradiegetic incompatibilities and unconventional page design) and readers need a means of explaining or coming to terms with the unnatural event that does not resort to generic convention.

In a later publication, Alber et al. (2012) list "conventionalization" as a form of "naturalization" (376–77) and/or "explanatory mechanisms of or ways of coming to terms with the unnatural" (381n5), and the authors distinguish between them on the following basis: "we draw a distinction between the process of conventionalization, which denotes the converting of the unnatural 'into a basic cognitive category' (Fludernik, "Natural Narratology" 256), and the process of naturalization in the interpretive sense of Jonathan Culler [in which he] argues that readers attempt to recuperate inexplicable elements of a text by taking recourse to familiar interpretive patterns" (378–79). In these two accounts, conventionalization appears to be the integration of the unnatural on the basis of a cultural shift in generic conventions and associated general reader reception—what Fludernik (2012) characterizes as existing on the "institutional level" (367)—and "naturalization" as a process of sensemaking by individual readers which must take place when the unnatural cannot be explained as a generic convention.

The different definitions of unnatural narrative have not necessarily been reconciled in unnatural narratology with the different theorists explicitly outlining their respective perspectives in both individual and collaborative publications. However, Alber et al. (2013) stress that, as unnatural narratologists, they are collectively interested in "the various ways in which certain narratives deviate from real-world frames by being highly implausible, impossible, unreal, or insistently fictional" (103) and that they "share a strong urge to interpret these narratives by addressing the question of what they might potentially mean" (103; cf. Alber et al. 2010). What we find particularly interesting about unnatural narratives and what drives our main understanding of them in this book are the ways in which they intentionally transgress "mimetic or nonmimetic conventions" (Richardson 2015, 5), thus achieving certain aesthetic effects in the audience, such as bewilderment, amusement, a reflexive and critical meta-stance vis-à-vis the medium and genre in question, or even outright frustration or anger. Furthermore, we would argue with Iversen (2016) and Richardson (2015, 2016) that those fictional artifacts that are "permanently defamiliarizing" in the sense of having extreme and cognitively unresolvable or challenging antimimetic effects on the reader/player deserve the greatest attention of unnatural narratologists, as their highly idiosyncratic and subversive forms are particularly prone to what Richardson (2015, xvii) calls the "end of spectrum fallacy." This is the assumption held by many conventional narratologists that their theories can easily accommodate antimimetic texts by simply situating them at the extreme end of a spectrum that nonetheless foregrounds mimetic texts, thereby rendering the considerable body of antimimetic texts near-invisible.

In this book, we seek to fill a gap within digital narratology, which has largely followed a similar, albeit medium-specific (non)mimetic bias as print and other medium-specific narratologies have done in the past. Thus, while we do not intend to discard Alber's broad, logically, physically, and biologically derived definition of unnatural narrative, which includes nonmimetic structures, we prioritize the concept of the antimimetic. This supports our transmedial methodology, which focuses on conventional vis-à-vis defamiliarizing factors of digital fiction in relation to other media.

Of particular yet not exclusive importance in this endeavor are logical impossibilities because they tend to challenge human cognition to a greater extent than, say, supernatural or fantasy elements. They typically include contradictions and cases of anticausality, exemplified in print fiction by the deviating yet co-occurring plots in Robert Coover's short story "The Babysitter." We suggest ways in which the digital context in which these unnatural narratives occur might mean that what are often unnatural, antimimetic, and unconventionalized (cf. Nielsen 2011) features in print fiction are often a conventionalized feature of digital fiction (and videogames in particular; see Ensslin 2015). In fact, while not engaging in unnatural narratology explicitly and chronologically preceding unnatural narratology, Bolter (cited in Landow 2006) goes as far as to claim that "what is unnatural in print becomes natural in the electronic medium" (2). Metaleptic interaction with the storyworld via an avatar, for example, is one of the most default ways of navigating a videogame (see chapter 2). We therefore argue that the conventionalized/unconventionalized distinction offered in Nielsen's account of the unnatural (cf. Alber et al. 2010) must be seen in relation to specific media contexts as well as (commercial or avant-garde) writerly practices and agendas. In particular, we suggest that the material and cognitive affordances of digital media must be considered when analyzing unnatural narrative in digital fiction so as to take into account the relative conventionality of particular narrative techniques within that context specifically.

A key aspect of unnatural narratology, when applied to and tested on digital fiction, is the consideration of story as opposed to discourse (Alber et al. 2013), or the traditional narratological distinction between the underlying chronological sequence of events (*fabula*) and the way it is organized through sequentialization, multimodal design, styles of writing, and so forth (syuzhet). Clearly, when dealing with multilinear stories that are not supposed to have one underlying chronological sequence of events, or one ending, but rather a multitude of different possible storylines and multimodal renderings which are enacted or performed differently in each read-through or play-through, the level of story becomes blurry or, at the very least, ambiguous (see Richardson 2013). Similarly, in narrative 3D environments, games and interactive fictions in particular, narrative experiences happen via exploration, decision-making, and simulation. Hence, narrativity happens in the present of the player rather than in the past of a narrated character, and therefore cannot be understood in terms of a story that has been arranged into a discourse (Juul 2001). In most narrative games, then, the story level as preconceived by the game designer is replaced by a broad narrative arc, often with several possible outcomes and numerous different branching paths that lead to them, unless the reader/player dies prematurely. The discourse is essentially the emergent sequence of events experienced by the player rather than a fixed authorial arrangement. Story time, discourse time, and narrative time are thus conflated into a present-tense experience, constructed by the player in interaction with objects in the game or storyworld.

To generate a framework of sensemaking strategies applied by readers of experimental digital fiction, we draw upon, critically engage with, and expand Alber's (2016) proposed reading strategies, which Alber argues help us create new cognitive frames that transcend our real-world knowledge. The basis of these strategies is that it is within our human nature that, when we encounter anything unfamiliar, or strange, as we do in unnatural narratives, we try to naturalize, or make sense of it in some way, by applying a range of reading strategies. As Alber puts it, we are "ultimately bound by [our] cognitive architecture, even when trying to make sense of the unnatural. Hence, the only way to respond to narratives of all sorts (including unnatural ones) is through cognitive frames and scripts" (2013b: 451–54). Hence, on the basis of cognitive theory, Alber proposes the following reading strategies employed by readers (in any combination and any order) to help them "make sense of impossible scenarios or events" (2016, 47–54):

1. The blending of frames: Drawing on the work of cognitive scientists (e.g., Schank and Abelson 1977; Nieuwland and van Berkum 2006), Alber uses the term *frame* in the sense of "specific [and dynamically evolving] knowledge to interpret and participate in events we have been through many times" (Alber 2016, 48; Schank and Abelson 1977, 37). Frame blending, then, refers to the human capacity to combine previously disconnected frames and, in relation to unnatural narrative structures in particular, to "conduct seemingly impossible mapping operations to orient ourselves within storyworlds that refuse to be organized by real-world parameters only" (Alber 2016, 48). In other words, "we are urged to blend pre-existing frames that we previously considered to be incompatible into so-called 'impossible blend[s]'" (Turner 1996, 60) and accept, for example, the fictional possibility that time may be running backward for one character while simultaneously running forward for another, as in *The Curious Case of Benjamin Button* (Fincher 2008);
2. Generification: This strategy involves "evoking genre conventions from literary and media history" (Alber 2016, 49) so that, in this case, "the process of blending has already taken place" (50). Thus, an impossible or nonmimetic narrative structure has been transformed into a perceptual frame and conventionalized in a given genre. Time travel narratives are typical examples of impossible structures that lend themselves to generification;
3. Subjectification: Here Alber attributes the unnatural to internal states of characters or narrators, such as "dreams, fantasies, visions, or hallucinations" (2016, 51). We know that it is perfectly natural for our unconscious mind to produce highly surreal scenarios, and therefore this option is part of our explanatory repository, especially when we are dealing with an unreliable narrator or a vulnerable, victimized protagonist. Alber's example of this kind of strategy is ascribing retrogressive temporality in Martin Amis's *Time's Arrow* to the dying protagonist's hallucinating mind and his desire to turn back time and undo his moral wrongdoings;

4. Foregrounding the thematic: Here Alber suggests that we identify specific thematic elements in the sense of "specific representational component[s] that recur[] several times in the [narrative], in different variations" (Brinker 1995, 33, quoted in Alber 2016, 51). Themes follow "the principle (or locus) of a possible grouping of texts . . . considered to have a common theme, which are importantly and significantly different in many other respects" (Brinker 1995, 33, quoted in Alber 2016, 51). Thematic questions relate to "the ideational function of the characters and [. . .] the cultural, philosophical, or ethical issues being addressed by the narrative" more widely (Phelan 1996, 29, quoted in Alber 2016, 51). A typical example of thematic foregrounding is the complex relationships between time and human experience, which can be thematized, for example, through experientially impossible representations of time, such as mutually incompatible, concurrent temporal speeds, foregrounding the subjectivity and affective quality of perceived time;

5. Reading allegorically: Here unnatural structures are understood as being part of an extended metaphor, or abstract allegory, representing elements of the human condition, or the world in general. As Alber explains, "allegory is a figurative mode of representation that tries to convey a certain idea rather than represent a coherent storyworld" (2016, 52). He offers the example of Sarah Kane's play *Cleansed,* which features inter-character metamorphosis, as an allegory about the danger of love;

6. Satirization and parody: This occurs when narratives employ unnatural and/or other structures to mock, ridicule, or satirize either other narratives or elements of the real world in general, mostly for didactic reasons. Alber shows that critique of such kind typically happens through distortion, exaggeration, caricature, and "grotesque images" of humiliation or ridicule (Alber 2016, 52). For Alber, "parody is a subcategory of satire that involves the mocking recontextualization of a prior text or style by a later one" (Alber 2016, 52). Philip Roth's (1972) *The Breast* is offered as an example of a satire that shows how someone can take fiction too seriously, thus turning into an example of his favorite object of teaching (human transformations as portrayed in world literature);

7. Positing a transcendental realm: Alber suggests that, in this case, we attribute the unnatural to some kind of supernatural setting, such as Heaven or Hell, where different and often superhuman or humanly incomprehensible laws are in place that shape the possible behaviors of its inhabitants. J. K. Rowling's highly realistic *Harry Potter* children's fantasy fiction series plays extensively with supernatural intrusions into the otherwise disturbingly naturalistic setting of Privet Drive, and showcases how the

supernatural may be naturalized to various degrees if viewed through the subjective lenses of diverse characters;

8. Do it yourself: Building on Marie-Laure Ryan's (2006b) work on narrative contradictions, Alber suggests that some narratives "can serve as a construction kit or collage that invites free play with its elements" (53), allowing them to use "contradictory passages . . . as material for creating their own stories" (Ryan 2006b, 671, quoted in Alber 2016, 53). Alber shows that narratives that employ this strategy are also known as "readerly" texts (Barthes 1990 [1974] 2001 [1970]) because they hide the author in collagelike constructions and instead lift the reader to some kind of *alter auctor*, or co-constructor of the text. He offers Coover's "The Babysitter," with its multivariant storylines, as an example of this kind of text;

9. The Zen way of reading: Despite the plausibility of Alber's strategies 1 through 8, and their applicability to a large corpus of unnatural narratives, they are also somewhat delimiting because using them potentially overrides the possibility of more finessed and complex readings of the highly idiosyncratic, nuanced narrative structures to which they are applied. Furthermore, there are numerous unnatural narratives which do not lend themselves to naturalizing readings. Such cases call for an unnaturalizing reading strategy (Nielsen 2013), which accepts the impossible as irreconcilable without trying to make sense of it. This approach can be described in terms of a "Zen way of reading" (Alber 2016, 54). Unnaturalizing readings require the "attentive and stoic" (54) position of accepting the unnatural as a given and embrace the feeling of confusion, frustration, discomfort, or even pleasure that the narrative experience may evoke in us.

Alber's framework represents an "extrinsic" (Richardson 2015) approach which considers the cognitive strategies that readers adopt to make sense of unnatural narratives. We suggest that Alber's frameworks can be separated into "internal" and "external" reading strategies. Internal strategies look to explanations within the storyworld (i.e., blending of frames; subjectification; positing a transcendental realm) and thus see unnatural elements as part of that domain. External strategies, on the other hand, work at a formal, genre-related, metafictional, or interpretative level (i.e., generification; foregrounding the thematic; reading allegorically; satirization; do it yourself; Zen) and require the reader to think about what the text is trying to say by deploying unnatural elements. Of course, readers can adopt more than one strategy—for example, noting the use of supernatural elements in an allegory.

In this book we propose a modified and expanded set of strategies for the reading/playing of unnatural narratives in digital fiction that takes into account the distinctive interactive, procedural, and heuristic qualities of the medium. A core observation that we arrive at, and that is evaluated throughout the book, is the way in which some unnatural narrative strategies are naturalized and even conventionally functionalized in digital fiction (e.g., multilinearity and second-person address) as opposed to other media, including print (Wolf 2013), because of the medium in which they appear. By the same token, our aim is to show which unnatural narrative forms in digital media defy naturalization, illusion, and/or immersion, and to examine why that is the case.

As an overall methodological approach, we analyze devices at work in digital fictions that lead to unnatural narratives, the effect of those devices on reader/players, and the strategies that reader/players adopt to make sense of them. We thus combine the intrinsic (text-centered) and extrinsic (cognition-centered) approaches while recognizing the medium-specific context in which texts are produced and received. In so doing, we give primacy to the intrinsic approach for decisions about what constitutes the unnatural, while turning to extrinsic reading strategies for coming to terms with the unnatural.

The book is divided into five core exploratory-analytical chapters, which focus on key features of unnatural narratology and examine both conventionalized and defamiliarizing elements of existing digital fictions. Our close readings examine texts that exhibit medium-specific conventionalized and antimimetic structures, and we have selected our material in such a way as to show a diversity of aesthetic approaches and technologies.

Our first theoretical-analytical focus, addressed in chapter 1, is on multilinearity and narrative contradiction. We investigate the distinction between contradictions in story and discourse and propose a new distinction between temporal and spatial multilinearity. We investigate narrative contradictions in Interactive Fiction (IF), hypertext fiction, and videogames and show that while some digital fictions hide or make no reference to their multilinear structure so that their readers cannot make informed choices about their pathway through the text, others empower the reader to influence the direction of the narrative. We also emphasize the importance of self-reflexivity in terms of its capacity for causing unnaturalness in what would otherwise be a natural narrative. In terms of the theoretical contributions of the chapter, we critically engage with cognitive and transmedial approaches to narrative contradiction and argue that the materiality of the reading experience must be central to any approach that seeks to understand unnatural elements in any narrative. Accordingly, this chapter establishes two new categories: a new *unnatural construction* reading strategy, and our new theoretical concept of *medium-specific antimimeticism*. While these new concepts are initially developed in this chapter on narrative contradiction, they are relevant to all unnatural narrative devices, and they are thus applied throughout the book.

In chapter 2 we focus on a particularly ubiquitous medium-specific unnatural device: interactional metalepsis. Metalepsis in all media denotes the movement of entities between what are normally seen as ontologically distinct spheres. As a specific type of metalepsis that occurs in digital media, interactional metalepses take place across the actual-world-to-storyworld boundary and exploit the interactive nature of digital technology either via the hardware through which the reader accesses the text and/or through media-specific interactive modes of expression such as hyperlinks or avatars. We analyze interactional metalepses in hypertext fiction, physio-cybertext, videogames, interactive drama, app-fiction, location-based mobile narratives, and Virtual Reality, and provide a conceptually open-ended typology of interactional metalepsis that comprises metaleptic breath, visual metalepsis, metaleptic hyperlinks, and convergent metalepsis. We also offer a new cognitive approach to metalepsis by considering metaleptic jumps as transgressions across worlds as opposed to narrative levels. Our new model accounts for the actual world of the reader/player, thus emphasizing the ontologically transgressive nature of this narratological device, and it also considers the user interface as an additional space in a digital storyworld. We show that while most studies of metalepsis in print observe an alienating or defamiliarizing effect, metalepsis can be and is frequently used in digital media to increase immersion. We thus exemplify the wide range of metaleptic devices that are possible in digital fiction, explore the effect of each type of metaleptic effects, and suggest whether metalepses can or cannot (or are meant to) be naturalized by readers.

Chapter 3 considers impossible spatiality and temporality in digital fiction. We explore how digital media engage with logical impossibilities related to space and time, and the effects of these types of engagement on users' experience of, relationship with, and immersion within the storyworld. In relation to game worlds that combine mimetic or even hypermimetic (photo-)realism with unconventional, nonmimetic elements, we introduce the concept of *environmental antimimeticism* to highlight the importance of impossible navigable spaces to unnatural narrativity. We discuss a number of "impossible corporeal spaces" implemented in digital fictions and explore how interior organs can become fully rendered, 3D navigable spaces for the reader/player, producing either more antimimetic and sociocritically evocative effects, or less antimimetic, immersive, and ludic effects. Our analyses further include an examination of surrealist and Escher-esque game spaces, where spatial dimensions are manipulated so as to cause logical incompatibilities. We show that these impossible spaces can be naturalized by a number of reading strategies. Indeed, we argue that the medium-specific qualities of videogames in particular encourage reader/players to not only naturalize but internalize and functionalize ostensibly unnatural mediated spaces (Nitsche 2008) for fast progress in the game. Conversely, we observe that, in some more experimental cases of what we call "multimodal and palimpsestic spaces," unnaturalizing readings lend themselves to the identification and analysis of "disorienting" rather than "orienting spaces" (Punday 2017).

In this chapter, we also broaden the methodological toolkit of extrinsic-cognitive unnatural narratology (Alber 2016) by introducing an additional, "metamedial" reading strategy to account for medium-specifically antimimetic experiences that draw the reader/player's attention to ways in which a text can subvert the conventions of its own medium. Furthermore, we introduce the concept of "impossible zooming world" to describe the way in which the app-fiction *Spot* affords an unconventional use of the touchscreen "spread," which implements an unnatural (in the sense of physically impossible) way of zooming punctually in on and out of individual, "primary storytelling spaces" (Punday 2017).

In the section on impossible temporality, we take Heinze's (2013) dual typology of unnatural temporality (story vs. discourse level), as well as commonly assumed intuitions of temporal logic, as a starting point and investigate the extent to which unnatural temporality at discourse and story level happens in digital fiction vis-à-vis other narrative media. We adapt existing concepts of unnatural temporality, such as antinomic temporality and anticausality, to digital fiction's medium-specific affordances, and expand existing theories by introducing medium-specific techniques like "multivariant chronology" and "cybertextual velocity."

Chapter 4 explores extreme forms of digital narration, examining a variety of medium-specific unnatural voices in digital fiction. We begin with a study of medium-specific unreliable narrators and the ways in which their psychopathological mindsets are implemented, for example, by hypertextual multilinearity. We also focus on the phenomenon of the reader-interlocutor in digital fiction and how it necessitates modifications of the standard, print-derived Chinese box model of narrative communication. We analyze the ways in which this form of narration metaleptically transgresses ontological boundaries in various types of digital fiction, and how it foregrounds and/or satirizes commonly unmarked system dialogue and feedback. We explore medium-specific forms of polyvocality, multiperson narration, and the "permeable narrator" (Richardson 2006), the latter of which changes spontaneously between different characters, minds, or voices, in more or less permanently defamiliarizing ways, depending on digital fiction genre and paratext. The chapter ends with an examination of machinic narration. We explore aspects of generative narrative and omniscience in digital media, and we particularly focus on the role of the "cybernetic narrator" (Ciccoricco 2015) that speaks through either real or fictional system messages and blurs the boundary between fictional world and the implied and actual world of the author-programmer.

Our final analytical chapter, "It's All About 'You,'" examines the use of the second-person pronoun in digital fiction, which has proved to be potent and ubiquitous in narrative digital media. In its most conventional forms, it occurs as reader/player address in interface messages instructing players what to do or giving them clues about what kind of text commands to enter. We explore the ways in which "you" occurs in more conventional, immersive forms in digital fiction, and how it is subverted and critiqued for specific critical, didactic, and emotive effects in antimimetic digital fictions. Our final analytical section focuses on doubly deictic forms of unnatural "you" and how they position the reader in an ontological hesitation between actual and fictional worlds. Again, we show how this conceit can have distinct emotive effects, such as unease resulting from being framed as an unwitting accomplice in sexual abuse and murder or as a dialogic partner in an emotional, empathic learning curve.

The conclusion consolidates the analytical, theoretical, and methodological contributions we have made in this book. We evaluate our unnatural narrative framework and provide pointers for future research needs in this area. We postulate more systematic connections between structuralist investigations of experimental narratives, empirical investigations of reader/player responses to these narratives, and the potential narratological advancements that can be made by analyzing unnatural narrative in digital media.

1

Multilinearity and Narrative Contradiction

> True freedom from the tyranny of the line is perceived as only really possible now at last with the advent of hypertext.
> —Robert Coover, "The End of Books"

1.1 INTRODUCTION

The epigraph to this chapter is taken from experimental writer Robert Coover's provocatively entitled article "The End of Books," which was published in the *New York Times* on June 21, 1992. Heralding a revolution in storytelling brought about by the development of information technology, Coover suggests that authors and readers have been adversely constrained by the inescapable linear structure of print. While Coover's prophesy about the end of books has not (yet) come to pass (and perhaps never will), the new narrative structures that digital textuality allows have changed the way readers can experience narrative.

In this chapter, we examine one of the most established forms of narrative play in digital fiction: the narrative contradictions and alternative readings afforded by multilinear narrative structures. We begin with an introduction to narrative contradiction and unnatural narratology, distinguishing between contradictions in story and discourse. We then move on to medium-specific considerations of narrative contradictions in Interactive Fictions (IFs), hypertext fiction, and narrative videogames. We show that unnaturalness in our examples is generated via a combination of different kinds of unnatural construction (Richardson 2016) *and* the attention that is drawn to the unnatural construction. We show that while some kinds of digital fiction—such as IF and videogames—contain different reading/playing paths, they do not necessarily produce an unnatural narrative. However, devices within the text can work with the multilinearity of digital media to construct a storyworld that is what we define as *medium-specifically antimimetic*: a form of antimimetic narrative which defies the conventions of an existing, established medium.

Analytically, we address a range of multilinear digital fictions and, using unnatural narratology as a cognitive framework, investigate ways in which readers might deploy strategies to naturalize them. We show that while early Storyspace hypertext fiction uses narrative contradictions antimimetically and self-reflexively, narrative contradictions in other, more recent forms of digital fiction can also contribute to the reader's feelings of immersion. In terms of theoretical contribution, we add to Alber's (2016) framework by developing Richardson's (2016, 391) concept of 'unnatural construction' to account for cases of the unnatural that we propose can be explained as 'accepted as an unnatural construction.' This chapter also suggests that while unnatural narratology has so far looked at the way that contradictions occur in print fiction from a temporal point of view, some digital fictions facilitate contradictions that have a largely visual and thus spatial basis. We thus show that digital fiction necessitates a reconsideration of narrative contradiction which considers the affordances of digital media.

1.2 CONTRADICTION, UNNATURAL NARRATIVE, AND DIGITAL FICTION

Contradictions occur in fiction when two or more mutually exclusive states coexist in the same novel, play, film, or other narrative fiction. In unnatural narratology, examples that are often analyzed include the mutually incompatible endings in John Fowles's (1969) novel *The French Lieutenant's Woman*, the multiple narrative possibilities presented in Robert Coover's (1969) short story "The Babysitter," and the three different possible outcomes to the story in Tom Tykwer's (1998) film *Lola rennt* [*Run, Lola, Run*] (see, for example, Richardson 2006, 2015; Alber 2016). Irrespective of the medium, these contradictions are unnatural because they are logically impossible. Like most narratologists, Alber invokes the law of noncontradiction to account for the impossibility of contradiction in fiction. For Alber, contradictions are impossible on the basis that they "violate the principle of noncontradiction by representing mutually exclusive story versions or event sequences so that time is fragmented into multiple (logically incompatible) itineraries" (2016, 172; cf. Thon 2016; Bell 2010). The law of noncontradiction states that the proposition p AND ~p is false, meaning that it is impossible to have a world in which two contradictory states occur simultaneously. Contradictions are logically impossible in the actual world and thus lend themselves to antimimetic uses when presented in a storyworld.

While Alber focuses on logical contradictions in a "story," Richardson distinguishes between texts that have contradictory stories and texts that have contradictory discourses (or what Richardson, adopting Russian formalist terms, defines as *fabula* and *syuzhet* respectively). While contradictory stories present mutually exclusive events, contradictions in discourse occur when the same story is presented in different orders; Richardson's archetype for this kind of text is B. S. Johnson's (1969) book-in-a-box *The Unfortunates*, in which individual pamphlets can be read in multiple orders but in which the overall plot is unaffected by those variable orders.

The distinction between contradictions in story and in discourse is important for this study because many digital fictions allow readers to choose their path through the narrative—that is, to determine the discourse—and, at the same time, their choices can also result in different stories. Thus, as Richardson (2011) notes, "some works [such as hyperfiction] where the reader chooses from different possible narrative paths have multiple fabulas and a variable sujet [sic]" (26). Indeed, while unnatural narratology has largely focused on contradictions in print and film, because digital fictions often allow the reader to choose their path through the text, they provide some of the most striking examples of texts that "test or defy the concept of narrative itself, of a single self-consistent story, of a fixed presentation (syuzhet) of the story (fabula), of beginnings and endings, and of the idea of a single story" (Richardson 2016, 51).

While contradictions can exist in any medium, the technological attributes that characterize digital fiction often facilitate multilinear narrative structures, which can result in narrative contradiction. CD-ROM-, floppy-, and flash-drive-based Storyspace hypertext fictions, which have been produced and distributed by Eastgate Systems since the 1980s, web-based hypertext fictions, and some of the more recent hypertextual app-fictions accessed on mobile devices are all composed of fragments of text, known as *lexias*, which are connected by hyperlinks. In these texts, the reader must choose hyperlinks to determine which path to follow through the text. Many narrative videogames also offer multiple and either contradictory or incompatible endings because the reader/player can, within limits, explore a storyworld according to their own agenda and/or their choices affect the outcome of the narrative.

While a finite number of narrative possibilities exist within a text, thus setting limits on its structural organization, reader/players are ultimately responsible for their journey through a multilinear digital fiction. They can choose to pursue a scene for as long as the reading path will allow or use hyperlinks or other navigational devices such as avatars to explore other diversions that interest them. A reader may read a path until they can continue no further or abandon a particular path through a game and return to the beginning of the text to choose another. Some reader/players might navigate back and forward through the text, retracing their earlier steps, or read hypertext in a less considered fashion by randomly following links. All of these reading situations in digital fiction can be utilized by authors to create narrative contradictions.

1.3 NATURALIZING NARRATIVE CONTRADICTIONS

Within unnatural narratology, theorists propose naturalizing strategies for narrative contradictions in particular, as a specific subset of unnatural narratives more generally. Alber (2016, 172–78) accounts for narrative contradictions by using only four of his eight-part model for explaining how readers deal with them: "subjectification," "satirization and parody," "do it yourself," and "the Zen way of reading."

Richardson (2015) suggests that readers will move from one reaction to another. He argues that the initial response of readers to narrative contradictions of any kind will be that they are "invariably frustrated, often extremely so" (46). This emotional response, he argues, will then be replaced by a more rational, logical approach as readers "try to find a recognizable meaning in the text, to latch on to one set of events as the real ones and disregard the other, contradictory versions as mistakes, delusions, or imaginings" (46), or "see it as an instance of authorial free play" (46), or "reject the mimetic conventions altogether and look for an entirely different ordering principle" (46). Like Alber, then, Richardson suggests that readers try to make sense of the contradictions either by "find[ing] . . . meaning" or by making practical decisions about how to treat the incongruities they find.

While Ryan (2006b) does not engage with unnatural narratology explicitly, in her exploration of narrative contradiction she proposes "several possible modes of rationalization for texts that report contradictory versions of events" (668). She thus implicitly proposes a typology for processing narrative contradictions as follows:

1. Mentalism, in which "the multiple worlds described in the story do not exist objectively: they are the products of dreams, hallucinations, the imagination or they are the symptoms of mental conditions" (669). Ryan

suggests that Michael Joyce's (1987) hypertext *afternoon, a story* can be rationalized this way because readers "imagine that . . . contradictory versions are representations that pass through the mind of the narrator" (669);
2. Virtualization, typified by "interactive narratives, such as computer games or the children's stories of the Choose Your Own Adventure series" (669) in which "the world shown by the current branch is the only actual one; the others are just nonactualized possibilities. . . . [A]fter a choice has been made, the branches not chosen become counterfactual and usually disappear from the readers' minds until they start all over again" (669);
3. Allegory and Metaphor, in which "the purpose of the multiple versions is to illustrate an idea rather than to represent objectively happening courses of events" (669). Ryan gives the example of the film *Run, Lola, Run*;
4. Metatextualism, in which the different versions are seen as "different drafts of a novel in progress, different developments that the author is contemplating" (670) and which she illustrates via the example of Fowles's *The French Lieutenant's Woman*;
5. Magic, in which "what is true at one time becomes false at another through an unexplainable metamorphosis of the fictional world" (670) and which Ryan illustrates via *La moustache* (1986), by Emmanuel Carrère;
6. Do it yourself, in which "the contradictory passages in the text are offered to the readers as material for creating their own stories" (671), which she suggests accounts for the contradictory fragments in Coover's "The Babysitter";
7. Plural realities, which are invoked "if all these [preceding] interpretations are eliminated" (671) but "the multiverse interpretation must be either explicitly suggested . . . or implicitly motivated by a thematic awareness of cosmological issues" (671).

Like Alber's and Richardson's reading strategies, Ryan offers a mixture of practical (e.g., do it yourself) and hermeneutic (e.g., allegory and metaphor) ways of engaging with narrative contradictions. There is some crossover between Alber's and Ryan's approaches: both propose "do it yourself" as a strategy, and Alber's subjectification maps onto Ryan's "mentalism." While Alber and Ryan each propose interpretative ways of understanding narrative contradictions—with Alber suggesting "satirization and parody" and Ryan "allegory and metaphor"—neither explicitly suggests that narrative contractions can encourage an otherwise thematic reading, with Alber's "foregrounding the thematic" notably absent from his approach to this particular narrative device.

While Alber focuses on unnatural narrative in print, Ryan also uses examples from digital media including hypertext fiction and computer games. While she suggests that Michael Joyce's hypertext fiction *afternoon, a story* is an example of a text that would be rationalized via "mentalism," she argues that the "virtualization" strategy is "typical of interactive narratives, such as computer games or the children's stories of the Choose Your Own Adventure series" (699). She thus suggests that some text types typically invite a particular reading strategy in general—what we might call a medium-specific, global form of naturalization—while other reading strategies depend on the nature of individual texts—what we might call a local form of naturalization.

Offering two ways in which viewers/readers/players deal with narrative contradictions, Thon (2016) maintains that recipients of film, comic, and videogame narratives will "routinely 'ignore' some aspects of narrative representation in order to intersubjectively construct the represented storyworlds" (60–61) or else they "will look for alternative external explanations related to authors' intentions or representational conventions before trying to imagine implausible or even impossible situations of storyworlds, which would be made necessary by insisting on internal explanations" (61). He thus suggests that viewers/readers/players will "exhaust every possible alternative explanation before trying to imagine" (61) a contradictory storyworld. Note that Thon suggests not that recipients of contradictions do not narrativize contradictions after experiencing them but rather that they "are not imaginable" (59). That said, Thon's pragmatic strategy of ignoring contradictions seems like an unsuitable approach in many cases because contradictions tend to be used deliberately; they are meant to be noticed. Thus, even if viewers/readers/players cannot imagine contradictions, it does not mean that they do not notice them or even look out for them. Looking to the author's intentions or representational conventions is a more likely strategy as viewers/readers/players search for meaning in the contradictions they find.

The preceding overview has shown that narrative theorists have proposed a range of ways of narrativizing (i.e., imposing narrativity on a text that is composed, for example, of textual chunks) or naturalizing (i.e., making sense of impossible narratives by aligning them with familiar interpretive patterns) contradictions across different media. Yet while Thon suggests that readers might look to "representational conventions" to make sense of narrative contradictions, none of the other theorists address the materiality of the reading experience. Importantly, however, the medium in which a narrative is produced will dictate how that narrative can be materially constructed. Drawing on Richardson's (2016) concept of *unnatural construction*, which Richardson uses to "designate texts constructed to be processed in surprising and unexpected ways, particularly those that invert or defy conventional reading practices" (391), we suggest that some readers might simply accept narrative contradictions as an inevitable part of a particular medium. This is because some media—such as digital media—have affordances—such as hyperlinks—that intrinsically lead to multiple pathways through a text which can then be harnessed to create narrative contradiction. While this does not mean that all narratives created in, for example, hypertext inevitably contain multiple reading paths or indeed that texts with multiple reading paths always contain unnatural contradictions, it does mean that some readers will be more used to contradictions occurring in particular media. It is a medium-specific convention that can lead to medium-specific antimimeticism. In the analyses below, we show how Richardson's concept of *unnatural construction* can be used as a reading strategy, and thus we add an additional cognitive frame—*accepted as an unnatural construction*—to Alber's framework.

Irrespective of the narrativization or naturalization strategy that is applied to explain them, narrative contradictions within print fiction and film at least are relatively unusual and thus usually, if not always, cause a defamiliarizing effect. For McHale (1987) this is because contradictions are inherently self-reflexive; they "lay bare the process by which readers, in collaboration with texts, construct fictional objects and worlds" (100). In digital fiction, narrative contradictions can also be self-consciously antimimetic and therefore defamiliarizing, but they can conversely be regarded as totally acceptable to reader/players, if not in fact expected; they can be a highly conventionalized form of medium-specific unnaturalness. As we will show, their abundance does not necessarily mean that they do not cause defamiliarization. However, it does mean that multilinearity and narrative contradiction in some digital contexts are conventionalized if not part of the expectations associated with particular genres.

Like Richardson's, our analyses pay attention to contradictions at both the story and the discourse level, and we also distinguish between texts that self-consciously draw attention to their multilinearity and texts that do not. We show that in some forms, such as Storyspace hypertext, narrative contradictions are used as a self-reflexive (postmodernist) defamiliarizing strategy, while in others, such as some narrative games, narrative contradictions are an integral and anticipated part of the reading/playing experience but can also be used antimimetically. We thus show that multilinearity and narrative contradictions in digital literary media differ in terms of the degree of agency or indeed illusory agency (MacCallum-Stewart and Parsler 2007) that they grant to reader/players. Moreover, while Alber and Ryan do not address the way in which narrative contradictions can be used thematically, we show that contradictions in digital fiction can certainly be used in this way.

1.4 NARRATIVE CONTRADICTION IN INTERACTIVE FICTION

One of the earliest forms of digital fiction is Interactive Fiction, also called text adventure games, and multilinearity is integral to this type of text. IFs were a highly popular type of interactive reading game in the 1970s and 1980s, with seminal works such as *Zork* (1980), produced by Infocom, but IFs continued to be produced throughout the 1990s and into the twenty-first century by prolific authors such as Emily Short, Adam Cadre, and Andrew Plotkins.[1] Some IFs are written in the third person (e.g., *Behind Closed Doors*, by John Wilson [1988]) and first person (e.g., *Arrow of Death Part 1*, by Brian Howarth [1981]; also see Jim Munroe's *Everybody Dies* [2008] in chapter 4). However, typically, IFs largely use the second person (see chapter 5) to describe a storyworld in which the player is a character—the "you" of the narrative.

As shown in fig. 1.1, the reader/player has to enter text commands, usually with the structure verb + object, or verb + complement, in response to fragments of text displayed onscreen. Typically, the "you" is situated in the storyworld using cardinal directions (i.e., North, South, East, and West). In the *Zork* example shown in fig. 1.1, the text also gives additional information about the environment—the "white house" and "windows" that are barred. Reader/player contributions are expected whenever a ">" symbol is shown. The narrative thus develops according to the response given by the reader/player, and IFs therefore create the illusion of the reader/player being present in a storyworld that they simultaneously construct in creative collaboration with the programmed text.

Since the reader/player is responsible for inputting text commands and thus for generating different textual responses, each reading of the text results in a different storyworld being generated and thus a different narrative which is produced using a different discourse. Indeed, Montfort (2003) defines IFs as "potential narratives" (13) insofar as they are not actualized until the reader/player unearths or co-constructs them during their interaction with the text. From a practical point of view, the IF program is able to respond to reader/player commands that cannot be parsed (e.g., responding with "That's not a verb I recognize"), and it also contains multiple potential responses to reader/

---

1. See the Interactive Fiction Database for an extensive list of IF works: http://ifdb.tads.org.

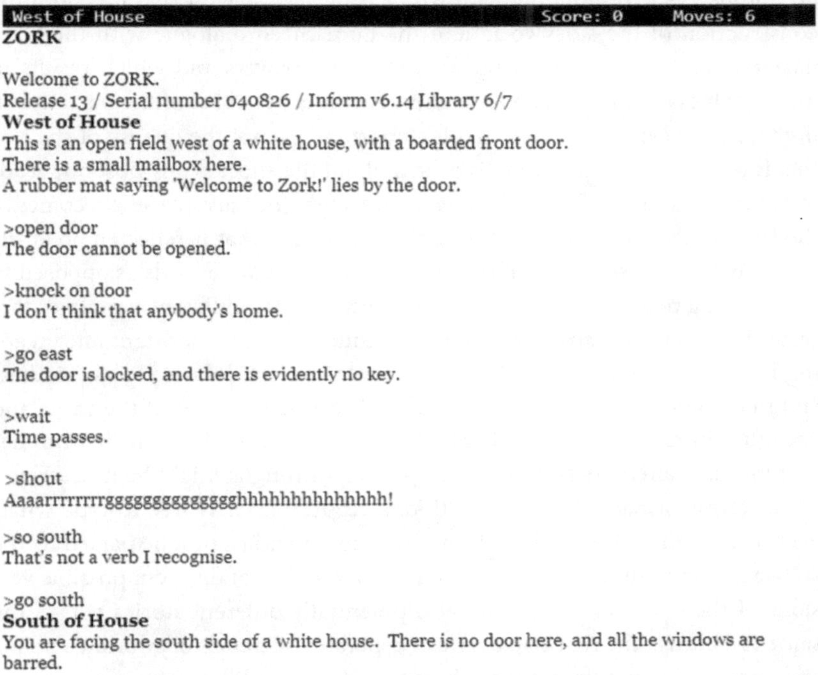

```
West of House                                    Score: 0        Moves: 6
ZORK

Welcome to ZORK.
Release 13 / Serial number 040826 / Inform v6.14 Library 6/7
West of House
This is an open field west of a white house, with a boarded front door.
There is a small mailbox here.
A rubber mat saying 'Welcome to Zork!' lies by the door.

>open door
The door cannot be opened.

>knock on door
I don't think that anybody's home.

>go east
The door is locked, and there is evidently no key.

>wait
Time passes.

>shout
Aaaarrrrrrrrrggggggggggggggghhhhhhhhhhhhhh!

>so south
That's not a verb I recognise.

>go south
South of House
You are facing the south side of a white house. There is no door here, and all the windows are
barred.
```

FIGURE 1.1. Screenshot from *Zork* (Infocom, 1980)

player inputs that can be parsed but which cannot advance the narrative at a particular point (e.g., in fig. 1.1, "time passes" in response to the input "wait").

Many IFs are narrated in an ironic, witty style that allows the reader/player to engage in an amusing dialogue with the text. For example, in fig. 1.1, when the reader/player enters "open door," the text responds with the rather pragmatic "the door cannot be opened." However, when the reader/player enters "knock on door," the text responds with "I don't think that anyone's home." Here the use of the epistemic modal construction "I don't think" introduces an element of uncertainty and the contraction in "anyone's" a level of informality. Thus, this response deviates from the formal omniscience of the previous line and to a more intimate form of dialogue. Likewise, the response to the command "shout" in fig. 1.1 (i.e., Aaaarrrrrrrrggggggggggggggghhhhhhhhhhhhhh!) offers a very literal and also humorous response to the reader's text command. Overall, these informal and humorous responses to the reader/player's input construct the narrator as a more personal yet disembodied interlocutor (see chapter 4), whose identity remains elusive throughout.

As the preceding analysis shows, readers experience responses to their input which rewards them practically—by generating more of the story—or humorously—by responding with wit or irony. We suggest that it is both the construction of the storyworld and the humanized dialogue with the text's narrator that creates enjoyment for the reader/players and which results in unnaturalness. Montfort (2003) argues that "it is the effect of the narrative *in the process of being generated* that is important . . . not the quality of the text that is output when the session is over, and not the effect of any post hoc reading of that output text" (13). He thus suggests that the narrative effect comes as the IF unfolds as opposed to it being an experience that is reflected on at the end. Montfort's assessment of IFs as having immediate rewards as opposed to encouraging post-reading reflections suggests that the different narratives that result from different readings are not considered to be important after reading has ended. At the same time, however, Montfort defines IFs as "riddles" (13) that reader/players seek to "solve" by learning the rules of the game and engaging in creativity via their responses—a conceptualization that implies that multiple attempts and thus multiple play-throughs might be necessary.

In terms of narrative construction, a reader/player is free to type whatever text command they like—even if that command cannot be parsed by the software—and thus there are an exponential number of different possible versions of the discourse. There are also potentially different stories within the same IF because the reader/player can generate different storyworld elements and events during different play-throughs. While multilinearity is an integral part of the IF reading experience, with each different play-through strictly speaking resulting in a new narrative, the reader/player does not typically experience mutually exclusive events in the same reading. Moreover, because reader/players engage in world-exploration-via-world-construction and thus create and explore a world at the same time, they may not conceptualize each play-through as a narrative that contradicts the others. That said, the style in which IFs are written draws attention to the fact that different versions of the story and the discourse are possible and thus to the inherent antimimetic potential of the texts. Irony is used to foreground the fact that the reader is co-constructing the storyworld with self-reflexive retorts in particular defamiliarizing the storyworld by drawing attention to the impossibility of the reader/player's co-constructor role.

On the one hand, then, reader/players of IF do not have to imagine an impossible scenario in which all the narratives exist at the same time (Thon 2016). On the other hand, the ironic style of the text foregrounds the unnaturalness of the experience by drawing attention to the reader/player's role in constructing one narrative from the many possibilities on offer. Reader/players thus might have to adopt a "do it yourself" (Alber 2016) approach, a "Zen way of reading" (Alber 2016), or a virtualization strategy (Ryan 2006b) in order to naturalize the many "potential narratives" (Montfort 2003) that are implicitly invoked by the text. IFs are not inevitably antimimetic, but the narrative style that has been adopted as a convention of the genre often makes them so.

1.5 MULTILINEARITY IN HYPERTEXT FICTION

While IFs create worlds that respond to readers' textual input and thus allow readers to co-construct worlds according to a set of learned conventions, narrative contradictions can be used in hypertext less predictably: the pathways through the text can be hidden by the software in which the text is produced and received, and readers can become lost in a maze of choices. It is for this reason that hypertext fiction provides the most narratologically significant examples of narrative contradiction in digital fiction.

All forms of hypertext have a branching structure in which chunks of text—known as lexias in hypertext fiction—are connected via hyperlinks. Thus, as in all forms of hypertext, readers select links in order to make choices about their journey through and experience of the text. For Ryan (2016) there is an almost inevitable relation between the hypertext form and alienation from the storyworlds they describe because of the choices the reader has to make when choosing a hyperlink. She notes that "every time the reader is asked to make a choice she assumes an external perspective on the worlds of the textual universe" (12). She thus argues that the reader is inevitably held back from being immersed in the narrative because the hypertext's "external/exploratory interactivity . . . promotes a metafictional stance" (2006a: 109). Ryan suggests that all hypertexts that allow readers "the freedom to choose routes through a textual space" (108) draw attention to their ontological status.

In what follows, we offer an overview of the formal features of hypertext that cause contradiction, examine the strategies that the hypertext reading community has adopted in order to account for contradictions, and examine the narratological features that are used alongside narrative contradictions to "promote a metafictional stance." We show that some texts use multilinearity as a means of disorientating the reader while others simply offer them an explicit and perhaps more empowering choice.

1.5.1 Narrative Contradiction and Disorientated Reading in Hypertext Fiction

Some of the earliest examples of both disk- and web-based fiction use hypertext's branching structure antimimetically. While hyperlinks allow the reader to choose their pathway through the text, as Landow (1997) points out, "hyperfictions are not organized in the way that informational hypertext is, so we may not be able to make empowered or informed choices in the same way" (185). Indeed, in many hypertext fictions, the multilinear potential of hypertext is harnessed by authors to present texts that self-consciously contain multiple narrative pathways and that result in readers feeling confused or alienated from the text (see Pope 2010). Thus, while hypertext fiction does use the structural attributes of informational hypertext, many writers of hypertext fiction have used the medium to subvert the attributes found within informational hypertext. For example, in an informational hypertext, the link is more often than not suggestive of what the reader will find at the destination, but in some web-based hypertext fictions, such as Shelley Jackson's (1997) *my body—a Wunderkammer* and Caitlin Fisher's (2001) *These Waves of Girls,* words used as hyperlinks are not always immediately indicative of the destination lexias to which they lead, so that they do not necessarily empower readers in their role as link chooser.

In pre-web Storyspace texts, which necessarily contain only internal as opposed to external hyperlinks, the reader can read as though in a linear text by clicking the "Enter" key on their keyboard to follow a default path through the text. Alternatively, they can follow hyperlinks which lead them to other parts of the text. While a finite number of hyperlinks exist within a text, thus setting limits as to its structural organization, readers are ultimately responsible for their journey through the text and thus partially determine the order with which the discourse is unveiled. They can choose to pursue a scene for as long as the default reading path will allow, or they can use the hyperlinks to explore other diversions that interest them. A reader may read a default path until they can continue no further, or they may abandon a particular reading path and return to the beginning of the text to choose another. Some readers might flick back and forth through the text, retracing their earlier steps. Others might use a "search" facility, which allows them to locate lexias that contain particular words or use a list of lexias from a drop-down menu. Readers can therefore navigate the text according to a particular agenda or read in a less considered fashion by randomly following links. In Storyspace texts, the same lexias can be read in a number of different orders, sometimes during the same reading, making it difficult for the reader to understand how a particular narrative works chronologically. Moreover, some Storyspace works also contain a key narrative contradiction; in Michael Joyce's (1987) *afternoon,* a car accident does and does not happen; in Stuart Moulthrop's (1991) *Victory Garden,* a character does and does not die in the Gulf War; in Shelley Jackson's (1995) *Patchwork Girl,* a character may be "real" or simply imagined by another character. Thus, in these texts, contradictions are caused by a combination of both structure and content.[2]

Alongside the emergence of hypertext fiction in the 1990s grew a healthy literary critical scene which sought to theorize the hypertextual form and associated reading experience. In what might be seen as an early attempt to naturalize narrative contradictions in hypertext fiction, a "first wave" (Bell et al. 2014) of hypertext theory, composed largely of hypertext fiction authors, sought to explain logically impossible structures in terms of a medium-specific and, crucially, empowering reading experience. Delany and Landow (1991), for example, define hypertext as "the use of the computer to transcend the linear, bounded and fixed qualities of traditional text" (3), and Bolter (2001) claims that "the role of the reader in electronic fiction lies halfway between the customary roles of the author and reader in the medium of print" (173). Readers are thus perceived to be empowered by the hypertextual structure, and, as Coover (1992) provocatively writes in the epigraph to this chapter, many commentators at the time felt that no other medium had facilitated this kind of flexibility before.

In addition to redefining the reader's role, first-wave theory used poststructuralist theory to claim that hypertext has revolutionized—or soon would revolutionize—textuality, reading, and writing. Bolter claimed that "the new dialectic of hypertext will compel us, as Derrida put it, to reread past writing according to different organization space" (Bolter 1991, 117). Moulthrop (1991b, 130) hypothesizes that hypertext "might come close to realizing Roland Barthes' vision of 'the Text.'" The term *lexia*, which is used to describe individual chunks of text in a hypertext, is also appropriated from Barthes's work. Because of its unfixed electronic form, hypertext was compared to Derrida's (1981) decentered text (e.g., Bolter 1991; Landow 1994, 2006). Since readers can choose which links to follow in a hypertext, they were considered "coproducers" of the text, and thus Barthes's (1990 [1974]) notion of the "wreaderly" text was invoked as a comparable model (e.g., Moulthrop 1991b; Delany and Landow 1991; Landow 1994, 2006). Hypertext was conceptualized as an embodiment of Deleuze and Guattari's (1988) *rhizome* (e.g., Landow 1994, 2006; Burnett 1993) because of its branching structure. It was also seen as a medium which might facilitate Cixous's (1991) *l'écriture feminine* because of the unfixed structures and unstable boundaries that it permits (e.g., Landow

---

2. Contradictions are so pertinent in Storyspace narratives in particular that *afternoon* is a rare example of a hypertext fiction that has notoriety beyond the field of digital literary studies (e.g., *Postmodern American Fiction: A Norton Anthology* [Geyh et al. 1997]) and/or is cited often as a representative example of hypertext fiction from within unnatural narratology (e.g., Richardson 2011).

2006; Guyer 1992). In first-wave hypertext theory, therefore, we can see reading strategies being adopted that implicitly naturalize hypertext according to its perceived conceptual, thematic proximity to poststructuralist theory.

Yet, while some poststructuralist models are seductively suggestive of the hypertext form, the utopian accounts of the first wave are not necessarily realized. If hypertext is, as Delany and Landow (1991) most famously declare, "an almost embarrassingly literal reification or actualization" (10) of contemporary literary theory, it is because it resembles a form of writing that was not available to theorists working with print. As Bolter (2001) points out, "if poststructuralist theories . . . seem to resonate with hypertext, it is important to remember that these theories developed among writers who were primarily working in and with earlier technologies. . . . To deconstruct a text, one used a vocabulary appropriate to the computer precisely because this vocabulary contradicted the assumption of print" (181). While conceptually alluring, therefore, hypertext does not fully possess the capabilities associated with the poststructuralists' ideals.

As the preceding discussion has shown, first-wave hypertext theory conceptualized hypertext reading at a largely conceptual level by talking about hypertext as a new form of textuality. When readers engaged with early examples of hypertext fiction on a concrete level—by reading individual works—as opposed to an abstract theoretical level—by simply theorizing their hypertextual form in general—many reported feeling alienated and frustrated with the reading experience as opposed to feeling empowered and liberated (see Gardner 2004; Pope 2006). Thus, while first-wave hypertext theorists perceived a high level of reader omnipotence in all hypertext manifestations, readers did not always experience them in that idealistic way, and, in fact, many readers found them to be so "permanently defamiliarizing" (Iversen 2016) that they did not actually enjoy reading them.

Reflecting the often challenging multilinearity inherent in many hypertext fictions, Ryan (2016) proposes five different ways of conceptualizing the reading experience:

1. a spatial metaphor in which "the reader is a traveler . . . , clicking is a mode of transportation, and the itinerary selected by the traveler is the 'story'" (195–96);
2. a supermarket experience metaphor in which "the reader browses along the links, takes a quick look at the commodities displayed on the screens, and either drops them in his shopping basket . . . or moves on to other screens" (196);

3. a kaleidoscope metaphor in which "the text consists of a collection of fragments that can be combined into ever changing configurations through the random choices of the reader" (197);
4. a jigsaw metaphor in which "the various lexias are the fragments of an exploded image that the reader tries to put together in a sustained effort" (198–89);
5. a possible worlds approach in which "every lexia is regarded as a representation of a different possible world" (199).

Ryan's spatial, supermarket, and puzzle metaphors suggest that readers have some insight into what choices are available to them. The kaleidoscope metaphor implies that the configurations are rather less informed. The possible world metaphor is, as Ryan notes, a way of "rationaliz[ing] texts which present a high degree of internal contradiction" (199) and thus represents a way of ontologically legitimizing narrative contradictions. While Ryan does not engage with unnatural narrative theory explicitly, each of her metaphors implicitly shows how she sees antimimetic contradictions as a device that can be naturalized as an "unnatural construction" because they suggest that readers will recognize that particular texts are "constructed to be processed in surprising and unexpected ways, particularly those that invert or defy conventional reading practices" (Richardson 2016, 391).

Ryan recognizes that the type of metaphor we adopt will depend on the "nature of the text" (200). However, she also suggests that it is the "reader's individual disposition" (200) that is as important in terms of which metaphor we apply because, she suggests, several schemes can likely be applied to one text. We might therefore see her metaphors as relating to the different narrativizing strategies—in terms of imposing narrativity (Fludernik 1996) on the fragments of text—that different readers might adopt for particular texts. The supermarket metaphor, for example, fits well with Ryan's "virtualization" and "do it yourself" strategies, and the possible worlds approach with Ryan's "plural realities." The completion of the hypertext jigsaw would surely lead to a sense of closure, but the jigsaw puzzle metaphor implies that there is one solution to the riddle, and, as the preceding discussion has shown, this is often not the case in Storyspace hypertext at least. Thus, while a reader might try and solve a puzzle, adopt a Zen way of reading (Alber 2016) by accepting contradictions, or simply give up in frustration, contradictions are a medium-specific convention very much entrenched within Storyspace hypertext fictions.

In fact, an additional strategy that we can associate with contradictory hypertext fictions in particular is a medium-specific acceptance of their multilinear structure. In this regard, our new reading strategy of "unnatural construction" can be deployed. Richardson (2016) explains that unnatural constructions "would qualify as unremarkable realism had they been presented in a conventional manner. What is unusual is their manner of presentation, which utterly transforms the experience of reading" (391). Many Storyspace hypertext fictions, including the aforementioned *afternoon, Victory Garden,* and *Patchwork Girl,* would not "qualify as unremarkable realism had they been presented in a conventional manner," either because they utilize self-reflexive elements or because, in *Patchwork Girl*'s case in particular, they contain supernatural elements. However, it is their narrative structure alone or in combination with their narrative style or contents that "utterly transforms the experience of reading." Indeed, narrative contradictions in some hypertext fictions occur precisely because the narrative is presented as fragments that the reader has to piece together. A fragmentary construction does not necessarily lead to narrative contradiction, as Richardson's reading of the book-in-a-box *The Unfortunates* shows. However, when used alongside features within the text that generate or at least imply a narrative contradiction, hypertextual fragmentation can be seen as an unnatural construction.

Since readers of hypertext fiction are aware of the form's capacity for generating narrative contradictions, it is likely that at least experienced readers of hypertext fiction would look to explain narrative contradictions as a medium-specific unnatural construction. We therefore add "accepted as an unnatural construction" to Alber's reading strategies to explain instances in which the materiality of the reading experience can be used to account for the unnaturalness of a narrative. This reading strategy is not often used to make sense of unnatural narratives in print because, as Richardson notes, very few print texts utilize unnatural constructions. However, digital fictions often utilize fragmentation as well as hyperlinks and other forms of interactivity to create texts that contain contradictions. Representing a subcategory of Alber's "Zen way of reading," this reading strategy would be employed by readers who are, to use Ryan's terminology, "predisposed" to hypertext and its metafictional games and thus will apply a medium-specific evaluative frame when reading this kind of text. This does not mean that the text in question is not antimimetic, but it allows the reader to see the unnaturalness of the text's structure as an inevitable part of the reading experience.

In some critical engagements with individual hypertexts, we can see critics implicitly outlining their individual naturalizing strategies. Douglas (1994), Landow (1997), and Walker (1999), for example, each keep rereading *afternoon* until their own personal curiosity has been satisfied and they have therefore assigned one particular ending as *the* ending to the story. The reader's response to narrative irresolution and ambiguity is thus narrativized and the contradictions naturalized by selecting a single and unambiguous ending from the multiple options on offer. While these scholarly accounts are based on personal experiences, they imply that contradictions can be resolved by finding satisfactory narrative resolution. They naturalize on the basis of finding a preferred formal structure (cf. Ryan's and Alber's do-it-yourself approach) rather than focusing on, for example, the role of the contradictions in the meaning of the text.

While some theorists advocate choosing one version from the multiple on offer, others argue that this approach defies and thus disregards the uniqueness of hypertext fiction. Miles (2003), for example, argues that selecting one version of the narrative as definitive attempts to squash the hypertext fiction into a form that is inappropriate. He argues that critics who encounter a hypertext's resistance to narrative singularity "punish the object because it doesn't give you the mastery and the pleasures that you have taken as your right." Instead of condemning the unconventional "because a work does not do what we think it is supposed to do" (Miles, 2003), he suggests that readers should try to evaluate how and why features such as contradictory narratives and resistance to deterministic closure are used in the text and thus contribute to its meaning. He thus suggests, implicitly, that a hermeneutic strategy should be adopted.

Somewhat inevitably, the naturalizing strategy that is adopted depends on the attitude and experience that readers bring to individual texts. If one knows that narrative contradictions are an inevitable feature of hypertext fiction and that they are meant to be noticed thematically, then a thematic or narrative construction strategy might be adopted, favoring seeing that as existing simultaneously for a reason. Conversely, readers who find it harder to adopt such a position will look to a do-it-yourself-style strategy, rereading the text to find a preferred story and/or adopting a reading strategy that favors particular narrative choices over others. Importantly, the attitude does not necessarily depend on the relative experience of the reader. Douglas (1994), for example, who is a very experienced hypertext reader and writer, claims that "while my readings of all these versions [of *afternoon*] are physically possible, I cannot accept all of them simultaneously" (167).

Even if readers wish to discount contradictions in hypertext fiction, once read, the reader cannot simply forget them. McHale (1987) suggests that texts that house contradictions create "worlds under erasure" (99) and sees them as analogous to a scripted word in a sentence that has been crossed out: "physically cancelled, yet still legible beneath the cancellation, these signs *sous rapture* continue to function in the discourse, even though they are excluded from it" (100). He thus suggests that once two contradictory alternatives have been posited, it is impossible to ignore either. From the moment of their discovery, they have a continuing presence, even if they are superseded with an alternative. Even in choosing one over the other, one cannot ignore the other possibilities. They are inevitably in readers' minds, simply because they have been read.

Following McHale and Miles, we argue that adopting a strategy that seeks to eradicate narrative contradictions will inevitably fail to accommodate contradictions in many hypertext fictions because they are meant to be noticed. While hypertext fictions do contain both story and discourse contradictions, what is often overlooked in brief citations or otherwise superficial engagements with many of these texts are the self-reflexive devices that are used alongside the main narrative contradictions and that draw attention to their unnatural status.[3] As the following analysis will show, stylistic and structural features that accompany the narrative contradictions are what prevent readers from adopting naturalizing strategies that rationalize contradictions and thus make many hypertext fictions archetypal antimimetic narratives.

1.5.1.1 Unnatural Multilinearity in *Victory Garden*

Stuart Moulthrop's (1991a) Storyspace hypertext *Victory Garden* is a historical fiction set during the first Gulf War, in the 1990s. Emily Runbird has been drafted to work on a Saudi military base, leaving her friends back home in the fictional university town of Tara in the US. Much of the narrative revolves around the two settings, with the text documenting Emily's experience of the war in the Gulf as well as the effect of the conflict on her friends, family, and colleagues at home and on the University of Tara campus. The motives behind and consequences of the Gulf War resonate throughout the text and are debated either explicitly between characters or implicitly through the various viewpoints presented. Offering a mediated view of the conflict, scenes from news broadcasts depict the off- and on-air discussions between two television war correspondents. Theoretical debates between University of Tara academics take place over the ideological and ethical motives of the war. Quotations from real-world figures such as George W. Bush, Saddam Hussein, and CBS anchorman Dan Rather are also scattered throughout the text that, while usually a product of Moulthrop's artistic license, remind the reader that the first Gulf War was an actual world event rather than a purely fictional construction.

---

3. See Bell (2010) for an extensive analysis of self-reflexivity in Storyspace hypertext fiction.

The various scenes and voices in *Victory Garden* are linked thematically, but the hypertext structure means that they are often encountered separately and/or sporadically. Readers are therefore required to draw associations between parts of the text that might not be physically connected. Moreover, the different reading paths in the text can sometimes result in mutually exclusive versions of events being documented. They are unnatural because the narrative contradictions they generate cannot be resolved according to real-world logic irrespective of how much more of the text is explored. Most strikingly, in some reading paths Emily Runbird dies during a bomb blast in the Gulf, but other parts of the text imply that she has survived the conflict to return home to her family and friends. In a less ruthless but equally prominent narrative incongruity, a heterodiegetic narrator self-consciously describes a scene three different times, with slight details changed in each iteration (see Bell 2010).

Alongside these narrative contradictions, the text uses self-reflexive devices throughout. For example, in the midst of a scene in which two characters, Boris Urquhart and Thea Agnew, are discussing a controversial curriculum review at the university (lexias "Insidious," "Motives," "What About Boris," "Chances"), a lexia entitled "Now Here This" appears and begins as follows:

> *Hear* it come again, riverRun past towering erections of five Cousins with but one muddle initial among them. I've seen The Best Minds of My Generation but I should've waited for the sequel. Revenge, renege, regain, once more around the bases.

The style of this text is very different from that which precedes it, where Boris's and Thea's conversation is marked as direct speech with speech marks and reporting clauses. The text in "Now Here This" could be attributed to an extradiegetic narrator who is observing the scene from a distance, or readers might infer that this is another scene entirely in which we have access to the direct thoughts of a particular character. Since readers are moved from one scene to another, however, they must reorientate to another part of the storyworld of whose ontological status they are unsure. The absence of temporal markers, which might otherwise locate this section of text in the wider context of the whole narrative, also causes disorientation. The deictic lexia title, "Now Here This," implies that this is a deliberate and calculated interruption to the narrative; the temporal "now" suggests immediacy, the imperative construction acts as a directive for someone to listen, and the second-person construction acts as an implicit address to the reader. This pseudo-pause draws attention to the artificiality of the storyworld because it suggests that story time can be stopped. Intertextual references in the first sentence to, for example, *Finnegans Wake* ("riverRun past") and Allen Ginsberg's *Howl* ("The Best Minds of My Generation") also act self-reflexively by "reinforc[ing] the notion of fictionality, and the reader's awareness of the construction of alternative worlds" (Waugh 2003 [1984], 113). Thus, there are several textual devices that act self-reflexively in this lexia alone.

In terms of structural self-reflexivity, there are three hyperlinks and a default reading path (i.e., by the reader pressing the "Return" key) that the readers can follow. One link leads to a concrete poem, one to a letter to Emily, and one to a scene that describes a scene in the second person and which begins "You always knew it would look like this" ("Slacktown" lexia). The default reading path leads to a further monologue whose ontological status is unclear before the text eventually states that "in some cases Return is simply impossible; this too is part of the American story" ("National Dick" lexia). Here, the text refers self-reflexively to the materiality of the reading context—that readers can use the "Return" key to advance the text—and also to itself—"this too"—as an artificial construction. Thus, while there are certainly parts of *Victory Garden* that allow readers to experience a coherent narrative, there are also intermittent interruptions that prevent them from being entirely immersed in the storyworld.

While contradictions in discourse and story are absolutely central to *Victory Garden* (and many other hypertext works), as the analysis above has shown, estrangement in hypertext is usually a consequence of several separate but integrally related characteristics. First, the reader's role outside the text draws attention to the artificiality of the narrative because the reader is always aware that they are involved in the construction of the text. Second, the reader is responsible for determining the discourse because they determine, within constraints of the text, the order in which lexias are revealed. Third, narrative contradictions emerge because there are deliberately conflicting scenes in the text. Last, self-reflexive devices within the text, such as the use of the second person, intertextual reference, and references to the interactive reading context, draw further attention to the ontological status of the storyworld.

Throughout *Victory Garden*, antimimetic devices are deployed, and thus the unnaturalness of the narrative is foregrounded. The text thus discourages an approach which seeks to locate narratives within neat ontological categories. Instead, it plays with ontology in ways that typify postmodernist fictions. As McHale (1987) argues, postmodernist texts typically use narrative devices to foreground their ontological status and ask the reader to contemplate "What is a world? What kinds of worlds are there, how are they constituted, and how do they differ?" (10). A number of analyses of *Victory Garden* note that metafictional devices, including narrative contradictions, are used as part of a postmodernist strategy in the text to question the ontological status of all narratives (e.g., Bell 2010, 95–100; Gaggi 1998, 126–30). It thus invites a thematic reading; to adopt a do-it-yourself approach misses the point of the text. At the same time, however, Storyspace hypertexts command a certain way of reading. Because contradictions and ambiguities are an integral part of the reading experience, they require that the reader tussle with their conflicting discourses and illogical stories. A reader can accept them as an unnatural construction, but the thematic message of foregrounding the fictionality of all narratives including those that claim to show the "truth" is hard to ignore.

1.5.2 Transparent Multilinearity in Web-Based Hypertext

While many Storyspace hypertext fictions deploy narrative devices that cause significant disorientation for the reader, other kinds of hypertext fiction use multilinearity in a far less alienating, but equally unnatural way. Texts such as *Same Day Test*, by Gavin Inglis (2002),[4] *Lucy Hardin's Missing Period*, by Stephen Marche (2010), and *Queers in Love at the End of the World*, by Anna Anthropy (2013), represent texts in which choice is very explicit, akin to the kind of agency granted to readers of Choose-Your-Own-Adventure print fiction. Deploying what Parker (2001) calls "blatant links" that "tell the reader exactly what information will be revealed when activated" (cf. Ryan 2006a, 110–11), such hypertexts use links denotatively, to signal in advance what readers will find when they follow them, and thus signal to the reader that they will experience different stories or different versions of that story within the same text.

 Lucy Hardin's Missing Period, by Stephen Marche (*LHMP*), is described as "an interactive novel with hundreds of possible storylines and multiple outcomes," signaling in advance that it is a multilinear narrative and drawing attention to the fact that it is meant to be read on those terms. The text always begins as Lucy wakes up beside her naked lover, Daniel. It is the anniversary of her father's death, and her period is late. Readers can make choices throughout the narrative, with links offering varying degrees of clarity as to what will come next. Choices can have an impact on which actions Lucy takes—for example, we can choose to either "sit self-pityingly on the curb for a minute" or "stumble defeatedly home," with each choice resulting in a different outcome for Lucy. In some versions, the narrator frequently asks "Was she

---

4. See Bell and Ensslin (2018) for an analysis of *Same Day Test*.

pregnant?" whereas in others it is an incidental possibility. In some versions, a baby, Maxwell Robert Hardin, is born; in others, Lucy has an abortion.

LHMP can be naturalized by reading it as a text that simply results in different stories, all of which can be seen as existing as separate storyworlds. Ryan's "mentalism" strategy can also be used to explain *LHMP* by regarding the different possibilities as Lucy's dreams, fears, or fantasies. Readers might also adopt a "virtualization" or a "do it yourself" strategy, in which one possibility is privileged over the others. However, the text explicitly discourages these strategies by drawing attention to its multilinearity. For example, readers can choose between "he blathers on about bombs" and "he blathers on about a blue spruce" as hyperlinks with syntactic parallelism via the repetition of "blathers" foregrounding the contradictory nature of the narrative. The path that the reader takes in *LHMP* determines not only events but also the type of story that readers experience. In one reading, Lucy works in a backstreet casino at an "illegal poker game." It thus becomes a tale of an oppressed woman working in a profession that she hates for a dominating and powerful man. In another, the narrative feels more like the tale of a young woman trying to understand the world as she moves from youth into adulthood. The hypertextual structure, which results in different discourses and completely different stories, is thus used to show readers that things could always be different.

Importantly too, before we begin reading the narrative, the instructions tell us that the text "allow[s] the reader to explore different aspects of Lucy's life and times and the city in which she lives, while following her through the labyrinth of her various futures. Lucy's fate, like our own, is up in the air, open to negotiation and sudden change." It therefore explicitly signals that the hypertextual structure is being used thematically to explore the unpredictability of the future. We thus read *LHMP* as an allegory (Alber, Ryan) and as a text that explicitly invites us to read it as something that "foregrounds the thematic" (Alber 2016). It presents life as something that is so easily affected by what might seem very trivial or otherwise superficial choices. The various versions of Lucy's life also show chance or luck to have a strong hand in everyone's destiny.

While *LHMP* allows readers time to reflect on the decisions they make, the short hypertext fiction *Queers in Love at the End of the World*, by Anna Anthropy (*QLEW*), enforces immediate decision-making. Written on the Twine platform, a free, open-source authoring platform that allows users to create hypertexts without having to code, *QLEW* represents a relatively new kind of literary hypertext that is more gamelike in style. Because Twine can be used by writers with relatively little technical knowledge, it serves, Ensslin and Skains (2017) argue, as "a platform for marginalized voices in the gaming industry, and . . . as a democratization of hypertext as a literary form" (300). Its popularity has opened up hypertext fiction to a wider readership and writership.

As soon as readers of Anthropy's Twine hypertext click the "Begin" link, the following text is displayed:

> In the end, like you always said, it's just the two of you together. You have ten seconds, but there's so much you want to do: kiss her, hold her, take her hand, tell her.

"Kiss," "hold," "take," and "tell" are hyperlinked and, if clicked, lead to scenes in which corresponding activities occur. For example, following "kiss" leads to a screen that reads "You kiss her: softly, slowly, fiercely, hungrily," with each adverb hyperlinked to another screen. What is significant about this text is that a timer, counting down from ten seconds to zero, also appears on the left side of the screen as soon as the reader begins the text. Once time is up, the current screen refreshes to display "Everything is wiped away," and the reader then has to begin the text again.

It is possible to reach the end of some of the reading paths, but, in order to do so, it is not possible to also read all the text. Instead, the ten-second limit forces a frenzied reading in which the text cannot be completed in one iteration; it must be reread again and again in order that all the text can be read over those multiple traversals. The text's construction thus invites if not enforces a form of reading in which we have to see the different versions as deliberately and self-consciously contradicting each other. The affordances of digital media are used to create a looping unnatural construction that asks to be read thematically. Read as an allegorical text that "tries to convey a certain idea rather than represent a coherent storyworld" (Alber 2016, 52), *QLEW* embodies the fervor of passionate love and sex in which time is both under our control and easily lost. The focus that the experience demands from the player means that everything except for the text and the sometimes incomplete storyworld it creates is blocked from the reader's attention. While an unnatural narrative insofar as it urges the reader to experience the scene again and again, it also acts as a ludic challenge in which the reader must learn to iteratively consume the text in order to reach a satisfying resolution.

Both *LHMP* and *QLEW* allow the reader to experience coherent narratives each time they are read. Unlike *Victory Garden*, they signal to the reader explicitly that they have a choice to make and that they are responsible for determining the course of the narrative. While the Storyspace hypertext reader is often thrown into an opaque form of multilinearity, the reader of what we call a transparently multilinear text is given much more information about where each hyperlink will lead. Thus, while hypertext is always composed of lexias and links, different uses of its form will require a different role for the reader and, moreover, potentially different naturalizing strategies. The medium itself does not necessarily dictate an antimimetic narrative experience, but, as we have shown, devices in the text can be used to create unnaturalness.

1.6 MULTILINEARITY IN NARRATIVE VIDEOGAMES

Most videogames allow players to play again and again; for example, their avatar might die and they may want to uncover more of the game world, or they might want to improve a previous performance or score. Whatever the motive, some narrative videogames, as a form of digital fiction, allow players to explore the same storyworld many times and in many different orders.

Acknowledging that any degree of exploratory agency can lead to different experiences of the same game world, Thon (2016) warns against seeing multiple explorations of the same game as an example of narrative contradiction. He stresses that "there is a narratologically significant distinction between the different playthroughs resulting from what can be roughly described as videogames' interactivity and the different playthroughs resulting from what can be abbreviated as their nonlinearity" (116). For Thon, only the latter "are arguably meant to represent . . . several different stories and storyworlds" (117), with the former simply allowing the player to explore the game world in different ways, creating "an arrangement of 'virtual storyworlds,' only one of which can be actualized in any given playthrough" (120). Like Thon, Juul (2005) also warns against "wrongly assum[ing] that since any game has multiple outcomes, any game is a contradictory world" (207n3). Instead, he suggests that "while a given game can have many different outcomes, it still sets up a dynamic fictional world that can be coherent within a single game session" (207n3).

Thon and Juul suggest that multiple play-throughs of a videogame do not necessarily result in a contradictory world, and this can be seen by exploring, for example, The Chinese Room's (2016) *Everybody's Gone to the Rapture* (*EGR*). In this game, players explore a three-dimensional game world in order to find out what has happened to an abandoned English country town. In the opening scene, players always find themselves standing outside at the top of a steep road from which the town can be seen below. There is a set of gates to their right and a small building ahead with its door ajar. If the building is entered, players find an abandoned office with a recording on a constant loop. Players who turn on the radio hear a broadcast from a character named Kate who tells us that "the event" has "left markers" but that "we don't understand it yet." She also tells us that "the answers are in the light." The function of the broadcast is thus to give contextual and navigational information to the player, to initiate the narrative, and to build suspense. Players who walk down the hill instead of entering the building are given different initiating information. This text thus has multiple points that can act as its "launch," "the first set of global instabilities or tensions in the narrative" (Phelan 2009, 195). When we explore *EGR* in multiple play-throughs, therefore, the storyworld might differ in the order in which we navigate the space, the order in which we receive information, and/or the various pieces of information that we choose to access (e.g., deciding whether to turn on the radio or not). These different experiences are a convention of the videogame genre; it is completely expected that players can have another go at the game. Thus, while impossible in the sense that the same scene can be experienced multiple times—something we cannot do in real life—this feature can be explained by reference to external factors and in particular the convention that videogame worlds can be explored multiple times, with each play-through seen as a different storyworld.

While *EGR* is an archetypical example of a videogame that offers multiple versions of the discourse each time it is played, as Thon notes, some games also contain contradictory stories and/or incompatible endings. Like the self-reflexive hypertext fictions above, contradictory videogames usually alert the player to the multilinear nature of the game explicitly so that the unnaturalness of the storyworld is flagged in advance via paratextual descriptions; on the videogame portal Steam, for example, games are tagged as "Multiple Endings" or as "Choices Matter." Within these games, however, reader/players can affect the discourse and story to various degrees, with some games using narrative contradictions self-consciously to create antimimetic experiences.

Orthogonal Games's (2013) *The Novelist* allows the player to affect the course of a family's destiny by making crucial decisions about the family's lives. The game focuses on Dan Kaplan and his family, who have recently moved to a remote coastal home in the US as Dan tries to finish writing his third novel. Players, referred to in the paratextual blurb as a "ghost," explore the family home with a first-person perspective, either as an invisible force or by hiding carefully from the family. Players can navigate the house by walking around, or they can transfer positions via occupying and switching between light-fittings. To uncover the story, players explore items such as diaries and letters. They can also access the private thoughts of the characters by standing near to them or by extracting personal memories via flashbacks. They thus assume an unnatural ontological and epistemological position in the storyworld throughout.

According to the instructions, "each member of the family desires a different outcome, and it's up to you to decide which path to take." The player's decisions thus determine the outcome of the unfolding story. In the "Writer's Block" chapter, either we can follow Dan's desires and find his notebook so that he spends the night working on his book, thus disappointing his son, Tommy, and wife, Linda, or we can satisfy Tommy and require that Dan play a board game with him, thus disappointing Dan, who needs to finish his book, and Linda, who wants to spend time with Dan. Rather than co-constructing the entire storyworld, as in an IF, players explore a world that already exists but whose development they partially determine. There is no ideal solution because each narrative resolution results in some disappointment for the other family members, with the result causing a lesser or greater degree of damage (e.g., Linda drinking a bottle of wine to numb her disappointment).

While *The Novelist* is "coherent within a single game session" (Juul 2005, 207n3) insofar as each play-through results in a coherent and logical story, to understand the work's thematic message we have to play the game multiple times. *The Novelist* teaches us that the choices we make in life always involve an element of compromise. However, players can only learn this message by seeing each play-through as them experimenting with the family's life. In real life, it is (unfortunately) not possible to try out different versions of the same life and have another go if we don't like what we experience. *The Novelist* relies on this feature of videogaming to draw attention to that idea. It defamiliarizes the basic constituents of a videogame narrative (cf. Richardson 2011) by drawing attention to the convention of multiple play-throughs. Players may well try not to be discovered by the family again and again in order to uncover more of the story and improve their overall performance in the game. It also defies the convention (cf. Richardson 2016) of multiple play-throughs because in order to see that each decision has a consequence for a different person, reader/players must play the game multiple times and thus see the different play-throughs as part of the same narrative experience as opposed to being new iterations that are separate from previous play-throughs. The game is thus what we define as a medium-specific antimimetic narrative—that is, it is antimimetic via defying the conventions of an existing, established medium. Yet, while it plays with the conventions of videogame mechanics, it does so in order to say something about the world beyond the game. Applying a thematic naturalizing strategy to *The Novelist* shows how the unnaturalness of the game world is used to give players a moral lesson about the ways in which individual actions can have an impact on other people in nuanced ways—consequences are not all bad or all good but involve a level of compromise. While the ludic challenge in *The Novelist* is to gather as much information as possible and to avoid being discovered in the house, the game is also ultimately didactic.

While *The Novelist* uses a multilinear structure to affect both discourse and story, in *Life Is Strange* (Dontnod Entertainment, 2015), multilinearity is also part of the game's central motif. In this third-person literary game, we play Max Caulfield, a shy and self-deprecating high school student in the US. The game opens with what we are led to believe might be a dream (but which turns out to be a premonition) in which Max is stranded on a cliff in the middle of a hurricane storm. Max then wakes up in her photography class. Players can read Max's journal and emails for back story and explore the school to progress the narrative. However, at key moments, players can choose to rewind time and thus revisit or revise particular events. For example, in "Episode 1: Chrysalis," we witness a fatal shooting in the bathrooms, but by rewinding time, we are able to rerun the scene and, the second time, prevent it.

As in *EGR* and *The Novelist*, discourse is always variable in *Life Is Strange* because we can explore the game world in different orders and with variable duration during different play-throughs. However, narrative contradictions are also experienced because the story is rewound and experienced again during the same play-through. The do-it-yourself or virtualization approaches are not appropriate naturalizing strategies in this case because scenes are rewound and rerun rather than a range of distinct possibilities being available to choose from. *Life Is Strange* thus embodies the "*sous rapture*" metaphor that McHale describes above in which contradictory narratives "continue to function in the discourse, even though they are excluded from it" (1987, 100). We explicitly see particular versions of the story erased, with unnatural temporality (see chapter 3) used in *Life Is Strange* to allow the player to reverse time and thus correct wrongs. Witnessing a storyworld that shows multiple and conflicting outcomes, reader/players are likely to naturalize the narrative contradictions by seeing them as part of a "magic" (Ryan) storyworld or as "plural realities" (Ryan) that the storyworld relies on. Narrative contradictions in *Life Is Strange* are thus explainable according to the unnatural logic of this particular storyworld, rather than as a convention of the videogame genre.

1.6.1 Temporal versus Spatial Multilinearity

In all three games discussed above, reader/players explore a 3D storyworld, and thus visual and spatial navigation is key to the experience. In defining narrative contradictions, Alber (2016) states that they are a form of "logically impossible temporalit[y]" (171) because when mutually irreconcilable narratives are presented by a text, "time is fragmented into multiple (logically incompatible) itineraries" (172). Alber emphasizes the temporal, as opposed to spatial, nature of impossibility with regard to narrative contradiction. Thus, while he indicates that narrative contradictions cause "ontological pluralism" (171)—and therefore produce multiple worlds—his analyses focus on contradictions as "incompatible storylines" (178) or "contradictory but coexisting events" (178).

Conceptualizing narratives in terms of temporality is fundamental to almost all definitions of "narrative" and "narrativity." However, the contradictory discourses and stories that occur as a result of players navigating a 3D videogame storyworld such as *The Novelist* and *Life Is Strange* can have a distinctly visual and spatial, as opposed to temporal, quality to them, so that a different visual representation of the same storyworld can be experienced each time. Clearly, the visual and spatial contradictions of videogames differ in degree rather than kind with respect to other nonvisual and non-ergodic media. As we have seen throughout this chapter, print, film, and hypertext can all produce narrative contradictions that can be described or represented using either text or visual images. However, the fact that a reader/player can navigate a 3D world means that multilinearity occurs through navigation of a graphically rendered storyworld. Contradictions are thus primarily experienced visually and spatially even though that experience is also ultimately temporal.

1.7 CONCLUSION

The examples of antimimetic narrative contradiction analyzed in this chapter are all unnatural because they present logically irreconcilable scenarios that, according to real-world logic, cannot exist within the same world concurrently. Importantly, however, neither the multilinear form nor the logical contradictions they can produce are intrinsically defamiliarizing, or antimimetic; the structural and aesthetic functions of each text must be judged on an individual basis to determine whether they do contain "events that are clearly and strikingly impossible in the real world" (Alber, Iversen, Nielsen and Richardson 2013, 102). *LHMP* and *QLEW* draw attention to their narrative contradictions, but these texts give the reader a strong sense of closure. The narrative contradictions in *Victory Garden*, on the other hand, cause greater ambiguity in terms of the discourse and story and often do not offer a definitive, single ending.

In narrative games and IFs, which intrinsically rely on the reader/player re-experiencing and thus co-constructing a new storyworld each time, multilinearity can be used simply so that the reader/player can have another go and improve on their previous performance or explore more of the storyworld. However, multilinearity can also be played with in videogames to generate an antimimetic narrative experience. In this regard, we have deployed and modified Richardson's definition of an antimimetic narrative to show that a digital fiction narrative can be medium-specifically antimimetic. This is achieved when a narrative defies the conventions of an existing, established medium (as opposed to an existing, established genre in Richardson's definition), such as when a videogame uses multiple play-throughs to deliver its overall message. Ultimately then, medium-specific antimimeticism can have varying degrees of alienating effects, with different kinds of texts alienating reader/players to a greater or lesser extent depending on the conventions they aim to defy.

Importantly, in most if not all cases analyzed in this chapter, narrative contradictions can be allied to the thematic concerns explored within the texts and thus relate to what Alber defines as unnatural elements that "foreground the thematic" (2016, 51) or the allegorical. That readers of all kinds of digital fiction have learned to expect that digital media easily facilitates, and therefore may well contain what are logically irreconcilable narrative contradictions, means that narrative contradictions represent one of the ways in which digital affordances, and the hypertext form in particular, might lead to a medium-specific conventionalization of what still remains a highly defamiliarizing unnatural narrative device in other media such as print.

In this chapter, we have argued that an acceptance of contradictions in particular forms of digital fiction can be seen as a medium-specific form of conventionalization or a medium-specific form of Alber's "Zen way of reading"—what we have defined as "accepted as an unnatural construction." Drawing on Richardson's (2016) category of unnatural constructions, we have added this strategy to Alber's framework to explain instances in which the materiality of the reading experience can be used to account for the unnaturalness of a narrative overall. In such cases, readers apply a medium-specific evaluative frame when reading a particular kind of text. However, to suggest that all contradictions can be naturalized via a medium-specific acceptance of them erroneously implies that all digital fiction readers are seasoned experts in this kind of reading experience. It also risks disregarding the enormously creative and experimental uses to which contradictions are put in digital fiction and the profound effect they can have on readers, whether novice or expert. While a reader might accept narrative contradictions as inherent in hypertext or games, it does not mean that they do not notice or think about their thematic purpose. As the analyses in this chapter suggest, therefore, the overall effect of any multilinear text ultimately comes down to how this challenging but flexible narrative device is deployed and to reader/player-specific levels of experience with and expectations of digital fiction genres and forms.

2

Interactional Metalepsis

> I got a lot more involved with what was going on on the screen and... the setting itself, exploring this house, I put myself into the mind-set of who I was,... looking at all the things, seeing what I could pick up,... it did get to a point where... I sort of situated myself as that first person view. Rather than playing the game... it sort of became like an automatic extension.

2.1 INTRODUCTION

The epigraph to this chapter is taken from a reader/player's post-play account of their experience of *WALLPAPER*, a digital fiction by Andy Campbell and Judi Alston.[1] The speaker moves from talking about being outside the text (e.g., referring to "the screen") to implicitly being inside the storyworld (e.g., "exploring the house") to deciding to become the avatar (e.g., "I [. . .] situated myself as that first person view"). At the end of the account, they describe how the avatar "became an automatic extension" as opposed to a role that they played. Their testimony exemplifies one of the ways in which readers of digital fiction can perceive that they are embodied in a storyworld and thus appear to move from one ontological domain to another.

In this chapter, we examine metalepses: the movement of entities between ontologically distinct spheres. We define interactional metalepsis in particular as a form of metalepsis that takes place across the actual-world-to-storyworld boundary and that exploits the interactive nature of digital technology via the hardware through which the reader accesses the text, such as the mouse, keyboard, or other navigational devices, and/or through medium-specific interac-

---

1. This data was collected as part of the Reading Digital Fiction project funded by the Arts and Humanities Research Council (Funding Ref: AH/K004174/1). The full data set can be accessed via http://doi.org/10.17032/shu-160006.

tive modes of expression such as hyperlinks or avatars (Bell 2016a). In terms of narrative theory, the existence of interactional metalepses means that some of the theoretical understandings of metalepsis need to be reconsidered in order to more accurately represent the ontologically transgressive nature of this narratological device. In particular, this involves the incorporation of the audience's "reality," that is, the actual world of the user, and also the emphasis on worlds as opposed to diegetic levels in the analysis.

Exploring the ways in which these medium-specific and unnatural forms of metalepsis manifest in digital fiction, we offer a typology of interactional metalepsis that incorporates metaleptic navigational devices, metaleptic breath, visual metalepses (including metalepses caused via webcams), metaleptic hyperlinks, metaleptic character interactions, and metaleptic locations. The chapter also considers metaleptic phenomena related to videogame "bleed." We show that different forms of metalepsis are likely to be conventionalized by readers of digital fiction to varying degrees that depend on the wider digital, cultural context to which they belong and also that, unlike most metalepses in print, which are typically very defamiliarizing, some forms of interactional metalepsis can also have an immersive effect. This chapter thus shows ways in which devices that may be unnatural in some media (e.g., print) can become highly conventional in a digital context.

2.2 METALEPSIS, INTERACTION, AND THE UNNATURAL

Originally defined by Genette (1980) as "any intrusion by the extradiegetic narrator or narratee into the diegetic universe (or by the diegetic characters into a metadiegetic universe, etc), or the inverse" (234–35), metalepsis is a term that describes the movement of fictional entities between what are, according to actual world logic, distinct ontological realms. Since Genette's original definition, narratologists have devised numerous typologies of metalepsis (see Pier 2005 for an overview) that seek to differentiate the various types and functions of the device.

Fludernik (2003), for example, proposes that a distinction must be made between what she calls "'real' and metaphorical metalepsis" or "between an actual crossing of *ontological* boundaries and a merely imaginative transcendence of narrative levels" (396). In further differentiating between the different kinds of metalepsis that Genette examines in his original exposition of the device, Fludernik (2003) proposes four types. First, she defines "authorial metalepsis," in which the author addresses the reader directly via the text and thus foregrounds the inventedness of the story. Fludernik uses Genette's example of Diderot's *Jacques the Fataliste* ("You see, reader, how considerate I am").

In authorial metalepsis, then, the author appears to speak to the reader but via the text rather than by invading another diegetic level. Indeed, Hanebeck (2017) argues that this "hardly constitutes a violation of the logic of diegetic levels" (95) and is instead "metafictional comment" (95).

Fludernik's second type is "ontological metalepsis 1: narrational metalepsis," in which the narrator moves "to a lower narrative level of embedded story world, or . . . a character to a lower (intra)diegetic level" (384). This kind of metalepsis, she shows, can be seen in Woody Allen's (1980) short story "The Kugelmass Episode," in which university professor Kugelmass hires a magician to help him enter the storyworld of Gustave Flaubert's *Madame Bovary*. Third, Fludernik proposes "ontological metalepsis 2: lectorial metalepsis," in which "the narratee [is implicated] on the story level or a character is raised from an embedded tale onto the superior (usually extradiegetic) plane" (385). Fludernik suggests that this form occurs in some forms of second-person narration when what initially appears to be an extradiegetic addressee turns out to be a character or when a "story-internal recipient . . . turns out to have some existential link with the extradiegetic story level as well" (385). However, this form also occurs in Flann O'Brien's (1939) *At Swim-Two-Birds* when the fictional author, Dermot Trellis, invents characters that subsequently check themselves into his hotel to torture him. Last, type 4, "rhetorical metalepsis or discourse metalepsis," occurs when the narrator provides the reader with some additional information during an apparent pause in the discourse. Fludernik uses Genette's example of the narrator of Balzac's *Les souffrances de l'inventeur*, who leaves a scene in which they are describing the churchman climbing the stairs in order to relate information about another part of the storyworld before coming back to the churchman again.

Fludernik's types 1 and 4 involve an address to the reader from either the author or the narrator (see also chapter 5), and types 2 and 3 involve fictional entities moving between diegetic levels. Ryan (2006a) affirms this distinction by discriminating between ontological metalepses, which "open a passage between levels that result in their interpenetration, or mutual contamination" (207), and rhetorical metalepses, which "open a small window that allows a quick glance across levels, but the window closes after a few sentences, and the operation ends up reasserting the existence of the boundaries" (207). Following Bell and Alber (2012), we regard authorial and rhetorical metalepses as metaphoric devices in which no actual boundary crossing takes place, and thus, in this book, we focus on ontological metalepses, or what Wolf (2005) defines as the "'genuine' type of metalepsis" (89).

As Fludernik's distinction shows, ontological metalepsis can be "descending" (Pier 2005), in which a fictional entity moves from a diegetic level to a hierarchically lower one per "The Kugelmass Episode" example given above, and also "ascending" (Pier 2005), in which fictional entities move in the opposite direction. Importantly, however, as this chapter will show, the nature of digital fiction reading is such that the emphasis of our discussion is on metalepses that take place across the actual-world-to-storyworld boundary as opposed to movements of fictional entities between levels within the storyworld.

Recognizing an underresearched area of metalepsis, Kukkonen (2011a) hypothesizes that "narrative research into hypertext forms, digital media and videogames will certainly reveal a wealth of what I would call 'interactional metalepsis'" (18), which, she conjectures, "might represent a special kind of metalepsis based on the actual interaction between the text and the reader" (18). Kukkonen's conceptualization of interactional metalepsis as involving an interaction between text and reader implicitly emphasizes the haptic and nontrivial nature of the ergodic reading experience. Since readers are involved in the construction of a digital fiction narrative via interactive interface elements, they are involved in what Aarseth (1997) terms a "cybernetic feedback loop" (65) in which "information flow[s] from text to user" via the modes of representation the text deploys "and back again" (65) via the various interactive functions the reader can perform. While the hardware through which readers access digital fiction does not necessitate metalepsis, the cybernetic feedback loop of which the reader is a part in ergodic digital fiction does because readers are required to interact with the text—via a mouse, keyboard, or their fingers on a touchscreen—to explore the screen and/or click interface elements (e.g., hyperlinks) to progress the narrative.

Crucially, however, the interaction with the text is not just a material part of the digital reading experience; it also results in a real or imagined ontological transgression. When the reader interacts with a digital fiction, using navigational hardware, their movements are symbolized visually onscreen either by an interactive interface element such as an avatar, a cursor, or, in the case of touchscreen technology, by a visual imprint of their haptic engagement with the text. The technology they use to explore the text thus causes a trace of the reader to appear onscreen and thus an imprint of them in a separate ontological domain.

Theorizing the cursor in digital fiction, Ryan suggests that it is "the representation of the reader's virtual body in the virtual world" (2006a, 122; cf. Ciccoricco 2015, 75). Ensslin's (2009) concept of "double-situatedness" in digital fiction also implies that dual ontology is an inevitable part of exploring a digital storyworld. She argues that "on the one hand, user-readers are 'embodied' as direct receivers, whose bodies interact with the hardware and software of a computer. On the other, user-readers are considered to be 'reembodied' through feedback which they experience in represented form, e.g., through visible or invisible avatars (third person or first person graphic or typographic representations on screen)" (158). Both thus suggest that the interface element is a version, copy, "proxy" (Klevjer 2012), or what we define as a digital counterpart (Bell 2014a, 2016b) of the reader in a digital space. In addition to interactional metalepsis relying on an interaction between "text" and reader and thus between the material object used to describe the storyworld and the reader, interactional metalepsis also causes the ontological boundary between the reader and the storyworld to be breached.

We thus define interactional metalepsis as a form of metalepsis that exploits the interactive nature of digital technology via the hardware through which the reader accesses the text, such as the mouse, keyboard, or other navigational devices, and/or through medium-specific interactive modes of expression such as cursors, avatars, or hyperlinks (Bell 2016a). Since interactional metalepses depend on the reader's nontrivial interaction with the ergodic text and associated storyworld as they are read/played, they are ontological transgressions that take place across the actual-world-to-storyworld boundary rather than transgressions across ontological levels within the storyworld. Since all forms of ergodic digital fiction require the reader to interact with the text and thus be visually represented onscreen, interactional metalepses are fundamentally built into and therefore an inevitable feature of ergodic digital fiction.

Digital media is not the only context in which actual-to-storyworld metalepses can take place. However, importantly, the nature of the actual-to-storyworld boundary violation is somewhat unique in an interactive digital context because of the cybernetic feedback loop of which the reader is a part and the associated multimodal manifestation of the reader onscreen that it facilitates. For example, in his analysis of the *Animal Man* comic, Thoss (2011b) examines a panel in which a character looks towards the reader and appears to acknowledge them, thus appearing to metaleptically cross the ontological boundary between them. Acknowledging the impossibility of the represented communication, Thoss calls this metalepsis a "feigned transgression" (198) because "fiction and reality cannot really merge in this way" (198). However, while he acknowledges that the metalepsis is only visually represented as opposed to materially manifesting, he does acknowledge that "there is no reason for a narrative not to claim the opposite, or for readers not to go along with such a claim for as long as they are engaged in the game of make-believe" (198).

Ryan (2006a), like Thoss, maintains that the actual world "remains protected from metaleptic phenomena" (209) on the basis that it is impossible for a reader to be physically implicated in a metalepsis. Wolf's (2013) transmedial definition of metalepsis as "the paradoxical violation of the outer border of a represented world" (117) is less restrictive and implies that domains outside the fictional world can be involved in metaleptic jumps. Of course, readers of digital fiction do not completely move into the digital storyworld; nor do entities from the storyworld completely move into the actual-world domains. However, this is precisely what readers are asked to imagine happens when any metalepses takes place, and, as we will show, it is particularly pronounced when readers are represented onscreen by navigational devices or when fictional entities seem to appear in the actual world, as in, for example, augmented reality.

It is perhaps more accurate to see metalepses in different media as involving the actual world to a greater or lesser degree of mimetic authenticity, or what Limoges (2011) calls having "a stronger or weaker coefficient of reality which in turn gives the impression, more or less convincingly, that they are indulging the extrafictional spectator" (207). In print, a text can verbally describe the involvement of the extratextual level such as when an author figure appears in the text.[2] The use of the second person can also be used as a prominent textual metaleptic device (see chapter 5). Pictorial media such as comics or paintings can visually depict metalepses—as Thoss's analysis above shows—and the visual nature of the media means that visual metaleptic jumps can have "a stronger coefficient of reality (a more realistic aesthetic)" (Limoges 2011, 206) than verbal descriptions. However, the capacity for representing metalepsis across the actual-world-to-storyworld boundary in pictorial images is still restricted because the images are obviously *representations* of a separate world. Film and television can present a strong coefficient of reality. Thus, they perhaps represent the next most authentic means of portraying metaleptic jumps between actual world and storyworld, such as when characters address viewers directly, as, for example, in Frank Underwood's frequent addresses to the viewers of Netflix's *House of Cards* (see chapter 5). As a multimodal medium, digital fiction can use visual, textual, aural, and filmic modes to represent actual-to-storyworld breaches, but it is the interactivity of the medium in particular that facilitates the crossing of that boundary because the reader-as-cursor/avatar is a fundamental part of digital fiction reading.

The fact that ergodic digital fictions are inherently interactionally metaleptic and that the associated ontological breach always takes place across the actual-world-to-storyworld boundary means that some narratological con-

---

2. As a textual medium, digital fictions can also represent metalepses verbally. In a comparable example, in Richard Holeton's (2001) hypertext fiction *Figurski at Findhorn on Acid*, emails are exchanged between several of the characters and a writer called "Richard Holeton." Thus, in an example of a descending metalepsis, the author is verbally depicted in the storyworld of *Figurski*.

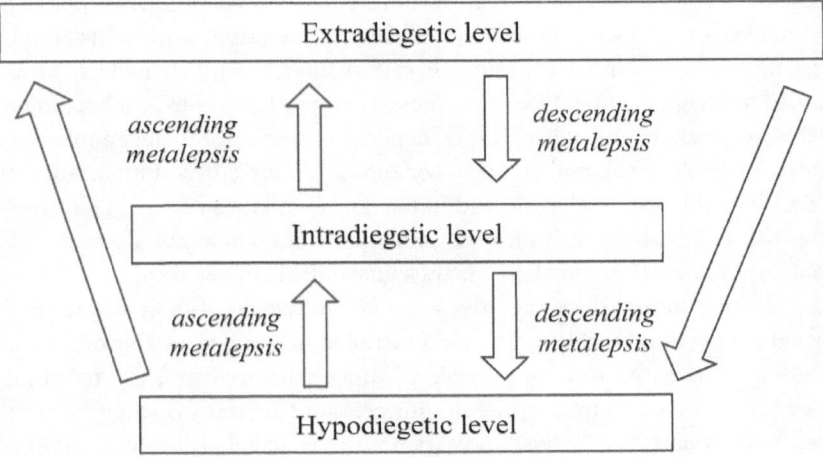

FIGURE 2.1. Klimek's (2011, 25) scheme of simple forms of metaleptic transgressions in fictional texts

ceptualizations of metalepsis, which are based on non-ergodic texts, cannot account for this medium-specific device. While accounts such as Ryan's and Thoss's explicitly emphasize the impossibility of an actual-world-to-story-world breach, others simply do not account for that form of metalepsis at all. More specifically, some narrative theorists (e.g., Fludernik 2003), following Genette, use the terminology of *diegetic levels* as opposed to *worlds* in their models and associated analyses. For example, Klimek's (2011) model (see fig. 2.1) adheres strictly to Genettian terminology and is based on the distinction between the "shifting but sacred frontier between . . . the world in which one tells [and] the world of which one tells" (Genette 1980, 236). She explains that the "'extradiegetic level' corresponds to the representation of a world that is regarded as 'real' within the novel" (24) and is thus where the narrator sits. She continues that "from this 'real world,' the 'intradiegetic level' emerges, which is regarded as a 'fictive world' within this reality" (24). This intradiegetic level is thus the world that the narrator describes. The third, hypodiegetic, level represents an embedded level such as a *mise en abyme* and can be added to as embedded stories occur.

Klimek justifies her terminological choice of *levels* as opposed to *worlds* on the basis that she "engage[s] exclusively with written and not visual fiction" (25). She thus implies that verbal narratives do not break the boundary between the actual world and the storyworld. However, while diegetic levels may be able to adequately model the ontological mechanics inside a storyworld and remain faithful to Genette's terminology, it does not accurately model what readers are asked to imagine happens when a metaleptic jump takes place—that is, it is a structuralist as opposed to a cognitive approach. Moreover, even in cases in which the reader in the actual world is not implicated, such as when heterodiegetic narrators interact with characters, we are asked to imagine that entities have moved from one world to another. Somewhat contradictorily, while Klimek explicitly rejects *worlds* terminology in favor of *levels,* when she explains her model she uses descriptions such as "fictive world" and "real world within the novel" and thus resorts to terminology that emphasizes the "worldness" of the different ontological domains. The ontological nature of metalepsis is thus unavoidable in her account.

In order to provide a cognitive approach to metalepsis and also to more accurately account for the ontological nature of metalepsis we, like other narratologists (e.g., McHale 1987; Wolf 2005; Kukkonen 2011a), use terminology that categorizes metalepses as transgressions between distinct "worlds" rather than narrative "levels." In cases where the actual-world-to-storyworld boundary is breached, such as when authors appear in their own works, when readers are directly addressed by characters, or, for the purposes of the present discussion, in interactional metalepses when a digital trace of the reader appears in the storyworld, world terminology is particularly important.

In our cognitive approach, adopting the term *world* as opposed to *level* seeks to address the narrative mechanics of metalepsis more authentically by emphasizing the ontological nature of the device and also, as analyzed in more detail below, by acknowledging the role of the actual world in some metalepses. However, it also allows the unnaturalness of metaleptic jumps to be explained more accurately. Several theorists note the impossible or "implausible nature" (Pier 2005, 90n19) of metalepsis. Ryan (2006a) also notes that "ontological transgressions cannot . . . occur in a fictional world that claims to respect the logical and physical laws of the real world" (210). Yet, within unnatural narratology, it is sometimes taken for granted, rather than explained explicitly why metalepses are unnatural.

Drawing on the concept of fictional "worlds" explicitly, Bell and Alber (2012) articulate why metalepses are unnatural. They suggest that "all metalepses are physically impossible because in the actual world, entities from two different ontological domains cannot interact" (167).[3] Thus, when entities move between ontological domains in fiction, a physical impossibility occurs. They also suggest that some metalepses are also "logically impossible because they violate the principle of non-contradiction whereby two contradictory states of affairs cannot be true at the same time, which means, for example,

---

3. This worldview is very Western and settler-colonial in nature. Some Indigenous worldviews, for example, assume more fluid boundaries between ontological spheres.

that the same character cannot exist in two ontologically distinct domains simultaneously" (167). The basis for the logical impossibility is that while some fictional entities move from one domain to another, in some instances and particularly when an author appears in the text, an individual exists in two domains at the same time. They explain: "When Martin Amis appears at the end of his novel *Money* to play chess with his protagonist, John Self, the text suggests that, ontologically, Martin Amis has moved from the actual world to the storyworld. However, even though readers can recognize Martin Amis as the figure with whom John Self plays chess, they must also recognize that Amis exists as an author in the actual world" (171). Using appropriate concepts and terminology from possible worlds theory, they suggest that the two Martin Amis figures exist as counterparts of one another.

While Bell and Alber focus on counterparts of author figures, Bell (2014a, 2016a/b) extends the notion to the reader of digital fiction. She suggests that when the reader is symbolized onscreen as a cursor or avatar, the interface element represents a counterpart of the reader. This means that while not all metalepses in print fiction result in logical impossibilities, interactional metalepses always do. Interactional metalepses are thus both physically and logically impossible. Since interactional metalepses are an inevitable component of ergodic digital fiction, it follows that ergodic digital fictions are fundamentally unnatural.

The preceding discussion shows how all types of metalepses are unnatural according to Alber's definition of the "unnatural," but Richardson's concept of the antimimetic can also be applied to metalepses. Richardson sees metalepses as "the most playful kind[ ] of . . . contamination [between fiction and nonfiction]" (2015, 69) but claims that "the fiction/nonfiction boundary is only breached within the fictional world" (69) and thus reserves the term for metalepses that take place within the storyworld only. In cases where authors appear in their own works and thus where descending metalepses take place between the actual world and storyworld, he discounts them as "a merely fictionalized version of the author" (81).

Yet while Richardson's examination of metalepses disregards the ontological transgressions that can take place between the actual world and storyworld, his definition of the unnatural as antimimetic applies to all cases of metalepses. In violating ontological boundaries within or across the storyworld, metalepses certainly "point out [their] own constructedness, the artificiality of many of its techniques, and its inherent fictionality" (Richardson 2011, 31) because in showing how the boundary can be crossed, the existence of the boundary is inevitably foregrounded. Inevitably different texts will draw attention to this violation in different ways and may or may not be naturalized by readers. Any analysis of metalepsis thus needs to pay attention to the context in which the metalepses take place as well as how readers make sense of them.

Indeed, while all ergodic digital fictions can be classified as unnatural on the basis that they are interactionally metaleptic, interactional metalepsis is used in a variety of ways, causing varying degrees of defamiliarization in individual works. In the analyses that follow, we exemplify the wide range of metaleptic devices that are possible in digital media, explore the effect of each type of metalepsis, and suggest whether metalepses can or cannot (or are meant to) be naturalized by readers of digital fiction. We show that while metalepses may be defamiliarizing in some media, they can also be highly conventional in a digital context.

2.3 METALEPTIC NAVIGATION

In this section we discuss the different degrees of metalepsis that are achieved according to the navigational device employed in the fiction. As we show, counterparts of the reader can appear in different parts of the text depending on whether a cursor or avatar is used to navigate the fictional space.

In the context of videogames, Juul (2005) makes a pertinent distinction between "world space," which is the entire fictional world that is projected, either explicitly or implicitly by the game, and "game space," which is the part of that fictional world in which the game actually takes place and thus to which the player has access when they are playing it (164–65; cf. Thon 2009, 281). The distinction between available and unavailable parts of a storyworld is also relevant in the context of digital fiction and metalepsis in particular because while some fictions allow readers to explore the storyworld in 3D and thus intrude metaleptically into the storyworld directly, others only allow reader access to the text and thus to the space that represents the storyworld verbally. In the following section, following Juul, we analyze examples of how metalepses work in the "text-spaces" and "world-spaces" in different kinds of digital fiction.

2.3.1 Metalepses between the Actual World and the Text-Space

In text-based digital fictions including Storyspace hypertext fictions, such as Shelley Jackson's (1995) *Patchwork Girl*, the cursor represents the reader onscreen as they select links, but the reader-as-cursor does not interact with the storyworld and the entities it contains. They cannot interact with, for example, characters or objects. The same is true for multimodal web-based fictions, such as *Flight Paths,* by Kate Pullinger and Chris Joseph (2007), and *High Muck a Muck: Playing Chinese,* by the High Muck a Muck Collective (Zhang et al. 2016). These works contain visual images of the storyworld as well as textual descriptions of it, and the reader-as-cursor can click on textual or visual links and thus the user interface. In multimodal digital fiction apps on tablets and smartphones (or app-fictions, as we call them), such as Steve Jackson's (2014) *Sorcery!* and Inkle's (2012) *Future Voices* collection, readers use a touchscreen to select links, and traces are shown onscreen either via a change in screen color or the visual impression when a button has been pressed. In all cases, the reader does not interact with elements within the storyworld as though they were present within it. Instead, in these text-based and 2D multimodal digital fictions, a counterpart of the reader—the reader-as-cursor—is metaleptic, but they are only able to interact with the "text space" of the storyworld.

That the reader only enters the interface of the storyworld in these cases does not mean that their influence on the storyworld is any less significant to the unfolding of the story. In the examples above, the reader-as-cursor still determines the order and pace of the narrative (see chapter 1). While this account might suggest that the reader becomes a narrator figure to some extent, insofar as they decide in which order the narrative unfolds, the metaleptic cursor does not mean that the reader intrudes into the extradiegetic space. An extradiegetic space houses the narrator, and, if a reader appeared in that space, the narrator would be aware of their presence. Rather, the text-space exists at a level above the extradiegetic level.

2.3.2 Metalepses between Actual World and Some Storyworld Elements

In some digital fictions, such as Christy Dena's (2015) app-fiction *Magister Ludi* (available for iPad), readers have a greater degree of influence in the storyworld than in the previous examples because they are able to interact with some items within that storyworld. However, their spatial access to the storyworld is still limited. *Magister Ludi* presents visual images of three different rooms: "The Schoolroom," "The Bedroom," and "The Room of Poverty." As shown in fig. 2.2, "The Schoolroom" contains a teacher's and a student's desk, bookshelves, a chalkboard, and a gym-kit store.

The reader must use a cursor to select items from an inventory on the left side of the screen and decide where to place them in the room. The text then responds with an analysis of where the reader has put the item. As shown

FIGURE 2.2. Screenshot from "The Schoolroom" in *Magister Ludi*, written and designed by Christy Dena and illustrated by Marigold Bartlett (2015)

in the screenshot, if the reader places the textbook in the trashcan, the text responds that this action "means you are rejecting what others want to teach you." Other choices receive an equally interpretative response until all items have been placed and an overall assessment of the reader's performance is delivered. At the end of "The Schoolroom," the narrator assesses the reader as follows: "You lift the Textbook above your head and then thwop it into the Trash Can. By rejecting what you're told is important, you are able to escape the schoolroom sooner." The reader's choices are critiqued by the sardonic, ironic narrator, who determines how long the reader must stay in the various rooms, but the apparent assessments make no difference to the time the reader actually spends in these spaces. Instead, the comments draw attention to, and moreover mock, quest games that use psychological assessments to determine the progress of the narrative. The metaleptic navigation can be naturalized as a convention of digital media, but it is still defamiliarizing in *Magister Ludi* because the narrator draws attention to the reader's presence.

2.3.3 Metalepses between Actual World and Storyworld

Some immersive, 3D-style digital fictions use visual modes to create digital storyworlds but the digital counterpart of the reader has a more pronounced spatial presence and thus greater metaleptic navigational agency. For example, the reader/player of Dreaming Methods's (2016) *WALLPAPER* experiences the 3D storyworld from protagonist PJ Sanders's first-person perspective and must navigate this storyworld using a mouse. As the reader explores the family house and its grounds, snippets of text emerge and reveal suppressed memories and facets of family history that were previously unknown to PJ.

WALLPAPER uses what Thon (2009) calls a "subjective point of view," in which the reader experiences the storyworld from both "the spatial and perceptual perspective of the player's avatar" (282). When PJ puts on or removes a computer headset, the visual presentation of the storyworld changes accordingly. *WALLPAPER* also deploys a "subjective point of action" in which "the action position of the player coincides with that of the player's avatar" (290), so that the player controls the actions of the avatar directly. They can choose to pick up items, such as old prayer cards, ornaments, and postcards that give insights into the family history. Thus, in terms of navigation, when the reader moves the mouse, the screen pans accordingly, determining the spatial point of view. In *WALLPAPER*, which is set during the hours of darkness, this spatial perspective is further pronounced by using light as a signifier of point of view. The direction in which the avatar looks becomes lighter, as though someone's eyes are adjusting to the darkness and then focusing once rested for a while. Thus, the reader is able to influence their view of the world by moving the mouse in the actual world, and we also get a digital trace of the reader within the storyworld via the subjective point of view and point of action.

There is clearly a difference both ontologically and experientially between readers being embodied as cursors, which can only access text, cursors that can affect the spatial point of view in a storyworld, and avatars that have fuller navigational access to a storyworld. As Klevjer (2012) notes, "The avatar is different from a cursor because it belongs to the simulated world of the game" (21). We might therefore think of a mouse-cursor as a "weak" form of interactional metalepsis and of avatars as a "strong" form. However, as the range of examples above suggests, the distinctions are not clear-cut, and the different navigational devices should be seen as existing on a scale of ontological intrusion as opposed to being seen in binary opposition.

Fig. 2.3 depicts our model of interactional metalepsis, which reflects the different kinds of interactional metalepses as they occur in different kinds of digital fiction. As in Klimek's original model, the white arrows in fig 2.3 show the metalepses that can take place within the storyworld. This is the case when, for example, a character moves to an embedded storyworld. As a cognitive model, which aims to capture the processes at work when a reader interacts with a digital fiction, the gray arrows represent metalepses that take place

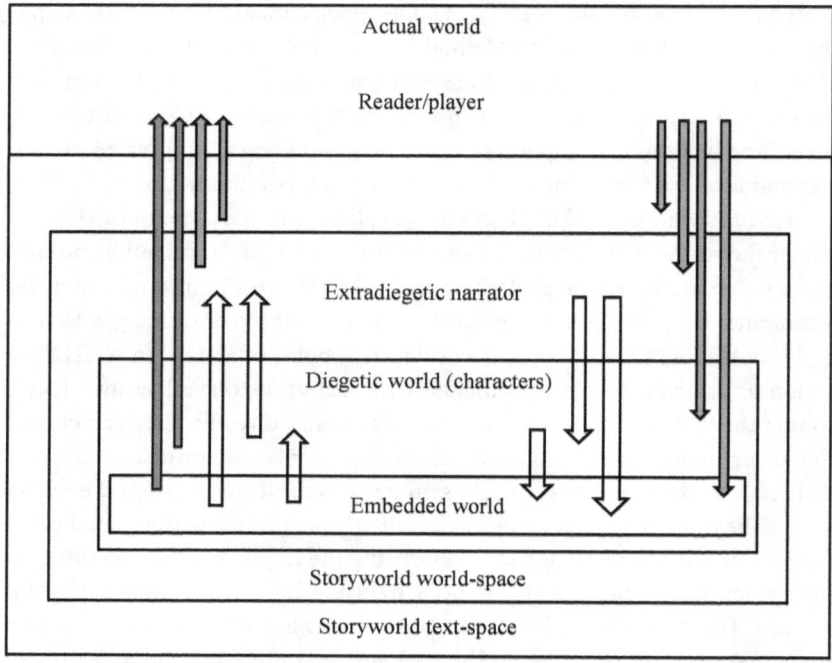

FIGURE 2.3. Model of interactional metalepsis

across the actual-world-to-storyworld boundary. Thus, our model, unlike Klimek's, explicitly accounts for the reader/player in the actual world. It also accounts for the fact that a counterpart of the reader can appear in the text-space or the world-space either in the primary diegetic world in or an embedded world. As discussed above, in digital fictions, such as *Patchwork Girl*, the reader is typically represented onscreen with a cursor, but they cannot interact with storyworld elements directly. The metalepsis thus takes place, as the shortest gray arrow shows, between actual world and text-space only. In other digital fictions, such as *Magister Ludi*, the reader/player can explore the storyworld and interact with objects within it. However, as a cursor they do not have the same ontological status as the other characters; other characters are not aware of their presence. In this case, the metalepsis takes place between the actual world and the diegetic world of the storyworld world-space, but the reader/player cannot not delve into all aspects of the storyworld, so that arrow is placed towards the top of that space. Finally, in digital fictions such as *WALLPAPER*, the reader is embodied as an avatar having the same ontological status as the other characters in the storyworld. Here, the metalepsis is at its most intrusive and takes place across the actual-world and storyworld boundary. The longest arrow shows how a metaleptic cursor or avatar could appear in an embedded storyworld.

Irrespective of whether the digital fiction uses a cursor in the text-space and/or world-space, or an avatar in the world-space, the reader in the actual world appears metaleptically in the storyworld as a digitally mediated counterpart. However, while such metalepses represent an unnatural device, they are also ultimately a conventional form of digital interaction. Analyzing the role of the mouse in human–computer interaction in general, Bizzocchi and Woodbury (2003) suggest that "we are so accustomed to this correlation [between hand movements and associated cursor movements] that it is perfectly transparent—we don't think about it, we don't question it, we don't even notice it" (558). Controlling an avatar in a storyworld is also an established and conventional feature of computer gaming. Thus, while ontologically transgressive, having the reader represented onscreen as a digital navigational device does not necessarily mean that the text is antimimetic. It can be perceptually unmarked because it is a standard and well-established aspect of digital-born textual interaction.

Moreover, depending on how a navigational device is used in a particular digital fiction, the effect can be somewhat different from the alienating or defamiliarizing effect of metalepsis as identified by many theorists analyzing metalepsis in print fiction (e.g., Fludernik 2003; McHale 1987). In his original conception also, Genette suggests that metalepsis "produces a strangeness that is either comical . . . or fantastic" (1980, 235). However, as transmedial investigations into metalepsis have developed, theorists have shown that not all metalepses have the same kind of effect on the reader/player/viewer. As Pier (2011) notes, "Originally noted for its disruptive, anti-illusionistic effects, metalepsis has since come to be seen as inherently bound to no specific effect, but rather productive of a wide variety of effects, in some cases even illusion-inducing" (273; cf. Wolf 2013, 125). In a digital context, rather than something that can be categorized as always causing alienation, metaleptic cursors and avatars can instead increase the reader's immersive experience of the text, especially when used alongside other immersive storytelling techniques.

Indeed, while metaleptic navigational devices such as cursors, avatars, or sensory imprints on touchscreen technology are always present within ergodic digital fiction, other additional forms of metalepsis can work alongside them to foreground their unnaturalness. These can be descending metalepses which show that the reader has an influence in the storyworld, or they can be ascending and thus suggest that elements from the storyworld intrude into the actual world. In the three types of metaleptic navigational devices discussed above, the particular texts discussed in section 2.3.1 (metalepses that take place between the actual world and the text-space) do not draw attention to the cursor onscreen. The same is true of *WALLPAPER* in section 2.3.3, which represents a metalepses between the actual world and storyworld. The interactional metalepses are therefore not foregrounded as antimimetic, even though they use an unnatural device in terms of a logical and physical impossibility. However, the narrator of *Magister Ludi*, as discussed in section 2.3.2 (metalepsis between the actual world and the storyworld elements), does draw attention to the unnaturalness of the interactional metalepsis by self-reflexively commenting on the reader's onscreen choices and foregrounding the antimimetic nature of the interaction. Thus, while a digital manifestation of a reader onscreen does not necessarily cause defamiliarization, aspects within the text can work to foreground the antimimetic. In the rest of the chapter we analyze how metaleptic techniques combine with digital fiction narratives thematically. We show the range and dexterity of metaleptic techniques in digital fiction, the medium-specific and thus relative conventionality of the different forms, and whether they can or cannot be naturalized by readers.

2.4 INTERACTIONAL METALEPSIS SUBTYPE I: METALEPTIC BREATH

While many digital fictions rely on a mouse, keyboard, or, more recently, touchscreen, for navigation, a relatively rare type of digital fiction, which Ensslin (2014a, 2009) has defined as *physio-cybertext,* also uses additional forms of human–computer interaction that result in physio-cybertextual forms of metalepsis working alongside more established forms of navigation. Physio-cybertexts are digital texts "that both integrate, through cybernetic interaction, and thematize and/or problematize functions and limitations of the human body" (Ensslin 2014a: 198). A physio-cybertext thus uses and incorporates the physiological functions of readers in terms of both their interaction with the text and their hermeneutic engagement with the narrative.

Using sound, text, and image, *The Breathing Wall*, by Kate Pullinger, Stefan Schemat, and Babel (2004, *TBW*) tells the story of Lana, who is dead and thus an unnatural in the sense of a nonmimetic narrator (see chapter 4), and her boyfriend, Michael, who has been falsely accused of Lana's murder and is in prison for the crime. In terms of navigation, the reader uses a mouse to select links within the "text space" but must also wear a headset with a microphone that sits under the reader's nose. In some parts of *TBW*, the text responds to and advances with the reader's breathing rate, but the narrative will only progress if the reader's breathing rate is slow and measured. Thus, the reader's experience of the storyworld is dictated by how their respiratory system interacts with the software with which the text is produced.

The sections of *TBW* that use the reader's breath for navigation are called "Night Dreams," and, rather than a textual narrative as found in other parts of the fiction, video and sound are used as the modes of representation. The opening screen in this section of the text displays a dark evening sky with clouds moving quickly across the vista, but the visuals contribute to the eerie atmosphere as opposed to documenting events in the narrative. As the reader breathes into the microphone, they can hear their breath through the headphones and see a small meter at the bottom of the screen that measures the depth and pace at which they are breathing. If the reader manages to breathe at a particular rate, the text releases segments of a first-person audio narrative in which Lana speaks to Michael and ultimately reveals to him (and us) how she was killed, and by whom. Thus, the reader's physio-cybernetic interaction with the text allows them to penetrate the ontological boundary of the storyworld to release information about the murder. More specifically, the fictional character, Lana, is prompted to speak by the reader's metaleptic physio-cybernetic interaction with the text and by their respiratory interaction in particular.

In the metaleptic "Night Dreams" of *TBW*, the reader who breathes successfully learns that Lana was murdered by asphyxiation. As Ensslin concludes, "By co-experiencing (with Michael) Lana's phenomenological death narrative, which merges her physical metamorphosis into 'thin air' with the reader's breathing motor, the reader reaches a maximum level of psychosomatic 'union' with the text machine and the characters within it" (2009, 147). The interactional metalepsis in *TBW* is thus used to connect the means of navigation with events within the text.

Physio-cybertexts that use the reader's breath as primary interactional means are rare, and the unusualness of this device does mean that this form of unnatural narrative has not been conventionalized. Moreover, because the reader must monitor their breathing rate in order to be rewarded with Lana's testimony, the interactionally metaleptic relationship between the reader and the text is foregrounded. However, at the same time, the respiratory metalepsis in *TBW* can also function as an immersive device. As Picot attests, "Where the technology works well [in *The Breathing Wall*], the feeling that the flow of images and sounds is controlled by our breathing makes the 'Dream' sequences authentically dreamlike and immersive" (n. pag.). Thus, while relying on an unconventional navigational device that ultimately draws attention to the antimimetic nature of the text, this form of interactional metalepsis is not necessarily so intrusive in the reader's experience that it prevents the meditative or hypnotic cybernetic feedback loop that the text aims to achieve. Rather, this medium-specific unnatural device, while relatively unconventional, can also result in an immersive experience for the reader. Indeed, *TBW* shows how an antimimetic narrative can be both defamiliarizing and immersive at the same time. The audiovisual design of the narrative and the hypnotic effects of the breathing-as-reading experience work in combination to produce a suspenseful narrative experience in which the relaxed and absorbed reader/breather can achieve narrative resolution.

While some readers may become more immersed in *TBW* as a consequence of their having to breathe slowly and calmly, the reader's breath is primarily used as the only way of advancing certain parts of the narrative and of ultimately resolving the narrative overall. Here, interactional metalepsis therefore has a navigational function that cannot be linked to either explanations within the storyworld (i.e., blending of frames; subjectification; positing a transcendental realm) or to strategies that work at a formal or genre-related metafictional level (i.e. generification; reading allegorically; satirization; do it yourself; Zen). The metaleptic breath can be read as an unnatural device that "foregrounds the thematic" because it contributes to the recurring motif of respiration, linked to the asphyxiation of Lara. However, it is used primarily as a navigational device.

Our new category of "accepted as an unnatural construction" can thus also be used to naturalize this device. Richardson (2016) explains that unnatural constructions "would qualify as unremarkable realism had they been presented in a conventional manner. What is unusual is their manner of presentation, which utterly transforms the experience of reading" (391). While it is very usual for a narrative to progress, it is not usual for a narrative to rely on a reader's respiratory system to progress. The reader-as-breather navigational device that is used in *TBW* foregrounds the antimimetic nature of this interactional metalepsis because it is not conventional and is in fact "unusual" and very much "remarkable." To use Richardson's words again, it "utterly transforms the experience of reading" and thus defamiliarizes this unique form of world-building.

Yet, while we can see metaleptic breath as a form of unnatural construction, this particular unnatural construction also deeply affects the physiological state of the reader/player. Some unnatural constructions in print, such as B. S. Johnson's *The Unfortunates*, materially implicate the reader because they have to, for example, arrange individual pamphlets that compose the narrative. However, *TBW* relies on an internal physiological process—breathing—for its antimimetic effect. In order for the narrative to progress, the reader must breathe differently, but, because breathing is such an integral physiological process, this particular unnatural construction is especially physically intrusive. The metaleptic breath "utterly transforms the experience of reading" but does so in a way that physically unites the reader with the text. *TBW* thus represents a significant example of how digital technology can be used to create very novel unnatural constructions, but it also shows that Richardson's original concept needs to be developed to account for medium-, text-, and/or technology-specific examples if it is to work as a transmedial category. Unnatural constructions in digital fiction do not just use the material affordances of the digital medium; they can also physiologically involve the reader/player in the construction of the text.

2.5 INTERACTIONAL METALEPSIS SUBTYPE II: VISUAL METALEPSES

Like the metaleptic breath analyzed above, some visual metalepses also rely on a peripheral computing device, but via a webcam and thus a more common piece of technology than the software-specific headset that we saw in *TBW* example. *Loss of Grasp*, by Serge Bouchardon and Vincent Volckaert (2010, *LoG*), is a first-person, multimodal narrative in which a contemplative protagonist considers the extent to which he is in control of his personal, professional, and spiritual life. He reveals that while he used to think "I control my destiny," he now feels "I have lost control" and asks "how can I have grasp [sic] on what happens to me?" Within the short fiction, the narrator finds a note from his wife, who appears to be leaving him, and is asked by his son to read his homework, in which he writes "I don't have a hero" and that by implication his father is not heroic to him.

The text combines static and kinetic text, colorful images, speech, sound effects, and moving images. Readers are instructed to ensure that their sound is on and to use a webcam. The reader must use pronounced physical movements to advance the narrative; they must click and hold the mouse button and/or make strong mouse strokes across the screen. Thus, the reader's physical gestures are integral to the navigation of this text (cf. Bouchardon 2014). However, the narrator's lack of autonomy is also reflected navigationally via the reader's frequent lack of agency in the text. The reader is given an illusion of control by seemingly being given choices, but they are subsequently revoked. For example, a female voice asks the reader whether they want a meeting now or later, but whichever the reader chooses, the same outcome occurs. Similarly, at numerous points in the narrative, the reading pace is determined not by the reader but by the speed with which the computer reveals the text.

In the fifth of six chapters, the narrator becomes even less confident about his circumstances and ultimately his existence. To navigate, the reader must move the mouse over chunks of text to receive more of the narrative. The narrator asks: "Am I so little here?" with the locative adverb "here" deictically anchoring the reader to the narrator's spatial point of view and thus to the world in which he exists. That he is asking such a question also signals a lack of confidence from the narrator. Readers then move the mouse to reveal "My own image seems to escape me." The narrator's hesitancy is signified stylistically by the hedged copula "seems." Grammatically also, the noun phrase "my own image," a depersonalized form of self-reference, appears in the subject position, with "me" as the object. The narrator's agency is therefore removed; something is done to "me" (him). Finally, his lack of control—or loss of grasp—is confirmed because the reader appears visually on the computer screen via the computer's webcam. The filmic image of the reader is, however, obscured, much like an animated distortion mirror. The accompanying text reads "It fails me." Here "it" is an anaphoric reference to "my own image," with "me" in the object position again. Combined with the reader's distorted image onscreen, *LoG* implies that they have taken the narrator's place in the storyworld.

LoG uses a descending interactional metalepsis to place a digital counterpart of the reader in the "text-space." It relies on the reader's interaction with the text via hardware—specifically the webcam—and it places the reader visually within the storyworld. In terms of unnatural narrative, this form of metalepsis remains unconventionalized. Not only do very few texts use webcam technology for storytelling, it is likely that the physical and logical impossibility of the reader being visually present via live streaming in the text is too affective for it not to be defamiliarizing. Moreover, the obscured image of the reader is not a faithful representation of them. Thus, the artificiality of the image draws further attention to its antimimeticism. It is used in *LoG* as a means of "foregrounding the thematic" (Alber 2016) by symbolizing the protagonist's lack of control. This visual metalepsis also functions somewhat playfully in the text because it shows the protagonist to be so hopeless that he cannot even keep control of his own testimony. Working alongside a narrative that is not primarily driven by events but instead by insights into the character, the reader's metaleptic insertion within the text offers a medium-specific surprise ending to the text.

In much the same way that the reader intrudes into the storyworld in *LoG*, visual features can also be used to cause metaleptic effects but in the opposite ascending direction. In Stuart Moulthrop's (1991a) hypertext fiction *Victory Garden,* set during the first Gulf War, a lexia entitled ". . . and . . ." describes the demise of a character named Emily as she slips into unconsciousness during a missile attack. In the succeeding default lexia, also entitled ". . . and . . . ," the same text appears as in the first, but the screen appears to have been smashed. Visually, therefore, the hypertext suggests that the storyworld has physically influenced the typographical materiality of the text that we are reading in the actual world. Importantly in this particular example, the reader clicks the mouse to reveal the cracked screen. By progressing the narrative, therefore, they are also responsible for revealing the violent act. This represents an unnatural construction because it is the visual manner of the presentation that causes the unnaturalness. It could certainly "qualify as unremarkable realism had [it] . . . been presented in a conventional manner" (Richardson 2016, 391). The ascending metalepsis suggests that the storyworld coexists ontologically alongside the actual world, with action unfolding in real time. This metaleptic jump is certainly defamiliarizing, but it is also used thematically. It serves to remind us that the Gulf War at the center of *Victory Garden*'s narrative is not simply a fictional construct but rather a phenomenon that did (and indeed continues to) have relevance in the actual world.

2.6 INTERACTIONAL METALEPSIS SUBTYPE III: METALEPTIC HYPERLINKS

Hyperlinks, Landow (2006) claims, are "the element that hypertext adds to writing" (13). Ensslin (2007) views them as "the crucial structural and aesthetic component of hypertext" (31). As an integral feature of hypertext fiction, hyperlinks can also be used metaleptically. Hyperlinks in any hypertext can be internal—leading to a destination within another part of the same document or site—or external—leading to an external website beyond the boundaries of the document or site. It is worth noting that, at the time of writing, while external hyperlinks are a conventional feature of informational hypertext (e.g., on the web) and internal hyperlinking is a conventional feature of hypertext fiction, external hyperlinking is not common in digital fiction. That is, despite being housed on the web, relatively few web-based digital fictions use external links.[4] However, because web-based digital fictions belong to the web's network of digital texts, when external links are used in fiction, they break the

---

4. Examples of works using external links include Lance Olsen and Tim Guthrie's (2005) *10:01*; Andy Campbell, Judi Alston, and Billy Johnson's (2008) *Clearance*; and Lyndee Prickitt's (2014) *We Are Angry* (see Bell 2018).

ontological frame of the fiction and can thus represent a form of ascending interactional metalepsis.

Deena Larsen's (2000) web-based hypertext fiction *Disappearing Rain* follows the family members of Anna, a first-year student at the University of Berkeley, California, as they try to discover what has happened to her following her mysterious disappearance. Third-person and first-person narratives describe the painful emotions the family feels and the plea from Anna herself to be left alone. Aside from a calligraphic symbol on the left of the screen and occasional photographic illustrations, *Disappearing Rain* is largely text-based, and, like most hypertext fictions, it contains internal links that lead to a destination within another part of the same fiction. However, it also uses external links that lead to websites that already exist on the web—they have not been created for the fiction—and thus lie beyond the boundaries of the *Disappearing Rain* site.

Some of the external links in *Disappearing Rain* are used to specify locations mentioned in the text. For example, the text tells us that "Sophie was watching and waiting for Anna to come home from Berkeley" (https://www.cddc.vt.edu/host/deena/rain/water/realities/urgentindex.html), and the proper noun "Berkeley" is hyperlinked to the official University of Berkeley website (http://www.berkeley.edu/) so that readers can get a sense from the official website of what that university is like or, rather, how it presents itself. In some cases, links are used to define items. When Amy is talking to her friend Sophie and refers to a "webcam," a hyperlink takes the reader to a webcam site (http://www.webcamworld.com) that is a directory of webcams around the world. Thus, the links are used to denote items or spaces referred to in the text and in all cases correspond to what Parker (2001) defines as a "blatant link" that "tells the reader exactly what information will be revealed when activated" (cf. Ryan 2006, 110–11) and function in the text to give "background information, explanations, supporting material" (Ryan 2016, 194). Importantly, then, while *Disappearing Rain*'s first- and third-person narrators describe and thus create the storyworld, the reader's knowledge of that domain is also provided via information that exists outside the physical boundaries of the text.

External links in *Disappearing Rain* have a primarily epistemological function insofar as they provide information about the storyworld, but they are also ontologically significant because they are metaleptic. When the reader follows a link, they move from the *Disappearing Rain* "text-space" and the storyworld it describes to sources of information that materially exist in the actual world. The ontological boundary between the two domains is thus transgressed by what is ultimately an epistemological device: the hyperlink. Since the reader is meant to use information they gather from the external websites within the storyworld of *Disappearing Rain*, they are asked to imagine either that the storyworld of *Disappearing Rain* is the same ontological domain to which they belong, or that the storyworld temporarily, but literally, reaches out to garner information from the actual world. The first case is impossible because the storyworld and the actual world are two different ontological domains, and the second case is impossible because an ontological boundary between the storyworld and the actual world would be breached.

While references to nonfictional entities, such as the University of Berkeley, in fiction are not metaleptic in themselves because they form part of the storyworld, references that are also hyperlinked and that are followed by readers to actual world websites are. As soon as the reader leaves the *Disappearing Rain* website, they are reading an external website that belongs to the actual world. While we always access our knowledge of the actual world cognitively when we read fiction, this text also materially, and ontologically, accesses the actual world.

This unnatural narrative relies on the hyperlink, a medium-specific device that has become a conventional tool of digital reading. To date, relatively few digital fictions use external linking (but see Bell 2014b, 2018, for examples), and it is thus not yet a conventionalized feature of digital literary reading. However, depending on how the links are used, they can be naturalized. A number of hypertext theorists have noted the anti-immersive quality that hyperlinks can bring to literary reading (e.g., Ryan 2015; Bell 2010; see also chapter 1). Bolter (2001), for example, suggests that the hypertext medium can cause feelings of estrangement because "whenever the reader comes to a link and is forced to make a choice, the illusion of an imagined world must break down, at least momentarily, as the reader recalls the technical circumstances of the electronic medium" (138). In the hypertextual reading experience of *Disappearing Rain*, hyperlinks do punctuate the reading experience, but the act of choosing and following links also resonates with the narrative itself; the reader must, like Anna's family and the police, digest and make connections between new and revisited pieces of information, taken from different sources.

The external links also connect thematically with the text by acting as a way of hiding information. As the reader uncovers the story in *Disappearing Rain*, we learn that Anna spent much of her time online, forging relationships with individuals unknown to Anna's family offline. Amy (Anna's sister) finds love letters on Anna's computer. Imagining what the man looks like, Amy reflects that "he could not look like any regular human. He would need to be something special to snare her sister. Only an avatar could have the stunning, shining muscles Anna required" (http://www.deenalarsen.net/rain/water/word/meaningindex.html) with "avatar" acting as an external link to the following URL: http://www.coyotesdaughter.com/azrael/pages/index.html. When followed, however, the link is broken. While this is likely an inadvertent consequence of linking to external pages on the web, in this case it works with the narrative; the broken link serves to intensify the mystery surrounding Anna's disappearance. Other broken links include a link to "Church" in the sentence "On a whim, Amy had driven down to the Church in Denver for Halloween" (http://www.deenalarsen.net/rain/water/particles/crowdsindex.html). When read at a metafictional level, the implication of this broken external link within the storyworld is that it may not actually exist or that it may have been deliberately hidden to prevent the family finding Anna as she herself may not want to be found; a letter from Anna to the police pleads, "Please don't search for me any more. I am happy where I am" (http://www.deenalarsen.net/rain/river/presence/partsindex.html).

The interactional metaleptic device on which the text relies allows the storyworld to intrude into the actual world in an uncomfortably familiar way because the text materially reaches out to the space to which the reader belongs. We can read the external hyperlinks as an unnatural device that "foregrounds the thematic" (Alber 2016) by seeing them as mirroring the search for information—or hiding of information—that takes place within the storyworld. The external hyperlinks are also medium-specifically antimimetic in that they act as means of "point[ing] out [the text's] own constructedness, the artificiality of many of its techniques, and its inherent fictionality" (Richardson 2011, 31) by defying the conventions of an existing, established medium.

Disappearing Rain was published in 2000, and the incorporation of external links in a hypertext fiction was even more unusual then than it is today. At the time of writing, while perhaps not as unusual, external links still function self-reflexively because they foreground the ontological boundary between the fictional and actual worlds. Metaleptic hyperlinks will perhaps therefore never be fully conventionalized, and their defamiliarizing effect may never be fully diminished. However, the fact that the relative familiarity of digital reading affects the extent to which external linking is noticed shows how medium-specific unnatural narrative devices may become more conventionalized over time.

2.7 INTERACTIONAL METALEPSIS SUBTYPE IV: CONVERGENT METALEPSES AND CHARACTER INTERACTIONS

The examples of metalepses analyzed so far have focused on the movement of entities from one world to the other and thus on a unidirectional ontological device. Some texts use the interactive affordances of digital media to

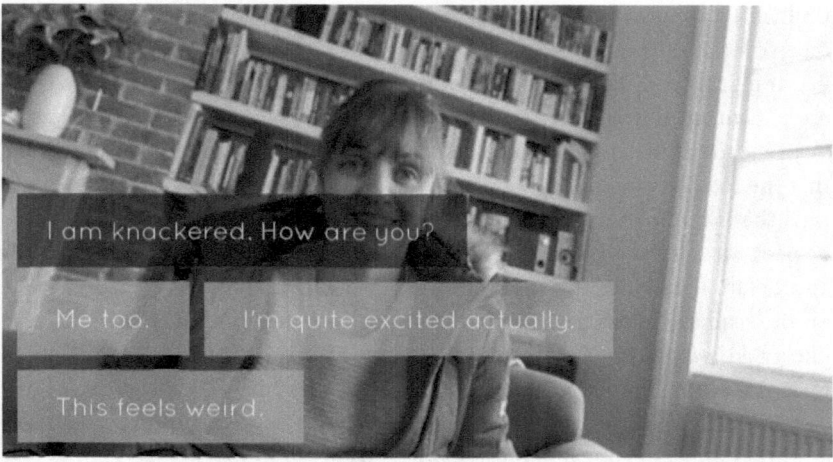

FIGURE 2.4. Screenshot from *Karen*, by Blast Theory, developed in partnership with National Theatre Wales (2015)

engage the reader in a bidirectional interaction. For example, in the "interactive drama" (Ryan 2006a: 172) *Façade*, by Michael Mateas and Andrew Stern (2005), reader/players must interact with Grace and Trip, characters from a 3D storyworld who are having marital problems. The reader/player observes conversations between the couple but is also asked questions to which they must respond by entering text on their keyboard. The reader/player thus builds a rapport with the characters, advising them and responding to their personal circumstances. The reader/player is therefore engaged in a two-way conversation with the fictional characters. The ontological boundary between the actual world and the storyworld becomes what McHale conceptualizes as "semipermeable" (1987, 34), a state that simultaneously enforces and breaks down the frontier between the two domains, making the worlds accessible to one another while also foregrounding the ontological disparity between them.

Façade takes place in a 3D animated cartoonlike storyworld whose affordances result in a relatively weak "coefficient of reality" (Limoges 2011). Representing a text with a much stronger coefficient of reality, *Karen* is an app-fiction for smartphones created by the UK-based experimental theater company Blast Theory (2015). *Karen* uses full-motion video and interactive interface elements to construct a storyworld around Karen, who is assigned as the reader's life coach. Over the course of eight days, readers receive video calls from Karen in which she divulges information about herself or else gathers information about the reader by asking them questions and requiring them to input text or select an answer from a number of options (see fig. 2.4). The entire *Karen* experience relies on the reader/player being in conversation with Karen, and, if the reader/player misses a scheduled interaction, they receive a text-message-style notification from Karen saying so, deployed with varying degrees of familiarity: for example, "I'm ready to get going when you are"; "Erm, yeah, we should do a session."

That the reader interacts with Karen via video and text responses means that the reader is in dialogue with a fictional character from a storyworld and thus that an unnatural metaleptic interaction takes place. However, various devices are in place that work to simultaneously immerse the reader/player and defamiliarize the experience for them. First, the interaction takes place on the reader/player's smartphone and thus on a device with which they will likely take part in the digital communicative methods that the app exploits in their daily life. The use of full-motion video feels like a Skype or FaceTime call, and the notifications mirror messages that readers would receive from any other app and appear alongside notifications from real people such as text messages or emails. Thus, the *Karen* experience exploits and blends into the user's more general interaction with their mobile device.

The content of the narrative also causes an uncanny level of familiarity. In our first encounter with the app, Karen walks through a street and up some stairs into her flat. She looks into the camera and says, enthusiastically, "I'm looking forward to getting to know you," with the use of second-person address directed at the reader/player. However, she undermines her authority as our life coach by adding "a bit nervous." As shown in fig. 2.4, which is taken from that first encounter with the app, the first question that Karen asks the reader/player to respond to is prefaced with "I am knackered," an overly familiar and perhaps inappropriate declaration in a professional life-coaching session. One of the answers from which the reader/player can choose—"This feels weird"—also pre-empts what they might be feeling in response to Karen's informal and overfamiliar style.

Of course, Karen is not real, and, because the actor playing her is performing a script, the reader/player cannot interrupt or guide the conversation as we would in a real conversation. However, the familiarity of the linguistic interaction, the way that Karen responds to the reader/player's input, and the accustomed conventions of digitally mediated communication on which the app-fiction relies combine to create an experience that feels uncannily real (Bell 2021). This form of metalepsis represents an ascending metaleptic intrusion from the storyworld into the actual world. However, the devices used to immerse the reader in the experience are deployed to make the reader/player think that Karen really does belong to the same world they do. It thus relies on the two worlds "converging" (Ensslin 2011a) so that the hardware through which the reader/player accesses Karen acts as a conduit rather than as an ontological barrier. Experientially, therefore, when the reader/player is engaged in this metaleptic experience, it results in an immersive experience.

As *Karen* progresses, readers are asked to give more information about themselves such as their personal goals and the names of people special to them. Karen meanwhile becomes increasingly erratic, and she and other characters in the narrative cross more personal boundaries. In the last interaction, reader/players see Karen's empty flat with all her items removed, as though she had never existed or else has left, never to return. However, she has taken with her all of the reader/player's responses to her questions and thus any personal information they have been coerced into giving. When the fictional experience ends, reader/players are invited to purchase a "data report" in which their actions are analyzed.

Ultimately, the digital technology through which we interact with *Karen* is the very thing this fiction teaches us to be cautious about. It models and problematizes the way in which we might readily give out personal information about ourselves in digitally mediated communication and datafied society more generally. Reality is shown to be an inevitable mixture of the actual and the virtual. However, stylistic, multimodal, and interactive techniques are ultimately used in this narrative experience to foreground the way that we might casually communicate across and with digital media in what might one day prove to have dangerous consequences. After all, the requests we get for personal information online are sometimes "fictional" insofar as they can come from fake sources (e.g., phishing; unauthorized data-mining).

While we can read convergent metalepsis in *Karen* as foregrounding the thematic (Alber 2016), the experience is antimimetic because it simultaneously foregrounds the ease with which we can interact with someone who is not what they claim to be and also the impossibility of interacting with a fictional character. Karen is not real, but interactions with her claim to be and can feel real. *Karen* shows such ontological ambiguity to be potentially very dangerous and therefore something that should not be uncritically conventionalized.

2.8 INTERACTIONAL METALEPSIS SUBTYPE V: CONVERGENT METALEPSES AND BLENDED WORLDS

Like *Karen*, other digital fictions exploit mobile technologies to create interactive experiences in which the actual world acts as the basis for and, crucially, merges with a digitally mediated storyworld experience. All fictional texts are based on the real world to a greater or lesser extent. Ryan's (1991) principle of minimal departure articulates how readers approach texts as though they are based on their immediate actual-world experience. She explains that when we read about a fictional world of any kind, we "project upon these worlds everything we know about reality, and we will make only the adjustments dictated by the text" (51). In effect this means that all fictional worlds are based on the actual world because our "world" schema is always based on our knowledge and experience of the actual world. When we read about entities or events that contradict that experience, we adjust our schema. While all fictional texts use the real world epistemologically, digital fictions can also use the actual world ontologically. In the analysis of hyperlinks above, we saw one such example, but mobile technology also allows actual-world spaces to be merged with fictional spaces.

34 North 118 West, by Jeremy Hight, Jeff Knowlton, and Naomi Spellman (2002), is credited in the *Electronic Literature Collection 3* as one of the "first locative-aware piece[s] of literature" (Boluk et al. 2016). It is a piece of site-specific fiction; readers used a portable computing device to explore an industrial quarter of Los Angeles while following an interactive map. When "hot spots" were found, readers heard fragments of the narrative via audio files that were location-specific, thus asking listeners to imagine the fictional stories alongside their current physical location in the actual world. Using what is now more freely available technology, *Story City* (2016) is an Australian-based app-fiction available for smartphones and tablets that relies on a similar location-based device. As readers walk through a number of Australian cities, including Brisbane and Adelaide, fragments of the narrative—as audio or text—are unlocked.

Representing a non-site-specific, but blended-world, storytelling experience, *Zombies, Run!,* by Naomi Alderman and Rebecca Levene (2012), is an augmented-reality narrative that allows users to listen to an "immersive audio drama" while they run. Addressing the user in the second person, the promotional material exemplifies the merging of storyworld and actual world: "While you run to the perfect mix of heart-pumping audio drama and pulse-pounding songs from your own playlist, you'll collect supplies to grow your base back home." This app-fiction thus combines storytelling and gameplay in a storyworld with the reader/player's exercise regime in the actual world.

There are currently eight "seasons" available, and each is divided into "missions" which are chapters of the story. Season 1 takes place over fifteen story missions whose default length is set at fifty minutes but which can be adjusted according to how long or how far the user wants to run. During the audio-recording, the user hears instructions from their comrades, who direct them through an imagined zombie-infested metropolis, and is occasionally warned when zombies are gaining on them (and thus when they should run faster). The world-building elements in *Zombies, Run!* are either sufficiently vague to allow the player to associate descriptions with themselves (e.g., "Hey, listen, I'm gonna call you Runner Five. Just 'cuz . . . I don't know your name, and we just lost a runner"; season 1, mission 1) or they ask the runner to associate elements that they might be able to see in the actual world with the landscape that is described in the audio (e.g., "You should be able to see Robinson Hospital now—one of the buildings, Gryphon Tower, is the tallest in the abandoned city"; season 1, mission 2).

Once each story mission is complete, the runner can click on an in-app map that shows their route in the actual world and the fictional artifacts in an inventory that they have collected on their mission (e.g., medical supplies, clothing). Another map of the "base" shows the area that the user and their fictional comrades must protect. The base can be explored further by zooming in on particular areas and also expanded by spending some of the supplies or materials that have been collected on previous runs. Although the user cannot interact with the other characters, other characters use the second-person address to talk to the user. For example, character Sam Yao is very reassuring and friendly to "Runner Five," while Sarah Smith begins to question the user's trustworthiness: "There's some pretty strange stuff going on out here and you turn up like a white knight" (season 1, mission 2). *Zombies, Run!* thus uses visual and audible storytelling techniques to merge the actual and fiction worlds.

As the enormous popularity of *Pokémon Go* has shown, augmented-reality experiences can cause the fictional world to have a significant effect on the actual world. Reports of people having serious or even fatal accidents while playing the game show how the metaleptic appearance of fictional entities in the actual world can have profound effects; a Pokémon becomes as much a part of the actual world as the tree the player might bump into while chasing it. *Ingress,* by Niantic, Inc. (2013), is a massively multiplayer online location-based game that uses augmented reality to connect players and tell its story. The premise for the experience is that the world has been split into two factions—the Enlightened and the Resistance—and the player must opt to be part of either one at the point of registration. When the reader/player opens the app, they see a map of their actual-world location but with additional fictional elements such as portals (currently controlled by either friend or foe), resonators (required to take over portals), and inventory items that have been dropped by and/or for others. Players can navigate to nearby portals, which are assigned varying levels of difficulty, in order to try to capture them for their faction. Portals are, according to the developers, "monuments, sculptures, unique architecture or publicly accessible art" (Ingress 2016a), and until

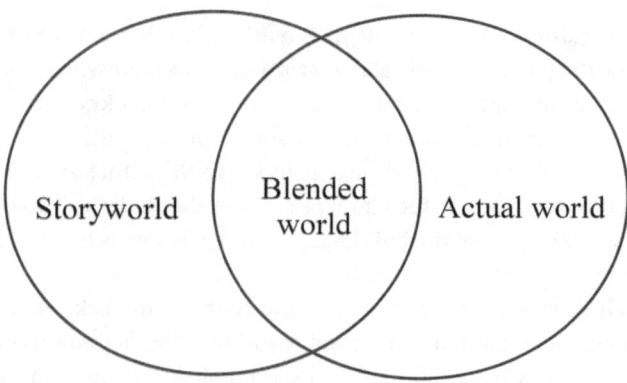

FIGURE 2.5. Convergent interactional metalepsis

recently players could propose particular actual-world elements to become portals (Ingress 2016b), thus contributing to world-building and the merging of ontological domains. *Ingress* thus turns the actual world into a playground that can be explored, added to, or colonized.

In the examples analyzed above, readers experience a digitally mediated storyworld, but, because that fiction is also based in and takes place in locations in the actual world, a blending of worlds occurs. Just as the interactions with the protagonist in the *Karen* app allow the storyworld and the actual world to come into contact for short periods, while the reader is experiencing the story in location-based narratives, the two ontological domains merge or blend. Rather than the model shown in fig. 2.3, metalepses that result in convergent or blended worlds are represented by the diagram in fig. 2.5.

Fig. 2.5 shows that there can be elements in the actual world that are not brought into the storyworld via convergent interactional metalepses. These include particular aspects of the reader/player's life in the *Karen* app or locations other than Los Angeles in *34 North 118 West*. In other fictions, such as *Zombie, Run!* and *Ingress,* the actual world and storyworld completely overlap while the player is experiencing the fiction. Each of the texts has a different thematic message—with *Zombies, Run!* more of a fun experience as opposed to a narrative with a deeper meaning. They all demonstrate the way that the actual and fictional worlds can be conflated in a way that is not necessarily unusual in a digital mediated experience. In fact, for some, talking about the separation of the digital and the nondigital is becoming increasingly problematic. Vial and Stimler (2014), for example, argue that we exist in a state of "Digital Monism" in which "the contemporary human world is inseparably digital and non-digital, online and offline or, in obsolete terms, virtual and real" (n. pag.). At the very least, our digitally mediated experiences can feel just as "real" as our offline experience and existence, and the boundary between the two can become blurred if not appear to be completely dissolved. Texts that use convergent metalepses are antimimetic because we know that the actual world cannot contain elements from or merge with the fictional world. However, because reader/players must merge the actual and fictional in order to process and become immersed in the narrative, they must also naturalize any antimimetic effects very quickly. Indeed, part of the fun of reading/playing these texts is pretending that such convergences do take place.

Examining additional ways in which a digital world can inflect the actual world is the phenomenon of "bleed" (Waern 2011). The term originates in role-playing communities and refers to situations in which feelings experienced by a fictional character are transferred to the player or vice versa. In this form of what we call *emotional metalepsis,* people can fall in love with fictional characters and use participatory media to enact their feelings (e.g., Barron 2011). As an extreme case, love affairs enacted in *Second Life* (Linden Lab 2003) have led to arguments, breakups, or even divorces in the actual world (e.g., Morris 2008). This form of what we call emotional metalepsis is "unnatural" in Alber's (2016) use of the term because entities from two different ontological domains cannot interact, and also because the same character cannot exist in two ontologically distinct domains simultaneously. However, this phenomenon is not antimimetic, because it is not defamiliarizing. In fact, it relies on the player feeling completely immersed in the experience and represents one of the ways in which the physical and logical impossibility of interactional metalepsis can go completely unnoticed.

2.9 VIRTUAL REALITY: THE ULTIMATE INTERACTIONAL METALEPSIS?

At the time of writing, virtual reality (VR) is becoming more ubiquitous as a technology for creating all kinds of digital worlds, from videogames to business meetings to training events. In any VR experience, whether accessed on a purpose-built system or a piece of ancillary equipment that turns a smartphone into VR, the user wears a headset through which they are visually enveloped by a digitally mediated world, typically supported by earphones and touch motion controllers. Users can explore the world by turning their head and looking around, by walking/traveling around the space, and by interacting with objects. Fully embodied by an avatar, they feel disconnected from the actual world while deeply immersed in a digital ontological domain.

What was once a "castle in the air" (Ryan 2015, 35) has now become a viable and, crucially, affordable form of storytelling, and digital fiction writers are experimenting with this technology. In November 2016 the British Broadcasting Corporation (BBC) launched *The Turning Forest* project, a "magical sound-led VR fairy-tale" (Pike and Watson 2016). The same year, Andy Campbell and Judi Alston (of One-to-One Development Trust's Dreaming Methods) also released a beta-VR version of the PC-based *WALLPAPER* analyzed above.

VR perhaps offers the ultimate interactional metaleptic experience. In a form of descending metalepsis, the user is not just represented onscreen as an avatar or cursor but instead fully embodied in a digital world. However, rather than being aware of the metalepsis, the user begins to experience the virtual world as though it were reality. We might even experience "presence," "a psychological state in which the virtuality of the experience is unnoticed" (Lee 2004, 32; cf. Steuer 1992). VR does not "defamiliariz[e] . . . the basic elements of narrative" (Richardson 2011, 34) but actually depends on the basic elements of narrative because the user experiences the narrative firsthand. VR is still a relatively new medium for storytelling. However, the extent of the deep immersion in VR means that the experience does not feel antimimetic—at least not in most currently available VR fictions. Although unnatural, the metalepsis is simply a very conventionalized part of the experience and one that we accept as soon as we wear the headset.

2.10 CONCLUSION

By offering a thorough exposition of the phenomenon of interactional metalepsis, this chapter has shown how hardware and software can be used to create metalepses in digital fiction in ways that are specific to the digital medium. The analysis of various subtypes of interactional metalepsis has shown how entities can move across ontological boundaries in ways that may or may not be possible in other media. It is certainly not possible in print, for example, for the reader to manifest in the text, and we have shown how some interactional metalepses, such as metaleptic breath in *The Breathing Wall*, constitute a form of unnatural construction that relies on computer hardware as well as software.

While we have focused on interactional metalepsis in digital fiction, we have also contributed to the understanding of metalepsis in narratology more widely. By offering a cognitive model of metalepsis, we move from a formalist model of narrative levels that does not always capture the way in which metalepses are conceptualized by readers to a world-based model that accounts for the ontologically transgressive nature of this narratological device. In addition to offering a generic cognitive model, we have also shown that inanimate and technologically driven entities, as opposed to characters, narrators, or readers, can act metaleptically. More specifically, visual and kinetic metalepses and external hyperlinks all suggest that inanimate entities have escaped the storyworld and had an impact on the actual world. The fact that digital media can facilitate inanimate components of a storyworld performing metaleptic jumps is significant from a theoretical point of view because most studies of metalepsis focus on the movement of a character and/or narrator between ontological domains.

This chapter has shown that while all types of metalepsis are unnatural in the sense of being logically or physically impossible (Alber 2016), they have become conventionalized to varying extents. This is because the medium-specific devices on which metalepses rely have been established within particular digital contexts to different degrees. Contrary to many analyses of print fiction which show metalepses as causing a defamiliarizing effect, the analyses in this chapter have shown that numerous interactional metalepses can also have an absorbing quality. Indeed, while ergodic digital fiction is defined by its reliance on interactivity, it has evolved from primarily using "antinarrative" devices such as fragmentation and multilinearity in text-based hypertext fictions such as *Disappearing Rain* to multimodal fiction such as *The Breathing Wall* and *Karen* in which interactivity is combined with immersion. Although interactional metalepsis relies on a highly conventionalized form of navigation in digital media, our analyses show that *unnaturalness* is a relative and potentially unstable term whose definition can change according to the temporal and medial context in which it is used.

We have focused on interactional metalepses in digital fiction specifically, but interactional metalepses can also occur in other forms of digital media. Metaleptic cursors and avatars are found throughout videogames, and they are used primarily to immerse the player in the game world. In videogames, ascending haptic metalepses can also be felt when the game controller vibrates to signify something such as an explosion that has occurred in the game world. Interactional metalepsis can occur in digital art installations. For example, in Chris Milk's (2012) "large-scale interactive triptych" *The Treachery of Sanctuary,* participants stand opposite a thirty-foot-high screen onto which their digitally captured shadow is projected. In the first part of the installation, the participant's shadow grows wings and the participant can fly by moving their arms in an upward-downward motion. In the second part, birds pick parts of the participant's digitally mediated shadow-body away, and in the third, birds spawn out of the participant's (shadow) body. In this installation, a digitally mediated counterpart of the reader metaleptically appears in the fictional world and experiences events that are impossible in the actual world but which can feel very invasive.

Given the ubiquity of metalepsis across digital media, it is likely that this ontologically transgressive device will become even more established and conventionalized within our increasingly digitally mediated lives (see Ensslin and Muse 2012). Interactional metalepses are already the immersive technique *par excellence* in digital-interactive media, and by using current or new technology, digital writers and artists will undoubtedly continue to experiment with metalepses, causing readers to reflect on their degrees of belonging, their shifting identities, and the increasingly blurring boundaries and changing priorities between the virtual and the actual.

3

Impossible Space and Time

> Leave the building you start in and the world is all immediately accessible, if a little far away, as every level is represented by an abstract shape floating in the surrounding emptiness. Learning how to get to them is tricky... and puzzles get infinitely more headache-inducing as you go. Simple move-the-block brainteasers give way to literally infinite pyramids, and long walkways turn into weaving skyscrapers you have to navigate through a series of impossible rooms.
> —Ashley Reed, "Relativity Is the Mind-Bending Cousin of Portal and Echochrome"

3.1 INTRODUCTION

In this chapter we explore how digital fiction engages with impossibilities relating to space and time, and the effects that these types of engagement can have on users' experience of, relationship with, and immersion within the storyworld. As exemplified by the game-review excerpt in the epigraph, players of spatially or temporally impossible games like *Manifold Garden* (Chyr 2017), which Reed (2015) talks about in the epigraph, are often led to describe their experience as "tricky," "headache-inducing," or "mind-bending." And yet, these players effectively naturalize, or learn how to cope with, perceived impossibilities, thereby integrating, internalizing, and functionalizing impossible spatiotemporal environments into highly effective play experiences.[1]

Generally speaking, unnatural narratologists distinguish between three large analytical themes: unnatural *storyworlds*, which are settings where impossible things happen; unnatural *minds*, typically pertaining to characters and narrators with impossible human qualities, such as omniscience or various kinds of psychopathological conditions (see chapter 4); and unnatural *acts of narration*, such as second-person narration (Alber et al. 2010; see chapter 5). Impossible spaces and uses of time form part of unnatural *storyworlds* in

---

1. Reed (2015) reviews a prototype of *Manifold Garden* called *Relativity*, for which reason the release date succeeds the publication of the review.

that they subvert reader/players' general, experientially derived assumptions of how possible worlds, including their own actual worlds, operate. In particular, the kind of Western reader/players we presuppose in this book will share the assumption that spaces are internally consistent in the sense that, for example, containers will have the same geometric dimensions and scope on the inside and the outside, and that looking at them from different perspectives will not affect this internal consistency. Similarly, we assume that interacting with objects is subject to the laws of gravity as we have come to know them, which means that an apple will fall to the ground when dropped, rather than float in midair. In terms of time, there is the shared assumption that we conceptualize time as moving forward, that we cannot stop or turn back time, and that time proceeds at the same objective, measurable speed for all human beings—regardless of how our subjective perceptions of the speed of time tend to differ and change depending on how immersed we are in an activity, for example.

The chapter is divided into two broader sections, which examine impossible space and time in digital fiction respectively. Section 3.2 explores the key importance and unique ambiguity of space in digital media arts. Digital narrative media, and in particular the kinds of 2D and 3D mimetic worlds we encounter in narrative videogames, offer reader/players unique, medium-specific spaces for experiencing stories. Even the more abstract, symbolic spaces of multimodal digital fiction make the reading experience distinctly spatialized in that readers must learn how to leverage the design and layering of the user interface to navigate and "play" the text.

Against this theoretical backdrop, we critically examine, in section 3.3, the work of Alber (2013a, 2013b) and Ryan (2012) on *unnatural* spaces and *impossible* worlds, and the ways in which these theorists apply cognitive reading strategies and possible worlds theory respectively to impossible spaces in prose fiction. We then develop our own, medium-specific theory of unnatural space and time in digital fiction, by offering analyses of unnatural spaces in digital fiction that both extend and modify existing concepts. In particular, we discuss what we define as "hypermimetic" 3D spaces that are used either mimetically or (partly) antimimetically to achieve a variety of effects in players. We also analyze impossible corporeal spaces navigated by reader/players as well as the way in which they can be naturalized as impossible yet highly immersive and potentially sociocritical reading and playing environments. We examine various kinds of spatial contradictions and incompatibilities that are naturalized through strategic game play and, simultaneously, "read" strategically as symbols or symptoms of higher-level textual meanings, such as characters' or narrators' internal states and psychopathological conditions. Similarly, our analysis of what we refer to as "impossible zooming worlds" in app-fiction and surrealist and Escher-esque game spaces examines impossible spatial designs that have to be mastered and internalized heuristically as a core game mechanic. Finally, we study experimental digital story spaces that employ highly multimodal and palimpsestic techniques of writing and semiotic arrangement so as to demonstrate the multifarious creative "writing spaces" (Bolter 1991) offered by digital media. We consider how cognitive interpretive strategies may be applied by reader/players to naturalize and/or narrativize the unnatural and integrate it into their overall ludonarrative experience. An important point we make is the relative ease with which highly logically impossible and contradictory mechanics and representations in videogames are readily embedded into the player's strategic and pragmatic repository, and we juxtapose this phenomenon with the kind of "permanently defamiliarizing" (Iversen 2016) spatial experiences typically encountered in experimental digital fiction.

In section 3.4, we examine an eclectic variety of unnatural uses of time—at both story and discourse levels—in digital fiction. Following a review of existing theories and concepts of unnatural temporality, we consider ways in which medium-specific uses of unnatural temporality require us to both adapt and expand the tools by theorists of unnatural prose fiction, drama, and film. We explore degrees of defamiliarization caused by antinomic temporality, temporal loops, anticausality, and co-deployment of different temporal logics. By inducing the concepts of multivariant chronology and cybertextual velocity, we develop our own, medium-specific concepts for digital fiction. We argue that, especially in immersive gameplay, unnatural temporality becomes not only naturalized but indeed internalized and functionalized as a means to successful game completion. By the same token, our analyses showcase how digital fiction writers may subvert the distinct possibilities of digital media design to create antimimetic experiences that play with agency and other medium-specific reader/player expectations.

3.2 SPACE AND DIGITAL NARRATIVE

There is little doubt that space and spatiality form core elements of digital media arts (Murray 2017; Aarseth 1997; Ryan 2001). In his seminal work on computers, hypertext, and the history of writing, *Writing Space,* Bolter (1991) explains that "all forms of writing are spatial, for we can only see and understand written signs as extended in a space of at least two dimensions. Each technology gives us a different space" (11). In other words, the very physical, material, representational, and medial affordances of any technology used for reading and writing (understood in a semiotically and medially inclusive, potentially overlapping way) are key for how participants of narrative communication understand the forms and meanings of the materials through which they interact. Importantly, in digital media, writing space becomes a multilayered, multidimensional, "deep" space (to adapt a concept from film theory; see Salt 1983), accessed and interacted with through screens. In this sense, reading space can assume a multitude of abstract and concrete, iconic and symbolical, representational and procedural manifestations.

Our focus on impossible spaces in this chapter is motivated by the ways in which the different spatial dimensions at play in digital fiction intersect to allow medium- and text-specific narrative experiences. As indicated in chapter 1, on multilinearity, videogames and other types of 3D immersive narratives in particular are more strongly anchored in spatial exploration than any other narrative medium. In relation to narrative games, Jenkins (2004) uses the term *environmental storytelling* to emphasize that games and other types of digital narratives are designed as simulated environments, as worlds full of characters and props for players to interact with (much like Disney World and other amusement parks). Players explore games spatially, in an episodic way, and this underlying, multilinear model is kept coherent by an overarching teleology and repetitive mechanic. Furthermore, players create their own emergent stories by exploring the game world. In doing so, they enact narratives autotelically (Ryan 2004b)—that is, they stage their own performance within the spatial constraints afforded by the game world without necessarily needing an audience.[2]

In his phenomenological theory of 3D game spaces, Nitsche (2008) distinguishes between "five conceptual planes for the analysis of game spaces" (15): "rule-based space" refers to the algorithms and mathematical rules that make up a game's source code and, combined with data and hardware restrictions, underpin and constrain the experience of gameplay. "Mediated space" relates to pictorial, cinematic, and other semiotic forms of representation of the game world we see on screen. "Fictional space" can be equated with imaginary space, and how players form mental images of game spaces, cued by stimuli they perceive and interact with in and through mediated space. "Play space" is the actual-world, physical space inhabited by the player as they interact with the hardware; and "social space" is the imagined and physically experienced,

---

2. Exceptions to this are recent public gaming and paratextual phenomena such as eSports, as well as Twitch and other Let's Play performances.

communal space that players share with others in mediated, fictional, and play space, most typically in multiplayer scenarios.

On a basic level, the ideas of mediated, fictional, and even social space may be considered as at least conceptually medium-unspecific because representation (in whatever form and style), the creation of imaginary worlds, and the assumption of social spaces shared by specific audiences (online or off) are shared across narrative media. Conversely, for digital, interactive media narratives, the focus on rule-based and play space is distinctive and necessitates analyses that take into account how the procedural, medium-, and site-specific qualities of digital fiction shape reader/players' experience and narrative comprehension. In fact, as we show in section 3.4, while many digital fictions use the same or similar kinds of rule-based or play spaces as commercial videogames, they may not integrate or accentuate action-driven ludic mechanics and, instead, spatialize interactive experiences in highly idiosyncratic and dynamic ways. Similarly, the unconventional ways in which digital fictions operationalize elements and functions in the graphical user interface may translate what is essentially a form of 2D interaction into an illusion of textual depth, layered complexity, pluri-dimensionality and pluri-directionality, architectural interaction, and topographical rather than linear progression (Bolter 1991; Ciccoricco 2007; Nitsche 2008) that can afford highly unique, surprising, immersive, and/or defamiliarizing experiences.

Although he does not engage with Nitsche's (2008) typology, Daniel Punday (2017) offers a complementary theory of space in digital narratives. He presupposes a concept akin to Nitsche's mediated space but breaks it into two different categories: "primary storytelling space" (which relates to the fictional world represented) and "orienting space." In filling an important gap in Nitsche's typology, Punday considers primary storytelling space as the space "in which gameplay or reading occurs" (92) and "where players can act" (93). "Orienting space" for Punday is the space "through which . . . primary spaces are encountered" (92), which encapsulates anything from a larger, nonplayable narrative world to interface items like "menu[s] from which game options can be chosen" (92). Thus, orienting space might be considered a category in between Nitsche's play space and mediated space that is key to a medium-specific understanding of space in digital fiction. Nonetheless, we argue that, from an ontological point of view, there is an important difference between fictional, unplayable game world elements and interface items. Whereas the former are part of the diegesis, the latter function at a meta level as they are placed in an intermediate, operational space between Nitsche's (2008) play space and mediated space. In Juul's (2005; see chapter 2) terminology, nonplayable in-game spaces are nonetheless part of the full, fictional "world-space," and interactive onscreen places, or elements, are part of the "text-space." As shown in chapter 2, the latter constitutes a key component in digital fictions' medium-specific spatial, ontological, and metaleptic qualities. In our ensuing analyses we engage with player experiences in and through the interplay between primary storytelling, world-space, and text-space.

3.3 THEORIES OF UNNATURAL SPATIALITY

In his print- and drama-oriented theory of "antimimetic spaces," Alber (2016) argues that "narrative spaces can be physically impossible (if they defy the laws of nature) or logically impossible (if they violate the principle of non-contradiction)" (186). These spatial impossibilities may range from situationally determined, spatial frames to entire socio-historico-graphical settings, and the story space (including imaginary elements conceived by characters) as a whole. They may "denaturalize our knowledge of space" (186); yet, in doing so, they always "fulfill a determinable function" rather than just being "ornamental or a form of art for art's sake" (187). The kinds of "spatial distortions" that Alber concentrates on include "manipulation of the extension of space . . . ; disruption of spatial orientation . . . ; destabilization of space . . . ; impossible creation or appearance of objects and changes to the setting . . . ; and formation of unnatural (i.e., non-actualizable) geographies" (187). Extensions of space are manipulated, for example, in unnatural containers, which are larger on the inside than on the outside. A straightforward example is Mary Poppins's seemingly bottomless carpetbag, the physical impossibility of which can easily be naturalized through a genre-specific, conventionalizing reading that situates the setting and props within the ontological possibilities of a fairy-tale world. A mixture of spatial-orientational disruption, spatial destabilization, impossible changes in setting, and formation of nonactualizable geography occur in Flann O'Brien's novel *The Third Policeman* (2001 [1967]). Alber (2013a) uses this example to demonstrate how, for example, a subjectifying or transcendentalizing reading can be applied to account for the narrator's perceived experience of a "'mysterious townland' . . . of bizarrely shaped police barracks and gigantic policemen" (Alber 2013a, 50), where a 2D police station can transform into a 3D one, and where buildings with impossible architecture are populated with dead characters and semihuman bicycles (50). Alber reads the unnatural elements in the novel as a "fantasy or hallucination that details the [dying] narrator's attempts to come to terms with the crime [he committed] and his feelings of guilt" (51) or, alternatively, as a transcendentalizing vision of the narrator's punitive afterlife, assuming he has already died.

Although not explicitly aligning with the work of unnatural narratologists, Ryan (2012) approaches impossible spaces from a possible worlds theoretical point of view, which focuses on the logical implications of such storyworlds. While she recognizes the commonality of the unnatural in the sense of physically or biologically impossible worlds, especially in fairy tales, medieval fantasy, and science fiction, she emphasizes that "an important form of experimental literature creates worlds that cannot satisfy even the most liberal interpretation of possibility. Such works transgress the logical laws of noncontradiction (not p and ~p) and excluded middle (either p or ~p)" (368; see chapter 1). She further notes that the increase in spatial (and other types of) experiments with the seemingly impossible "coincides with developments in science that replace the Newtonian vision of a clockwork universe—predictable, knowable, and deterministic—with a world full of paradoxes" (368), such as "non-Euclidean geometry; elastic time and space that shrink and expand depending on the speed at which the observer travels; . . . undecidable issues; . . . and either incompleteness or contradiction in mathematical systems" (368). It is therefore unsurprising that, especially in the area of narrative media that experiment with space (see section 3.4), we have seen a sharp increase in the production of artifacts that "rival the power of modern science to challenge the imagination" (368).

3.4 IMPOSSIBLE SPACES AND DIGITAL FICTION

It is important to note that unnatural—in Alber's sense of physically and logically impossible scenarios—uses of space are ubiquitous in digital fiction and narrative videogames in particular. In fact, if we begin from this rather broad, extrinsic definition of unnaturalness, we might say that it is partly because of the impossibilities afforded by games that they are so attractive to vast, global audiences of players (see Ensslin 2015). They enable us to escape into realms of what is normally thought to be humanly impossible or unthinkable. They "allow players to crawl, jump, run, fly, and teleport into new worlds of unheard-of form and function" (Nitsche 2008, 2), thereby "stag[ing] our [wildest] dreams and nightmares" (2) and making spatial impossibilities and other types of nonmimetic structures a *sine qua non* of game design.

Games and other types of immersive digital fiction are also arguably the most readily naturalized of all narrative media because they integrate in their procedural mechanics the very structures (unnatural or not) and "ecological" interactions (Linderoth 2011) that players are meant to internalize as effectively as possible for fast progress and high levels of satisfaction. We argue therefore that physical and logical impossibilities are not only more easily naturalized in games but indeed more easily conventionalized than in other narrative media. As we showed in chapter 2, we inhabit game worlds—no matter how mimetic, nonmimetic, or even antimimetic they are—by placing our own avatar alter ego within them. Thus, we must learn very quickly how to interact with the often highly idiosyncratic physical and logical laws of the game world and their spatiotemporal renderings, regardless of how unusual the scenarios they depict are. We internalize, functionalize, and naturalize unnatural spaces not just in Alber's sense of frame blending through observation; we actually learn how to "live" and operate within them, through procedural and experiential learning.

Yet, while reader/players can easily adapt to physically and logically impossible digital spaces, there is no denying that spatiality in some digital fictions is more intrinsically unnatural, in terms of being antimimetic (Richardson 2016), and more permanently defamiliarizing (Iversen 2016) than in others. After all, as we have established, defamiliarization is gradable rather than absolute. The following analytical sections are structured accordingly, in that they move from generally illusionist, immersive (3.4.1 and 3.4.2) to intentionally antimimetic types of unnatural spatiality (3.4.3 and 3.4.4).

3.4.1 Environmental Antimimeticism in Non- and Hypermimetic Game Worlds

In an interview with the *Guardian* (Parkin 2012), Nintendo's legendary auteur designer and director, Shigeru Miyamoto, explains that, in game design, "the key thing is surprising people. Video game development is actually a very easy tool to use to surprise people and to offer new, unexpected things to players." He confesses, however, that surprising players is becoming increasingly difficult, when "we have experienced players and players with no experience and we must accommodate the needs of both groups." In other words, conventionalization of initially antimimetic elements is far advanced in experienced players, while novice players routinely experience defamiliarizing effects vis-à-vis subjectively perceived, antimimetic effects. That said, it is within videogames' general, medium-specific mandate to stretch the boundaries of human imagination for purposes of entertainment and "surprise" (Miyamoto, quoted in Parkin 2012). Their appeal often lies in giving players the kind of agency and supernatural powers that actual life denies them, such as defying gravity and achieving superhuman jump heights, respawning and living multiple lives (simultaneously and successively), and mastering nonmimetic scenarios such as navigating highly complex fantasy worlds and beating seemingly invincible bosses (top-level enemies). For this reason, Ensslin (2015) describes videogames as "unnatural narratives *par excellence*" (43).

However, this proposition only holds true if one adopts a primarily nonmimetic concept of unnaturalness, which defines it as physically or logically impossible when measured against the foil of real-world cognitive frames. After all, commercially produced games are only meant to surprise to an extent that does not overly alienate the player, and as long as nonmimetic features remain within medium-specific genre boundaries, they minimize entrepreneurial risk and help retain large, popular player bases. This is particularly pertinent in relation to game spaces that allow avatars to implement what their human players could only dream of, such as warping, or teleporting, between distant geographic places and thereby violating the limitations of earthly physical movement as we know them. Similarly, many blockbuster games feature highly dexterous and often gravitationally unfeasible types of movement that are more akin to those of (some very light, insectoid) animals than human beings: the wall runs in *Prince of Persia*, for example, allow reader/player(s) to move along vertical surfaces for superhuman amounts of time without any visible support other than speed and thrust. The jumping art of *Super Mario* and other Nintendo-style platform characters has become a standard nonmimetic feature of the side-scroller genre. Finally, the fact that fatal interactions with space, such as falling off cliffs and other high-rise settings and props, do not normally result in reader/player(s) permadeath, or even the slightest degree of physical harm, has become a default and thus a medium-specific, widely expected ontological feature of narrative game worlds.

An exception to this nonmimetic illusionism is the Infocom Interactive Fiction *Trinity*, published by Brian Moriarty (1986) for the Commodore 64. Written during the peak of the Cold War, the work is a ludoliterary commentary on the potentially devastating effects of nuclear war. A fictional take of atomic history, it was specifically intended as a critique of the 1945 Trinity atomic bomb test in New Mexico. The opening scene, or primary storytelling space (Punday 2017), is set in a highly mimetic everyday environment: a fictional, future version of Kensington Gardens in London, where the reader/player (an American tourist) is spending the final day of their vacation. The rules governing the world around them seem to be perfectly familiar in the sense of obeying the laws of the actual world and therefore predictable up to the point when a Soviet nuclear missile, heralding the beginning of World

War III, is about to strike, and the physical environment begins to assume surreal dimensions. Not only does narrative time begin to slow down directly before the bomb hits, but the previously realistic narrative space begins to become unhinged: the exits to the gardens are suddenly being blocked by "hordes of nannies," and the grass of the lawns quite actively (and impossibly anthropomorphically) blocks the protagonist from walking across it.

In order to make an escape from likely vaporization, the reader/player must find various unconventional ways of interacting with in-game props, such as getting in the pram they have been pushing around the park (which, in itself, is a highly unlikely activity for a childless tourist to perform), opening the umbrella they have previously obtained (albeit for no particularly obvious reason at the time), using the resulting transport scenario to zoom across the inimical lawn, and finally escaping through an open door that has unexpectedly (as well as physically and logically impossibly) appeared in midair. This "Omega Door" leads to "The Wabe," a fantasy world set upon a giant sundial "peppered with toadstools" (Welbourn 2015a) and surrounded, spatiotemporally, by toadstools with doors leading to different historical nuclear explosion settings, such as Nagasaki (1945) and Siberia (1949). As suggested by the intertextual reference to Lewis Carroll's "Jabberwocky" ("'Twas brillig, and the slithy toves Did gyre and gimble in the wabe . . ."), the world unfolding around "The Wabe" follows its own, surreal logic, where "time and space will behave with their own intricate and mischievous logic" (Welbourn 2015b), and the player needs to come to terms with "the logic behind [their] newfound universe" (Welbourn 2015b). Thus, the physical, ontological, and logical boundaries of the reader/player's cognitively construed primary storytelling space (Punday 2017) are broken down in a multidimensionally impossible way that transcends their conventionalized way of mentally creating fictional space from IF interaction.

While unnatural, the sheer appearance of a door in midair is not something intrinsically antimimetic in a narrative game world. However, it does assume antimimetic dimensions in *Trinity*, the opening of which frames the storyworld in a highly mimetic setting, thereby deluding the player into a false assumption of everyday life and safety. The looming nuclear disaster, which, at the time the game was produced, was a very real political and historical possibility, transforms the physical and logical laws underlying human perception in the IF, thus creating an antimimetic diegetic challenge that the player must tackle through unconventional, creative command input (e.g., get into the pram rather than push it).

Similarly, *Trinity*'s version of a mushroom kingdom (toadstools on a giant sundial) is one that does not lend itself to the kind of smooth naturalization evoked by its cognate nonmimetic *Super Mario* settings. Contrarily, the mushroom imagery here alludes to the mushroom clouds typically caused by nuclear detonations and may thus be read as a playful but powerful satirization or parody (Alber 2016) of nuclear weapons. Thus, *Trinity* uses spatial (and temporal) antimimeticism to stage a poignant and "deeply serious atomic-age tragedy" (Maher 2015), communicating its author's "grim determination that it's only a matter of time until these Pandorean toys of ours lead to the apocalyptic inevitable" (Maher 2015), a mood that is disquietingly closer to today's political reality than it has ever been since the end of the Cold War.

Another case study in environmental antimimeticism are specific instances of what we shall here refer to as *hypermimetic game worlds*—game worlds that display extreme degrees of photorealism, overaccentuating environmental detail so that they appear to be beyond real. This hyperreal aesthetic stands in stark contrast to a game world that is, despite being set in and around a rural village with clear symptoms of being inhabited in the near past, devoid of human life. Yet what happened to the village and its inhabitants is left completely unexplained to the player as they embark on their journey through the dazzlingly overtextured game world. The latter cues players to interact with specific environmental elements (such as notes, radios, and other informational sources) to find out what happened, thus filling the gaps opened by character and plot erasure. Walking simulators such as *What Remains of Edith Finch* (Giant Sparrow 2017) and The Chinese Room's *Everybody's Gone to the Rapture* (*EGR*) and *Dear Esther* fall into this genre, as they depict visually hyperrealistic 3D worlds that evoke high levels of environmental immersion despite being practically devoid of actual (living) human beings (except for the player's first-person avatar).

Yet the effects of hypermimetic game worlds on players' levels of alienation differ according to the degrees in which the worlds' contents resemble players' real-world and fictional genre schemas. Whereas the abandoned house in the gothic world of *What Remains of Edith Finch* and the desert island in the Hebrides featured in *Dear Esther* are credible scenarios for the reader/player's trip down memory lane, the humanless setting in *Everybody's Gone to the Rapture* is alienating because of the eerie atmosphere afforded by a village that seems to have been evacuated not too long ago, with doors and windows left open as if everyone had left in a hurry, and rendered during bright daylight on a beautiful summer's day. The village, which appears to have been taken right out of a tourist promotion clip or documentary about an English countryside setting, is teeming with voices and fleeting, animated light swirls and human-shaped light effects that superimpose a symbolical, supernatural layer of meaning onto the otherwise hypericonically represented game world. Put differently, the idealized representation of the spatial environment in *EGR* follows an antimimetic strategy: it renders the pastoral-inspired mediated world (Nitsche 2008), including its setting and props, as a narrative agent, if not the main character and ludonarrative informant, of the story. In its morbidly blinding perfection, the storyworld seems to carry the curiously alienating symptoms, or rather aftereffects, of an epidemic caused by an unknown incident, which leaves hardly any physical traces of human death or suffering (except for sporadically encountered, bloodstained tissues in former residents' living rooms). The village setting thus represents an almost antiseptic form of pastoral idyll that easily leaves the player overwhelmed and somewhat numbed by the overpowering effects of this immersive hypermimetic experience.

It is a convention in narrative games to provide players with a back story to the reader/player's current situation as they enter the storyworld of a game. This can happen, for example, via written or voiced-over narrative discourse, factual news reports, or character speech, and it serves as a vital contextualization aid to the player and their understanding of what motivates their reader/player(s) in the game world. In *EGR,* by contrast, players are deprived of any worldly or otherworldly factors or information that might help them formulate a reliable explanation for what happened to the village residents. Instead, players are led to apply a range of their own strategies to understanding the background, meaning, and purpose of their experience. While a transcendentalizing strategy lends itself to making sense of the paradoxically hyperrealistic and simultaneously mystical storyworld, positing a superhuman realm is not enough to understand the unconventional lack of meta-information via backstory omission. It becomes clear during interaction with the game world that the player's main task is to find out what happened to the residents of the village, and the fact that the game itself does not provide an explicit reason for the village's utter desertion yet lack of physical devastation leaves them with an unconventionalized narrative and metaludic riddle to resolve as their key antimimetic challenge.

We refer to this medium-reflexive stance as *metamedial*: it refers to a medium-reflexive and/or medium-critical reading strategy that tests the reader/player's knowledge and experience of existing medium-specific conventions and/or the technological biases underpinning them and seeks to locate the digital writer's or game designers' intent in an attempt to subvert and innovate those conventions and/or ideologies. Thus, metamedial readings identify and expose medium-specific antimimeticism (see chapter 1) vis-à-vis medium-specific conventions. In a videogame context like the above, metamedial reading becomes metaludic as players recognize that they are playing a game that seeks to subvert or transcend conventions and techno-teleological ideologies of photorealism. Thus, our medium-conscious unnatural narratological framework demands a further expansion of Alber's reading strategies, which reflects the need to include author-designers' attempts to break genre conventions and innovate reader/player experiences without necessarily satirizing or parodying existing conventions.

3.4.2 Impossible Corporeal Spaces

In this section we look at impossible, navigable corporeal spaces in digital fiction as a form of Alber's (2013b) "non-actualizable geographic spaces." This relates to parts of a human body that become an element of the story- or game world and that have to be navigated and interacted with as primary storytelling spaces (Punday 2017) in highly idiosyncratic ways. As is the case with most uses of nonmimetic spaces, however, the phenomenological experiences of play-reading impossible corporeal spaces can be either more or less defamiliarizing.

The 3D adventure game *Psychonauts* (Schafer 2011) features a young boy called Raz as protagonist and player-character, who participates in the Whispering Rock Psychic Summer Camp, where he undergoes "psychonautic" training: a ludically implemented, heavily allegorized kind of psychoanalytical therapy helping him come to terms with the fraught relationship he has with his father, the problematic relationships with and between other characters in the game, and the struggle to survive in a psychologically and socially challenging environment. Throughout his training, Raz must solve various mysteries surrounding his coaches and fellow trainees, and he must earn specific psychic powers such as invisibility, telekinesis, pyrokinesis, and levitation, in order to progress in the game. His main training modules appear in the form of his having to physically enter the brains of his three coaches and other characters, which assume gigantic internal dimensions in order to become navigable worlds. The mental landscape of Coach and scientist Sasha Nein's brain, for example, confronts Raz with a world of geometric shapes that only partly follow the law of gravitation. The basic cube structure that serves as the platform of interaction in this level is constantly turning and shape-shifting, and can be walked upon on all sides without characters sliding or falling off the edges and planes. In fact, this impossible spatial arrangement forms the main mechanics and ludic challenge in this level and thus has to be internalized as a heuristic strategy of play.

Eccentric though the entire game world and its characters may appear, the experience of playing different brains in the sense of different levels in *Psy-*

chonauts is not permanently defamiliarizing. In actual fact, the multifarious references to Freudian psychoanalysis and the metaphorical representations of commonplace psychological concepts like *emotional baggage* and *mental cobwebs* plainly suggest to the player how they are intended to be read: as a foregrounded thematization of character subjectification, or, a combination of Alber's (2016) subjectification and thematic strategies. Furthermore, each level ends with a metaphorical boss fight that symbolizes each brain's main psychological challenge, the mastery of which materializes itself in Raz beating various types of figurative supermonsters such as the Mega Censor in Sasha Nein's brain. Thus, despite the pervasiveness of corporeal, physical, and logical impossibilities, the game is distinctly playable and immersive throughout, and it rewards players with a satisfying, happy ending, suggesting overall closure and coherence. In other words, *Psychonauts* does not cause any sense of permanent ludonarrative alienation in the player other than the commonly experienced frustration caused by fiendishly difficult puzzles and levels.

A very different walkable corporeal space is presented in *Inkubus* (2014), a 3D immersive digital fiction by Andy Campbell and Christine Wilks. *Inkubus* thematizes and problematizes, in a mixture of iconic and symbolical representations, issues surrounding young women's body image and the social pressures emanating from contemporary ideals of beauty, power, and belonging. The nameless protagonist is a teenage girl who has been grounded in her bedroom and begins chatting online with her friend, Beccy. The conversation takes the form of a partly abusive cross-examination about the protagonist's perceived popularity and the extent to which she thinks her looks contribute to it. She must choose between different conversational options, which can earn her hearts with her interlocutor (depending on how socially compliant her answers are) and allow her to come across as more or less self-confident vis-à-vis Beccy's increasingly abusive and manipulative language ("You warty meathead"; "I know your popularity. Better than you").

Towards the end of the increasingly uncomfortable and one-sided chat, the protagonist's nervous breath becomes audible to the player, who has previously only been able to see a reflection of the protagonist's face on the fictional *mis-en-abyme* screen. The heavy breathing evokes an impression of discomfort and panic, which then becomes paralleled visually by the camera fading from a surreal disfiguration of the bedroom setting into the tunneled interior of a human body. The wallpapered tunnel walls gradually transform into the walls of greatly magnified blood vessels (see fig. 3.1), which can be navigated from a first-person camera angle.

As the reader/player, alias the dreaming protagonist, moves along the red-stained channels, she is bombarded with snippets of text resembling the pre-

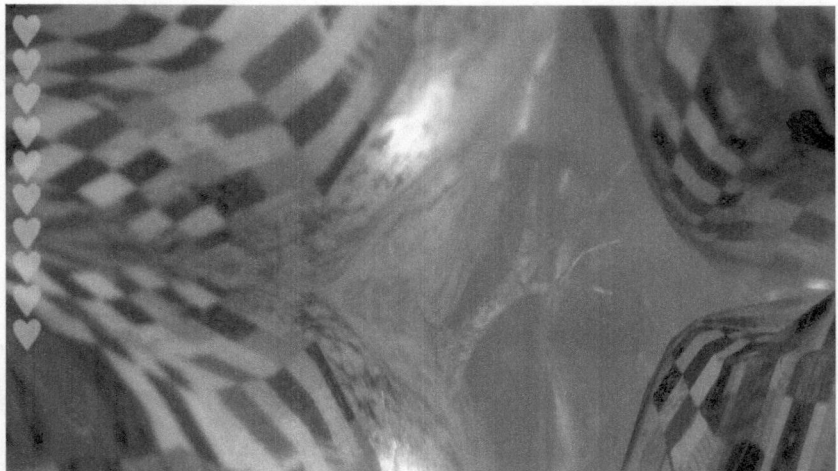

FIGURE 3.1. Surreal 3D navigable body space in *Inkubus*

FIGURE 3.2. Binary navigational choices in *Inkubus*

ceding online chat. The different options she is given take her down different chosen pathways through the body maze (fig. 3.2), making her choose between ideals of physical appearance and body image versus intellectual abilities—an unconventional semantic opposition (Jones 2002) frequently encountered by (cyber)bullied female adolescents (e.g., Peterson and Ray 2006). And indeed, choices that favor intellectual capacities result in further abusive onscreen responses, such as "dumb answer." The reader/player then receives a light that she can use as a weapon to defend herself by metaphorically shooting (or enlightening) floating representations of the beauty ideal, such as high-heeled shoes and portraits of manga-style female beauties, combined with empty slogans such as "Be an individual copy" and "Don't walk, pose!" (fig. 3.3). The

FIGURE 3.3. Enemy symbol to shoot, or throw light at, in *Inkubus*

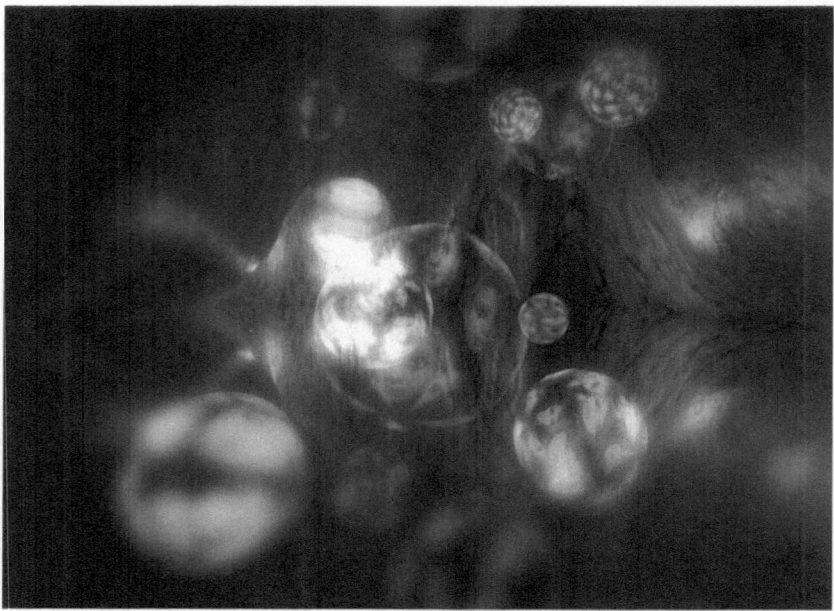

FIGURE 3.4. Identity bubbles in *Inkubus*

reader/player can escape the fight against the beauty ideal "baddies" by moving through a white onscreen swirl, which will lead her to an empty part of the tunnel system, where her pace slows and she is led to a cluster of bubbles that depict aspects of her own identity (fig. 3.4). Moving through the bubbles triggers audible cries of fear, pain, or panic, and once all bubbles have been removed, the camera returns to the screen of the computer in the protagonist's bedroom, this time reflecting an image of a girl's face distorted to intertextualize that of Edvard Munch's *The Scream* (1893). The painting, originally titled *Der Schrei der Natur* (*The Scream of Nature*), symbolizes the existential struggle of modern humanity at the turn of the twentieth century. The reference to the crisis of human nature in this subtextual link corroborates the medium-specific, antimimetic construction attempted by Campbell and Wilks.

The navigation of and interactions with impossible corporeal space as presented by *Inkubus*, paired with an open, neo-expressionist ending, thus leaves the reader/player bewildered and concerned about the realities of teenage bullying and the psychological repercussions of social pressure and unhealthy body image among young women in particular (Wertheim and Paxton 2011). Rather than being rendered playable spaces of entertainment, achievement, and willing suspension of disbelief, as is the case in *Psychonauts*, impossible corporeal spatiality is thus rendered antimimetically in *Inkubus*. Experiencing *Inkubus* likely causes a reflexive and critical attitude in the player, who is made to read their 3D interactive experience thematically and in terms of subjectification (Alber 2016), as a visceral phenomenological struggle against social pressures and counterproductive, unhealthy body image. The defamiliarizing experience further leads to didactic effects as reader/players are led to reflect on the gender politics embedded in the text's procedural rhetoric.

3.4.3 Spatial Contradictions and Incompatibilities

Recent years have seen a sharp rise in the production of narrative games that explore the ludic possibilities of spatial contradictions, non-Euclidean geometry, and Escher-esque spatial paradoxes. Games (series) such as *Monument Valley* (Ustwo Games 2014, 2017), *Antichamber* (Bruce 2013), *Back to Bed* (Bedtime Digital Games 2014), and *Portal* (Valve Software 2007, 2011) are essentially puzzle-solving platformers where players must stretch the limits of their imagination of what is geometrically feasible, possible, or logical to such an extreme degree that creative mastery of unnatural spatiality becomes their main strategic challenge. These challenges typically include shifting between, defying, and/or recombining multiple gravitational centers; connecting geographically remote, geometrically incompatible levels, platforms, pillars, and dead ends; exploring reconfigurable spaces; and working against optical illusions of spatial impossibility.

The level of narrativity employed by non-Euclidean games, however, can vary greatly. *Antichamber*, for example, features hardly any narrative elements other than its complex and confusing spatial arrangements. *Monument Valley*, by contrast, combines abstract geometric and architectural scenarios with one or more schematized characters (abstract and/or concrete) and a minimum of (albeit powerful) emotive potential. *Back to Bed* displays a Magritte-inspired, semisurrealistic representational world where the reader/player (a dog with devil's horns for ears) acts as a tritagonist, or sidekick. Our in-game actions are motivated by antagonistic spatial arrangements facing the sleepwalking protagonist, whom we must save from falling off lethal edges, by placing supersize green apples in his way. Finally, the *Portal* series arguably displays the most narrative agenda of the above-mentioned list in that the reader/player faces an antagonist—a counterforce that, albeit robotic, is to be reckoned with and adds an important psychological component to the puzzle genre. Moreover, as Moulthrop (2017) suggests in relation to the player's spatial interactions,

> We play by folding the geometry of the virtual world upon itself, creating an uncanny hyper-interiority. In choosing more or less freely to shoot connective holes in floors, walls, and other surfaces, we rearrange what in conventional games would be pre-ordained conditions of play—in effect over-folding not just the stuff of the game level, but domains of action as well. (125)

Players thus turn into co-creators of the spatial environments they are meant to overcome, which adds yet another level of productive creativity to their dealings with impossible space.

A distinctly psychological, character-driven approach to spatial contradiction is taken by Tale of Tales in *The Path* (2009), an experimental, gothic gamification of the Perrauldian "Little Red Riding Hood" myth. Players can choose between six sisters age nine to nineteen, who have to be exposed to different types of trauma—the wolf in disguise, so to speak—and tailored to their age. The game world and the player's interaction with it are designed to evoke notions of horror and premonition of what may happen, and the game's contemplative effects are partly created through slow movement through the game world (Ensslin 2015). Whenever a girl has met her wolf and experienced spiritual (or other kinds of) death as a result, she ends up lying in front of Grandmother's house, which on the outside looks fairly small. As she enters the house, however, it obtains gigantic dimensions and the semi-cut-scene after her "fall" takes her through seemingly endless corridors with countless doors and oversized interiors displaying and staging objects evocative of her nightmarish experience. Hence, the storyworld represents a medium-specific, antimimetic space where spatial extensions are manipulated to "denaturalize our knowledge of space" (Alber 2016, 186) in order to "fulfill a determinable function" (187).

The logically and physically impossible spatial dimensions of the house can be read in terms of either Alber's (2016) subjectification strategy, where players are led to attribute spatial incompatibility to character trauma, or, in an extreme reading, even to positing a transcendental realm, in which they are led to envision characters' experience of transitioning into an afterlife. However, the game also defamiliarizes in terms of its mechanics as players are forced to walk through the house in a unilinear fashion, proceeding step by step without experiencing conventionalized, medium-specific agency and exploratory freedom. The effects of this mechanics add to the subjectifying reading in that they augment players' impression of living through the girls' traumatic experience, but they also operate on a metamedial level (see section 3.4.1) as they metaludically subvert the medium-specific affordances of 3D gameplay.

Finally, we turn to a spatially impossible phenomenon in app-fictions, which we define as *impossible zooming worlds*. David Wiesner's (2015) children's app-fiction, *Spot*, plunges its readers into a multiply embedded universe of anthropomorphic insects, robots, and other nonhuman creatures, which must be navigated by using the pinch (open and close) and slide gestures. Each pinch-open zooms so far in on an object or organism that its surface becomes a new, fine-grained environment. Zooming in on a spot on a ladybug, for example, generates the image of a green island, which then enlarges into a house containing an insect robotics workshop. Various objects on a desk can then be used to zoom in on, for example, a bug family having a picnic in a park, a group of snowboarding and sledding bugs in a ski resort, and/or a group of bugs sitting underneath their umbrellas on a rainy day. Each zoom-in thus opens up a completely new, evocative narrative space, rich in nonmimetic elements and antimimetic in its interactive affordances. Each pinch-close reverts the zoom-in and returns the reader to the previous scene, or world.

The spaces we are dealing with in this app are thus exponentially deep, permeating spaces, multiply layered and each complete in its own cohesive boundaries and systemic logic. An effective reading strategy would be a combination of generification, attributing the unnatural to children's fantasy fiction, and the blending of frames. The former happens against the conventionalized foil of physical and logical impossibilities in children's fiction. However, this specific digital fiction inevitably bears, for its novelty, the connotations of a medium-specific, unnatural construction (see chapter 1), which is only possible on a gestural touchscreen interface. The medium-specific blending of frames, then, is grounded in the observation that touchscreen devices may afford experimental uses of conventionalized gestures, thus producing immersive (rather than antimimetic) storytelling scenarios that were previously held to be technically impossible, namely the movement between scenes within a primary storytelling space (Punday 2017) via zooming in on points on a map that, as a result, turn into self-contained mediated worlds (Nitsche 2008).

3.4.4 Multimodal and Palimpsestic Spaces

Contrary to the immersively oriented examples discussed in the previous section, digital fiction obtains its most antimimetic forms and effects from experimental, conceptually alienating uses of its multimodal, dynamic, and palimpsestic writing and reading spaces (Bolter 1991). These uses are mostly situated within the discipline of electronic literature, which generally presents its creative agenda as avant-garde, thus following in the footsteps of its conceptual and artistic precursors (e.g., Baroque poetry, futurism, dadaism, and Oulipian constraint; see Simanowski 2011). The multimodal affordances of digital technologies and the executable nature of code enable digital fiction authors to experiment with different combinations of written text (still or animated), verbal and nonverbal sound, film, animation, and other types of visual representations. Thus, fiction can be represented in and against a variety of settings and backgrounds, with iconic and symbolic features layering, overlapping, mixing, and mashing to an extent that makes experimentation a fundamental element of digital literature.

A prime example of such a marked multimodal and palimpsestic semiotic space is Samantha Gorman and Danny Cannizzaro's app-fiction, *Pry* (2015). The work is described by its developers as "an app hybrid of cinema, game and novel that reimagines how we might move seamlessly among words and images to explore layers of a character's consciousness" (Tender Claws 2015). As opposed to the zoom-only affordances of *Spot*, readers of *Pry* use a variety of touchscreen gestures to navigate the text's multilayered content, which involves prying open lines of text to obtain movie footage of the protagonist James's memories of his experience of the first Gulf War. James is about to lose his eyesight, and the sensory implications of this development are enacted by readers as they move their fingers across lines of braille and as they look beyond the visible text into the protagonist's subconscious dreams and associations.

The unnaturalness of the reading experience lies in its unconventional and symbolical uses of touchscreen gestures, where the conventional gesture of swiping symbolically enacts unconventional touchscreen practices such as braille reading, which is not currently available to general touchscreen users and is therefore medium-specifically antimimetic. However, the medium- and text-specifically unconventional uses of otherwise conventional gestures are readily naturalized using a variety of cognitive strategies. Prying open the protagonist's eyes through symbolic finger spread subjectifies (Alber 2016) the reading experience as entering James's subconscious musings. At the same time, a thematic foregrounding strategy (Alber 2016) allows readers to understand their interactive-palimpsestic experience as embodied insight into the long-term, destructive physical and psychological effects of war that require therapeutic interventions to engage the patient's subconscious. Finally, our proposed metamedial reading strategy shows how readers can understand their experience critically, in terms of the access restrictions and ableist ideologies underlying contemporary touchscreen design.

The idea of palimpsestic writing, or writing across conceptual and/or spatial layers, has also been explored in Jason Nelson's web-based *Dreamaphage* (version 1, 2003). The text presents readers with a 3D zoomable and clickable interface that symbolically represents the interior of a person's mind that has been infested by the imaginary Dreamaphage virus. The work consists of multiple layers of "stories, poetry, science, and multimedia playthings through a turning page interface" (Nelson 2006). The blurb invites readers to explore the dreams to find a cure for the condition, which will eventually lead to "life becoming a [fatally] looping dream" (Nelson 2003). The strongly antimimetic character of the work lies in its deliberate failure to grant readers the satisfaction of solving the riddle and finding the cure. The "orienting space" (Punday 2017) of the reader/player's interface, or "text-space," becomes a "disorienting space," with reader/players finding themselves eternally looping and zooming through the psychopathic palimpsest, trying to read meaning into seemingly incoherent clues and to navigate a space that defies any kind of teleological interaction. Thus, *Dreamaphage* invites a combination of unnaturalizing and potentially thematic reading strategies, whereby the latter may be seen in the work's symbolic hint at human failure to keep track of its own multifarious dreams. An unnaturalizing Zen reading (Alber 2016) renders *Dreamaphage* as permanently defamiliarizing (Iversen 2016), as a conceptual, avant-garde digital fiction that seems to invite problem-solving yet subverts the reader's expectations repeatedly, with every failed attempt at obtaining closure.

In recent years, palimpsestic 3D *immersive* fictions have become a trademark of a particular group of digital writers and artists, namely Judi Alston, Mez Breeze, Andy Campbell, and Christine Wilks. In forensic-mnemonic works such as *Consensus Trance II* (Campbell and Alston 2010), *All the Deli-*

cate Duplicates (Breeze and Campbell 2017), and *WALLPAPER* (Campbell and Alston 2015), mimetic 3D environments are superimposed with lines, chunks, and circles of writing, which lend the environment an atmosphere of supernatural literary orality.

All the Delicate Duplicates (*ADD*) deploys palimpsestic text to render interior monologues and dreamlike associations of the protagonist, John Sykes, a single father who experiences moments of his past life, his subconscious mind, as well as imagined and written utterances from other characters, most importantly those of his daughter Charlotte. Palimpsestic text appears in different shapes and fonts, on different surfaces, wrapped around trees, or as ribbons floating through the air like wafts of wind. This adds a strongly defamiliarizing element to the more "naturally" occurring textual material—for instance, from computer and cell phone screens, as well as written notes and books.

In *ADD*, palimpsestic text becomes a constituent element of the temporally and spatially layered, primary storytelling space (Punday 2017), combining navigational functions with narrative clues, character speech snippets and purely decorative items. In fact, we argue that the text synthesizes various medium-specific impossible spatialities. Similar to *The Path*, the interior of the house that forms the major backdrop of the storyworld assumes near-indefinite dimensions as the protagonist meanders through recursively arranged interiors in a seemingly delirious or psychedelic state. This seems strangely paradoxical, as the 3D game world follows principles similar to those of the hypermimetic game worlds mentioned in section 3.4.1, except that the textual layering and infiltration strongly distracts reader/players from the more mimetic elements in the storyworld. The further the reader/player progresses in the narrative, the more the game world seems to turn into some kind of audiovisual representation of a mental rather than physical landscape—similar yet decisively more alienating than the brain worlds of *Psychonauts*, for example. Furthermore, during the dreamlike outdoor scenes, the projected phrase "You're not here. This isn't now" adds a level of linguistic defamiliarization. It suggests a logical paradox of impossible spatial and temporal deictic negation seemingly denying the narratee (or metaleptically addressed player) their very real experience of the protagonist's surreal, dreamlike traversal.

In line with the narrative's focus on quantum physics and multiverse theory, here and elsewhere in *ADD*, impossible spatiality is combined with impossible temporality. The game world consists of different, spatially represented time periods (e.g., the years 2006 and 2011), which reader/player(s) navigate and explore in the tradition of time travel to obtain clues—from different phases of John's life and different places inhabited by him. Yet, while time travel is a regular and conventionalized feature of a variety of sci-fi narratives, here the logical and physical impossibility becomes defamiliarizing, as we are experiencing an interactive medium that resembles the mechanics and narrative representations of a 3D game world and yet refuses to ease player/readers into a straightforward, immersive ludonarrative experience. Rather, spatiotemporality is used antimimetically to subvert player expectations of a coherent, (non)mimetic game world that uses text sparingly for illustrative and navigational purposes, rather than as a key, pervasive and forensic and simultaneously distractive storytelling device. This inspires a metamedial reading strategy, which causes reader/players to reflect on the ludoliterary strategies they must develop to play a game that defies ludic conventions while calling for unconventional, medium-specific literary-linguistic engagement.

3.5 IMPOSSIBLE TEMPORALITY IN DIGITAL FICTION

As our discussion of *ADD* in the previous section indicates, unnatural spatiality can be chronotopically combined with unnatural temporality in digital fiction. Not only are spatial representations in the game distorted into grotesque, surreal mixtures of physical and visionary landscapes; the reader/player is literally thrown back and forward in time and space at numerous stages throughout the game. The experience of reconstructing traumatic memories is rendered in nonsequential form, and players are led to piece together, by interacting with textual and nontextual objects in the game world within their historical contexts, the contextual puzzle of who the mysterious person Mo is, or was, and what role she plays/ed in the main characters' lives. The narrative experience of *ADD* hence contradicts three of our most basic human intuitions: that time flows forward, "in a fixed direction," that "you cannot fight this [linear] flow and go back in time" (Ryan 2009, 142), and that, ultimately, "the borders between the past, the present, and the future are fixed and impenetrable" (Alber 2012, 183).

In a subjectifying reading of the game (Alber 2016), of course, this multilinear and multilayered experience of time can be narrativized to an extent at least by following reading strategies that we know from print fiction and film, where we are used to construing a chronological fabula from a nonchronologically arranged syuzhet. However, the complete and precise chronological order of how events evolved during the years documented in *ADD* remains obscure to the reader. In fact, it is part of the intended aesthetic effects of the narrative to leave at least some aspects of the story up to the reader's imagination and speculation. The diegetic opacity evoked by the chronotopic arrangement, or unnatural construction (Richardson 2016), of the game parallels the protagonists' confusion and visceral experience of trauma and amnesia. Similarly, the textual fragmentation and disarray experienced by the reader/player can be naturalized by means of subjectification: by ascribing it to the phenomenology of the protagonists' traumatic musings. However, the aesthetic experience and disorientation resulting from the game's deliberate elision of any instructional material or metacommentary leave the player in a bewilderingly empathic state vis-à-vis the traumatized main characters, thus contributing to *ADD*'s antimimetic aesthetic.

To the two above-mentioned general human intuitions about time—that it flows forward constantly and cannot be reversed—further logical assumptions can be added: first, there is a shared belief (at least among Western audiences) that "causes always precede their effects" (Ryan 2009, 142), which means there is a monolinear logic underlying causal chains that cannot be reversed (e.g., a bruise must be the result of an accident rather than vice versa). Another assumption is that "the past is written once and for all" (142), which means what happened in the past cannot be undone. Furthermore, humans in Western cultures tend to share an understanding that, objectively, "the flow of time cannot be sped up or slowed down" (Alber 2012, 183) and that this flow is reflected by globally agreed, mechanical time measurement. Alber (2012) explains that, from a logical point of view, "it is not possible for an event to happen and not happen at the same point in time" (184; see also chapter 1), which implies that if someone denies the proven, historical facticity of an event (such as the Holocaust), they are generally assumed to be liars. Finally, people in Western societies tend to agree that "eternity is unreachable and ungraspable" (184), which has generated religious and philosophical myths and visions surrounding apocalyptic thought.

Against this logical-ontological backdrop, Alber (2013b) explains that "unnatural temporalities challenge our real-world ideas about time and temporal progression" (n. pag.) and cause us to apply reading strategies that either naturalize temporal aporias as part of a frame blend or subjectification narrative, or unnaturalize them as cognitively unresolvable. As Heinze (2013) suggests, "Narratives that subvert one or more of [our human] axioms about time are almost inevitably situated in the realm of the physically and logically impossible by readers" (33), and this is despite the fact that human assumptions about time do not necessarily align with the laws of actual physics and the experimentally verified postulations of relativity and quantum mechanics.

In relation to the effects of unnatural temporality, Heinze (2013) shows that an important distinction must be drawn between temporalities at the level of fabula (story) and the level of syuzhet (discourse). As detailed in chapter 1, fabula refers to the underlying sequence of events as they happen in chronological order, and syuzhet is the way these events are arranged and reordered at the plot level. Narrative audiences are likely more used to piecing together a storyline that has been chronologically rearranged at plot level than to being confronted with a temporally disarranged story. Typical examples of plot-level desequentialization are crime fiction novels that use nonchronological arrangement to create suspense, as well as experimental films like Nolan's (2000) *Memento*. In fact, syuzhet-level reorganization and desequentialization using pro- and analepses is a fully conventionalized narrative technique across narrative media and has been used as a highly effective storytelling technique across narrative media history.

When it comes to unnatural experiments with time, the assumption that a consistent story can be pieced together by engaging with discourse-level material is often subverted. Indeed, as Alber (2016) suggests, "in unnatural narratives the story is no longer the sacrosanct chronological sequence of events that can then be represented in different ways at the level of the narrative discourse. The story itself can also be unnatural, that is, physically or logically impossible" (151; cf. Richardson 2002, 52). Thus, readers' logical intuitions about time are undermined, causing them to reconfigure their cognitive frames and scripts, at least in relation to the rules of the storyworld they are presented with by the narrative in question.

Unnatural narrative theory has shown that these cognitive challenges include a range of different unnatural temporal techniques. Firstly, retrogressive, or antinomic, temporality occurs in narratives that reverse the scripts of everyday life (Richardson 2002; Alber 2013b). An example often mentioned by unnatural narratologists is that of Martin Amis's novel *Time's Arrow* (1991), in which "intradiegetic time (time within the story) moves backward . . . at the level of story [rather than discourse]" (Alber 2016, 153–54) and presents us with a narrator that experiences his life from death to birth in reverse, thus lending the represented actions different meanings: "for instance, the narrator thinks that taxi drivers and prostitutes pay their clients . . . ; that patients become sick after being treated . . . ; and, most disturbingly, that [the protagonist] Odilo, a former German Nazi doctor, is creating Jews at Auschwitz (here 'exterminating' becomes 'creating')" (154).

A second, typical scenario of unnatural temporality are eternal temporal loops, or circular temporalities (Richardson 2002), where the narrative, or a character, seems to be going around in circles, as in a Moebius strip. As Alber's example demonstrates, in Samuel Beckett's play *Play* (1963), the characters, M, W1, and W2, are caught in an eternal loop of having to retell their lives "in a strange purgatorial world" (Alber 2012, 183). A slight variation of the loop can be found in multivariant film narratives like Harold Ramis's (1993) *Groundhog Day*, where the narrative returns to the same scene again and again: a morning in the life of the protagonist Phil Connors, who is made to relive the same day repeatedly, until he manages to transform his life and to fall in love, at which point he succeeds in escaping the loop.

Third, so-called chronomontages (Yacobi 1988; Alber 2012) are conflated timelines conjoining different, incongruous temporal zones and mixing incommensurate elements from different time periods. In Gilliam's (1981) fantasy film comedy *Time Bandits*, for example, time traveler Kevin is catapulted into the historical past of ancient Greece, wearing his own, late twentieth-century clothes and taking photos with his Polaroid camera. Another example mentioned by Alber (2012, 2016) is Ishmael Reed's print novel *Flight to Canada* (1976). It is "set in the United States and Canada of the 1860s (or what the slaveholder Arthur Swille calls 'the pre-technological pre-post-rational age' . . .)" yet combines "numerous forms of [twentieth-century] technology and commodity culture" (Alber 2012, 175). Thus, the novel conflates early and late forms of capitalist modernism and accentuates that "there has been technological progress but no real spiritual or moral development" (Alber 2016, 167) between the two time periods.

Fourth, in narratives of reversed causality, the present is caused by the future, thus contravening the principle that causes always precede their effects as well as our logical assumption that "we remember the past but not the future" (Hawking 1988, 144). An example of reversed causality from print fiction, according to Alber (2012), is D. M. Thomas's magical-realist novel *The White Hotel* (1981). The narrative contains "another unnatural time line," where the protagonist Lisa (alias Anna) Erdman's "feelings of pain in the present are (impossibly) caused by a maltreatment that happens in the future" (Alber 2012, 178). Hence, the causality lies in a paradoxical premonition about the future and the physical (yet perhaps not entirely psychosomatic) impossibility of a body "literally feel[ing] the future, namely Lisa/Anna's brutal murder at Babi Yar, a ravine in Kiev, in 1941" (178–79).

A fifth type of unnatural temporality is contradictory temporality (Richardson 2002), which aligns with concepts of contradictory multilinearity as discussed in chapter 1. Here the narrative presents the reader with several mutually exclusive events or sequences, which could not have happened at the same time because they logically contradict each other. Coover's (1969) short story "The Babysitter," for example, presents the reader with hierarchically equivalent yet mutually exclusive plot options, which suggest that, for instance, the baby's father, Mr. Tucker, both did and did not go home to have sex with the babysitter, that the babysitter did and did not answer the phone, and even that the sitter and all the children did and did not die.

Finally, Richardson (2002) lists differential temporality and multiple timelines as typical cases of unnatural temporality occurring in more than one element of plot at the same time. Differential temporality, which Yacobi (1988, 95) refers to as "telescoping," relates to timelines that move in different directions or at differing paces, such as the divergent aging speeds of the characters in Woolf's *Orlando* (1928), and the juxtaposition of a gradually aging protagonist with another one that keeps getting younger in F. Scott Fitzgerald's short story "The Curious Case of Benjamin Button" (1922; adapted to a namesake Hollywood blockbuster in 2008). Multiple timelines occur in narratives where different plotlines proceed at different speeds yet converge again towards the end of the story. This happens, for example, in Shakespeare's *A Midsummer Night's Dream,* "a play replete with sly allusions to skewed chronology" (Richardson 2002, 51), where the duke and his entourage experience the time span of four days and three nights, whereas, for the lovers in the enchanted forest, only two days and one night pass during the same time.

In the analyses that follow, we both adapt existing theoretical concepts, such as antinomic temporality, temporal loops, and anticausality, and introduce new, medium-specific ones, namely multivariant chronology and cybertextual velocity. We explore the extent to which these unnatural uses of time lend themselves to narrativization, naturalization, and conventionalization and demonstrate that, once again, in the case of rule-driven, ludic digital fictions, any initial antimimeticism has to be naturalized if not internalized swiftly by players in order to succeed and progress in the game. The most permanently defamiliarizing forms of unnatural temporality, however, are again found in experimental forms of narrative electronic literature.

3.5.1 Antinomic Temporality

As demonstrated by the example of Amis's *Time's Arrow,* antinomic temporality used at the level of fabula can deliver a powerful account of human subjectivity that can take readers on a reverse-linear journey down memory lane. Rendered in 16-bit pixelated retro-graphics, Freebird Games's (2011) role-playing adventure game *To the Moon* features scientists Dr. Rosalene and Dr. Watts, who are hired by the aged Johnny Wiles on his deathbed to reconstruct his memories in reverse order, thus enabling him to remember the reason for his final wish, to go to the moon. The player, represented in the game world by the two scientists, embarks on a reverse biographic journey to bring back

Wiles's memories of his deceased wife, River, including details such as how they met and how they spent their life together, as well as the tragic events that ultimately caused his amnesia. Level by level, the reader/player thus unveils elements of Wiles's past, jigsawing together his complex biography (Ensslin 2014a, 156–57). To do so, players have to retrieve mnemonic, psychologically energizing objects from Johnny's house and other places where he spent parts of his life. Thus, the game uses a similar type of object-oriented mnemonic storytelling featured in *All the Delicate Duplicates,* except in a decisively less antimimetic, disorienting manner for the player. The most likely reading strategy employed by players in order to naturalize the unnatural in this game would be generification (Alber 2016), which attributes the supernatural to a sci-fi conceptual framework.

Whereas antinomic temporality is employed mostly at a narrative level in *To the Moon,* other games implement it at the level of mechanics, thus making it a core element of actual gameplay. As discussed in chapter 1, the graphic adventure game *Life Is Strange* allows players to rewind time and undo what they just did for a short timespan ranging from a few seconds "to a couple of minutes depending on the context . . . [b]oth when making large-scale narrative decisions and also when just walking around and exploring" (Albin 2016, n. pag.). However, there is a limit to the number of rewinds, thus committing the player to one (conceptually corrective) rather than indefinite changes of mind.

A game that embeds a number of unnatural temporalities in its key mechanics is Jonathan Blow's 2D platform game, *Braid* (2009). In a subversive take on a frequently critiqued videogame trope, the game's protagonist, Tim, is on a quest to save the princess, beg her forgiveness for a mistake he made, and live happily ever after. However, towards the end of the game, he has to learn that she does not actually want to be saved and prefers to stay with the monster instead, to escape the burden of marriage. Thus, the game turns out to undermine some of the key phallocentric and misogynist tendencies dominating mainstream game culture in which macho male characters save stereotypically feminine female characters, which usually results in their romantic union.

Braid comprises six levels, rendered as self-contained worlds with unique temporal logics and mechanics. Players must understand, internalize, and ludically operationalize these temporal mechanics, often against their real-world and genre-specific intuitions, in order to be successful. In the "Time and Forgiveness" level, players can rewind time by holding the shift key, thus empowering Tim, for example, to "un-die" (rather than respawn) indefinitely. Indeed, certain achievements become possible only through this rewind function (e.g., unlosing a key in a situation that then enables Tim to reach the door he has to unlock), and the level can only be completed if players learn to master its antinomic mechanics in an environment that is riddled with proliferating enemies and environmental challenges. On the whole, then, impossible (in the sense of unconventional) ludonarrative temporality in *Braid* can be read thematically (Alber 2016), as a way of engaging with the relativity and subjectivity of temporal experience. Second, a metamedial reading as introduced earlier in this chapter can be applied specifically to the medium-specific antimimeticism of the game. In this case, the game can be seen to foreground and subvert players' medium-specific expectations and to showcase how videogame mechanics might stretch and rewire human imagination and logic reasoning, by demonstrating how readily players internalize and master seemingly counterintuitive concepts of time and temporality.

A third possible strategy is an allegorical reading (Alber 2016), critiquing Faustian hubris and in particular the gravity and irreversibility of human error and suffering in the nuclear age. Intertextually, then, *Braid* can be seen to reference Moriarty's Interactive Fiction *Trinity* (see section 3.4.1; for Blow's own explanation of being influenced by *Trinity*, see Bentley 2012). Both games reference, explicitly or implicitly, the Trinity nuclear bomb test of 1945, directly preceding the destruction of Hiroshima and Nagasaki. *Braid*'s complex, diverse, and unconventional treatment of unnatural time alludes to the surreal experience of "time [standing] still" (Moriarty 1986) as the bomb strikes, and especially to the kind of phallocentric heroism that renders humankind godlike, often with horrendous consequences. In relation to the subtextual parallelism drawn to the Trinity test, Bentley (2012) comments that the game's protagonist, Tim, may well be seen as "a childlike version of [J. Robert] Oppenheimer (the hollow cheeks, the thin face and nose)," as the character reflects Oppenheimer's "personality, his life, his relationships, triumphs and failings." Thus, metamediality as a reading strategy is here mixed with allegorizing intertextuality on a fictional, biographical, and historiographical level.

In all three games discussed in this section, players are made to attribute the nonmimetic possibilities they have in relation to time to the "magic" (Ryan 2006b, 670) inherent in the ontological parameters of the primary storytelling space (Punday 2017). This "magic," as discussed above, is conventionally embedded (Alber 2016; Ensslin 2015) in fantasy role-playing games, and players easily normalize, functionalize, and internalize the mechanics that allows them to rewind time, thus optimizing gameplay efficiency and/or narrative-philosophical depth. In *Braid* in particular, antinomic temporality is further interwoven with otherwise highly challenging gameplay mechanics, thus increasing its antimimetic effects on players who have to both expand their conceptual framework as well as implement its resulting rules and required actions in effective gameplay.

3.5.2 Multivariant Chronology

This section examines different ways in which chronology at story level is broken up and remixed in more or less narrativizable ways, thereby disrupting the chronological linearity of the underlying story or indeed its reverse, antinomic temporality (see previous section). Multivariant chronology, as we shall refer to the phenomenon of fragmentation and rearrangement at story level in digital fiction, is frequently used to represent the ungraspable nature of human memory. We distinguish the term *multivariant chronology* from Genette's (1980) cognate concept of *anachrony*, which applies to the rather more fixed plot and time arrangements we know from print fiction. Multivariant chronology, by contrast, is distinctly medium-specific, as readers and players of digital fiction are often required to create their own pathways through the storyworld (see chapter 1), thus experiencing different degrees and varieties of temporal rearrangement that affect their understanding of what happened in the story, who experienced these events, and in what order.

As argued earlier in this chapter, the rearrangement of chronology at discourse level is a fully conventionalized element across narrative media, including digital narratives. Indeed, it has been implemented effectively in blockbuster videogames such as *Beyond Two Souls* (Quantic Dream 2013). In this first-/third-person action adventure, the protagonist's biography is broken up and rearranged, thus causing a crisscrossing of prolepses and analepses. Her fragmented and confused subjectivity adds to the overall supernatural atmosphere of the game. Nevertheless, the aesthetic effects of this storytelling technique do not leave players permanently defamiliarized—unlike in Nolan's movie *Memento*, for example, which also uses discourse-level fragmentation and rearrangement. On the contrary, the game implements highly immersive levels of interactive narrativity that make psychological confusion, telekinesis, and other nonmimetic, superhuman powers both highly playable and narrativizable.

A digital fiction that uses multivariant chronology at discourse and story level, and to considerable antimimetic effects, is Sam Barlow's interactive crime mystery, *Her Story* (2015). The player's main goal in the game is to find out, by watching video snippets of a police interrogation, whether the protagonist, Hannah Smith, is guilty of murdering her husband, Simon. Adopting a concept used in linguistic typology to describe the morphology of specific types of synthetic languages, Hussey (2017) uses the term *agglutinative* to describe the way in which players activate individual videos of the culprit's interrogation in a seemingly random, quasi-hypertextual fashion and arrange them into highly individualized discourse-level sequences. Not only does this play style evoke different versions of who might have killed Simon; it also inspires different temporal sequences, and even different possible lives and character constellations of the protagonistic "Eve-Hannah complex" (i.e., the question of whether either of the twins, Eve or Hannah, committed the murder, or indeed both, or whether either one of them is a fantasy construct). As Hussey (2017) shows, unnatural, multivariant temporality therefore resides within the game's

> non-temporal organization[, which] resists any given player's impulsive urge simply to view the tapes in chronological order. Instead, the player queries the database through a search engine, using keywords gleaned from the transcriptions. (173)

The player's mental framework of the circumstances within which the murder happened, as well as the protagonist's longer-term biographical background, thus shape-shifts around a variety of temporally rendered, "agglutinative formations." These formations may be conceptualized as a labyrinthine structure, with different emergent timelines leading either to a more coherent imaginary storyline, or indeed to a dead end. Overall, this narrative arrangement lends itself to a subjectifying reading strategy, which renders the protagonist ontologically ambiguous and fundamentally unreliable, thus leaving the actual answer to the murder mystery open throughout.

An older example of antimimetic, multivariant temporality is Rob Swigart's (2002) web-based hypertext, *About Time*. Subtitled *A Digital Interactive Hypertext Fiction, Two Braided Parallel Paths, A Double Helix*, it eponymously implements the idea of a DNA helix to interweave two story "'times' that are, on the surface, far removed, but nevertheless continually bumping up against one another" (Ciccoricco 2010, n. pag.). These story times relate to two temporally far removed characters: Crockford (Cro) de Granville, a greedy businessman living in the present day, and Mouth, an Indigenous figure who lives 40,000 years before de Granville. Readers can choose which character to follow by choosing one of two sequentially organized, yet hypertextually crisscrossable strands.

The blurb explains *About Time*'s underlying, impossible temporal assumption, "that all of human time is now, though, some aspects of now are more distant than others, temporally speaking. While some files may be very far away, they are available with a click." The "click" refers to an icon at the bottom of each page that multimodally connects both strands. The perceived spatial proximity of the click, implemented via the user interface, is thus conceived as both removing or diminishing human historicity and as making the present appear more distanced, so much so that, as the blurb explains, "all time is equal. History is merely one possible ordering of event for the convenience of temporally unidirectional beings." Thus, we may apply a didactic reading strategy that focuses on the thematic foregrounding (Alber 2016) of the complex and subjective relationships between time and human perception, as well as ideologically charged hegemonial conceptualizations of modern capitalism vis-à-vis Indigenous civilizations.

3.5.3 Cybertextual Velocity and Temporal Loops

An important distinction made by narratologists is between "discourse time," the time it takes to read a story, and "story time" (also called "diegetic time"), which represents real time as it unfolds in the storyworld (Chatman 1978, 62). Clashes between discourse and story time, or anisochronies (Genette 1980, 86), need not necessarily appear alienating to readers. In fact, techniques such as summary, where fictional events are condensed so as to shrink story time vis-à-vis discourse time, or scene, where the time it takes to narrate a fictional event exceeds the duration of the event, are used ubiquitously and are fully conventionalized in fiction writing and other narrative media.

In digital fiction, however, antimimetic uses of discourse time often affect readers' perceptions of story time, which is partly an effect of the dynamics and fluidity of textual material displayed on interactive screens. In this section, then, we discuss texts that reduce reader agency to a degree that makes intentional and controlled interaction either futile or indeed impossible and, as a result, impedes the incremental generation of mental models of story time. In digital fiction as in print, story time is real time as it unfolds in the storyworld. However, discourse time can either be the time the reader takes to read the text (as in print) or, in particular cases, the time given to read and interact with the textual material onscreen. In texts like Stuart Moulthrop's web-based hypertext fiction, *Hegirascope* (1995/1997); Anthropy's Twine game, *Queers in Love at the End of the World* (see chapter 1); and Young Hae Chang Heavy Industry's (YHCHI) Flash fiction, *Dakota* (2001), text is displayed only momentarily onscreen. Thus, the reader is forced to read the text at a pace dictated by the software in which the fiction is written. Adopting terminology used by Ensslin (2007, drawing on Aarseth 1997) to describe works of electronic literature that empower the underlying program code at the cost of reader agency, we use the term *cybertextual velocity* to describe this aesthetic process. More specifically, cybertextual velocity manipulates the time given to readers to peruse discourse-level textual material, thereby diminishing their agency and ability to read at their own pace. Instead, the reading experience turns into a counterintuitive, quasi-ludic race against time, which can have permanently alienating effects on the reader.

Cybertextual velocity gives the reader more or less agency depending on the text. *Hegirascope* allows readers some degree of agency: its interactive screen refreshes and changes every eighteen (in the first version) and thirty (in the second version) seconds, thus forcing readers to choose their next link within the given time frame, and decisively more forcefully so in the first than in the second version. Although, strictly speaking, thirty seconds is long enough even for a slow reader to cover all the textual material on screen, the fact that reading becomes a timed performance distracts readers from becoming fully immersed into the diegesis of the story (if indeed there is one). Even more antimimetic is the approach followed by YHCHI in *Dakota,* which essentially consists of animated onscreen text that allows no reader interaction and, instead, changes the pace of changing text chunks to speeds that border on illegibility. The hammering soundtrack augments the hectic pace at which the narrative unfolds before the reader's eyes, and the fact that readers cannot rewind and replay individually chosen sections for enhanced understanding turns the text into an antagonistic force. In both *Hegirascope* and *Dakota,* it is near-impossible to apply any naturalizing reading strategy. Instead, a Zen approach to unnaturalizing experimental, avant-garde electronic literature (see section 3.4.4), as well as to rereading and re-viewing likely yields deeper understanding, appreciation, and memorization.

Temporal loops—the second topic covered in this section—are a common feature of digital fiction. They are used in various ways by digital writers and game developers, and to different degrees of antimimetic defamiliarization. A highly conventionalized form of temporal looping is common in videogames, where reader/players regularly have several if not infinite lives and therefore respawn, or come back to life, in numerous places throughout the game. Respawning does not necessarily have to throw players back to the beginning of the game; over the years it has become rather more common for narrative games to teleport avatars back to earlier positions in the same game level that are nonetheless within easy reach of where they met their (temporary) downfall, or to positions immediately following save points. Avoiding having to start from scratch (also called *permadeath*) is generally seen to enhance player motivation and to reduce levels of frustration. That said, recently there has been a countertrend to raise the stakes of player investment in gameplay and to introduce more permadeath games (Allison et al. 2015; Falkenstern 2013). Generally speaking, however, respawns as forms of temporal loops are fully conventionalized and tend to be seen as part of the challenge of making progress and maximizing player performance in all kinds of videogames.

The expectation of temporal looping in the interest of skill improvement and progress, garnered by players from exposure to blockbuster narrative games, is parodied in Davey Wreden's experimental first-person walking simulator, *The Stanley Parable* (2013; *TSP*). The game's first-person protagonist is Stanley, an office worker in a Kafkaesque bureaucratic environment, whose day-to-day existence is marked by monotonous, nonautonomous labor. Stanley's main quest is to find out what happened to his co-workers, who have vanished from the premises. On his way through labyrinthine office corridors and deserted workspaces, he is accompanied by an invisible third-person voiced-over narrator, who seems to play the role of an omniscient, authorial narrator claiming to have created every aspect of the game and thus adopting the role of an intrusive, fictionalized author-programmer. Projecting overall control of the pre-scripted goals and narrative options of the game, the narrator dictates his own navigational preferences for Stanley and comments on Stanley's and the player's actions and decisions throughout (Thoss et al. 2018; also see chapter 4).

TSP is antimimetic in that it has nineteen different endings, the pathways to some of which are extremely short and satirical, thus parodying players' need for choice, agency, and narrative richness in gameplay. At the end of each pathway, players are thrown back to the opening scene of the game, which sees Stanley drudging away in his solitary office. The loading message following each ending runs "the end is never the end," thus foregrounding the thematic, antimimetic significance of the loop and, figuratively, of the rat-race futility that Stanley (in his working environment) and the player (in their ineffective quest for agency) are exposed to. However, despite the fact that *TSP* experiments with a range of ludonarrative conventions, thus running the risk of alienating potential, action-driven player bases to the point where they refuse to invest financially in a download, the game has been extremely popular, with over one million copies sold as of 2014 (Karmali 2014).

Even more extreme cases of antimimetic looping, which contribute to reader/player confusion rather than to cohesive plot construction, can be found in hypertext and other types of experimental electronic literature. In hypertext fiction, for example, readers frequently become "stuck in a loop," experiencing for example "the 'same' utterances recur[ring]," yet with very different meanings "because of where and when they are encountered" (Thomas

2007, 358). This recurrence phenomenon is mirrored in and symptomatic of characters' perceived incapability of "finding out who they are and what has happened to them" (357). This, for example, is the case in Michael Joyce's (1987) *afternoon, a story,* where the homodiegetic narrator Peter is unsure whether a deadly accident happened or not, and whether he caused it or not (see also Ensslin 2012; Bell 2010; and chapter 1). In a subjectifying reading (Alber 2016) of this highly antimimetic use of temporal looping, we can attribute it to Peter's trauma-induced confusion and dissociation from the tragic events that he actually experienced or even caused to happen—the fatal car accident of his wife and child. The looping might further suggest periodically revisited memories of the repressed event in successive therapy sessions.

Finally, William Poundstone's narrative Flash animation, *3 Proposals for Bottle Imps* (2002), combines cybertextual velocity and temporal looping. Playing with the automaton metaphor of "person as machine," the text alludes to Raymond Roussel's 1914 novel, *Locus Solus,* featuring a wealthy scientist who has built a range of absurd automata, including seven bottle imps, or Cartesian Devils—little gas-filled figurines moving up and down in a sealed container of water, depending on the fluid pressure of the container.

The text consists of three "Allegories," of "Genius," "Ambition," and "Envy," which readers run as noninteractive, animated text loops and which cannot be stopped at any given time. Cybertextual velocity in *3 Proposals* does not significantly pressurize the reader in terms of pace of reading—readers have plenty of time to peruse the material. Yet the ways in which music, morphing images, and dynamic words "pulse along together" put "the machine in control of the reader's experience of the text, and thus in control of the reader. The reader's time must be the machine's time" (Fletcher 2015, n. pag.). Thus, the way in which *3 Proposals* foregrounds machinic superiority subverts readers' expectations of interactivity and agency. This disempowering effect defamiliarizes the reading experience and calls for a thematic (Alber 2016) and metamedial reading that reflexively and medium-critically highlights the increasing influence of artificial intelligence on human life and projects the rise and potential fall of *homo cyberneticus* (Duus and Cooray 2015) in an age dominated by AI and algorithmic culture.

3.6 CONCLUSION

In this chapter we have examined transmedial and medium-specific uses of unnatural space and time in digital fiction. In the section on space, we explored narrative game worlds in particular and observed that game spaces, no matter how mimetic, nonmimetic, or antimimetic, lend themselves to speedy naturalization and conventionalization, by virtue of the way that reembodied players inhabit them as secondary worlds with internally coherent ecologies. We also showed that some of the most hyperrealistic game worlds—what we define as *hypermimetic* spaces—can have what we refer to as *environmentally antimimetic* effects on players, due to the ways in which they deploy semiotic processes of erasure and stylization, or by virtue of the ways in which they combine realism and fantasy in medium-specific, antimimetic ways. To this end, we introduced *metamedial* reading as a medium-specific addition to Alber's cognitive naturalization strategies, to account for instances in which reader/players are prompted to reflect on internalized medium-specific conventions and to widen the scope of what they consider possible in the area of narrative media design.

We further explored unnatural, corporeal 3D spaces and the degrees to which reader/players might be able to naturalize them through immersive gameplay. We argued that, in *Inkubus*, a combination of symbolical, intermedial, and sociocritical aspects leaves players in a critical state of mind vis-à-vis contemporary body-image issues. The internal body becomes an imaginary space where binary social and psychological conflicts are enacted, and the unconventional way in which the Unity game engine is deployed evokes ideas of narrative nonclosure and unresolved identity crisis that underscore the didactic, politicizing effects of medium-specific antimimeticism. By contrast, the physically impossible yet highly navigable and playable brain spaces in *Psychonauts* can be narrativized far more easily and functionalized for highly fantasy-driven game play. Thus, the degree to which impossible corporeal reading and writing spaces lend themselves to naturalizing readings depends on the authors' intent to immerse or defamiliarize the body space created for ergodic reading and play.

In the section on spatial contradictions and incompatibilities, we explored how a range of non-Euclidean games and experimental-immersive story apps employ spatial impossibility as a core mechanic for strategic game play and, in some cases, invoke subjectifying and other types of naturalizing readings, such as characters' or narrators' internal states and psychopathological conditions. Here as well as in the later section on unnatural uses of time, we emphasized the relative ease with which players subvert some of their most basic assumptions about how the world around them operates and thus how they can operationalize these subversions into systematic, effective gameplay.

Our discussion of palimpsestic writing spaces in digital fiction demonstrated how unconventional uses of conventional touchscreen gestures can lead to different degrees of medium-specific antimimeticism, as well as metamedial and technology-critical readings targeting ableist technology design. Furthermore, our analysis of Nelson's *Dreamaphage* as a palimpsestic work of avant-garde electronic literature allowed us to expand and modify Punday's (2017) distinction between "orienting space" and "primary storytelling space." In the unnatural, antimimetic absence of a coherently structured and (non)mimetically represented, primary storytelling space, "orienting space" becomes "disorienting space." In *Dreamaphage* in particular, disorienting space is suggestive of a dreamlike world, yet the mediated "text-space" onscreen (Nitsche 2008; Juul 2005) eludes the reader/player's actual construction of and teleological interaction with a coherent, primary storytelling space.

In the section on impossible time in digital fiction, we established that unnatural temporality is often connected with antimimetic representations of space, thus reconfirming the contemporary significance and transmedial relevance of the Bakhtinian chronotope. Impossible temporality at story and/or discourse level can encourage reader/players to engage critically with subjectively perceived time, or memory. Reader/players may be led to imagine and experience aspects of amnesia through medium-specific antinomic temporality that will allow them to go back in time via ludic mechanics. However, as our analyses of unnatural time in *Trinity* and *Braid* have established, antinomic and other types of medium-specific unnatural time may also be used didactically and politically, to expose a more general human concern about the dangers of Faustian ambition in a nuclear age and the risks involved in potentially drastic and irreversible interventions in global political affairs.

Finally, we introduced multivariant chronology and cybertextual velocity as new, medium-specific concepts of unnaturalness. Multivariant chronology often co-occurs with multilinearity and narrative contradiction (see chapter 1). In our discussion of *Her Story*, we demonstrated how multivariant chronology can be employed agglutinatively, at discourse and story level, in digital-born detective fiction, thus leaving the reader/player permanently defamiliarized over the apparent coexistence of several possible chronological sequences, culprits, and character constellations. In a more cultural-philosophical application, exemplified by *About Time*, multivariant chronology offers didactic ways of reading postcolonial-critical meanings into diversely experienced and lived time that exposes and undermines settler-colonial hegemonial thought. Finally, we proposed the concept of cybertextual velocity to explain medium-specific ways of programming discourse time for antimimetic effect. We discussed the crucial role of reader/player agency in the perception of antimimeticism in these types of unnatural uses of time and concluded that reduced agency does not necessarily reduce immersion: player subjugation to illusory agency is employed antimimetically as a highly immersive theme and mechanic in *The Stanley Parable,* while radically avant-garde, noninteractive animations such as *Dakota* leave reader/players exposed to machinic agency, thus evoking metamedial, technocritical readings regarding the growing importance and ethical implications of artificial intelligence in our digitalized society.

4

"Extreme" Digital Narration

> Thomas couldn't fall past this block. Think, damn it, think. What if there was some other kind of inverted fall, some way to "jump"? . . . It worked! Thomas had solved the great inverted fall mystery. . . . A big jump. But Thomas noted that there was no real danger in missing it. The world didn't want him to fail here. It was pushing him, but gently.
> —Mike Bithell, *Thomas Was Alone*

4.1 INTRODUCTION

At first glance, the narrative discourse in the epigraph may seem like a standard case of free indirect discourse: there is a character named Thomas, whose internal thoughts are represented in the past tense by a heterodiegetic narrator from a third-person point of view. Strictly speaking, this could be a section from a children's book about an adventurer, or an anthropomorphic animal, that is beginning to explore their environment and to test out their possible interactions with it, mostly in relation to vertical movements (falling and jumping). Having said that, the narrative exhibits some distinct lexical items that are strongly suggestive of the inventory and action repository of a typical platformer game that allows, for example, "jumping," "falling," (puzzle) "solving," and "failing." And indeed, this passage is an excerpt from a narrative indie game called *Thomas Was Alone* (Bithell 2012), which consists of simple geometric shapes as characters and playable environments. Thomas is a vertical, red rectangle that the player adopts as avatar. His aim is to explore possible movements and interactions in an abstract world whose rules partly emulate but also curiously deviate from the laws of the player's actual world. Similarly, the narrator adopts the developing, impossible mind of a geometric shape as it naively yet eloquently reflects the player's strategic intuitions and reasoning while progressing in the game world.

Surely, the presence of a narrator as such is not unusual, or antimimetic, in narrative games. Narrative voices occur in games in various communicative forms and semiotic modes. Yet there is something alienating about having the narrator provide an ongoing commentary on the player's actions because, in games, players tend to become their own narrators, or rather the experiential instantiators of their own personalized narratives—a phenomenon that Henry Jenkins (2004) refers to as emergent, environmental storytelling. Therefore, having a commentator-narrator accompany personalized gameplay is unconventional (Thoss et al. 2018) and creates a critical, metamedial stance in players. As a medium-specific antimimetic strategy, the pervasive voice of a commentator-narrator in a game that is primarily experienced by a player according to their own exploratory agenda lends itself to ludonarrative experimentation, as we shall see in section 4.7 in relation to cybernetic narration and the curious case of a would-be omniscient yet ultimately unreliable narrator-opponent in *The Stanley Parable*. What the example of *Thomas Was Alone* shows is the key significance of medium-specific storytelling conventions that derive from the specific affordances of digital interactivity and the ways in which fictional worlds are designed to allow stories to unfold through reader/player interaction with graphical user interface (GUI) elements and players' execution of the underlying source code algorithms.

With this in mind, we dedicate this chapter to an exploration of various medium-specific unnatural (in the sense of antimimetic) narrative voices in digital fiction. We begin from Richardson's definition of *extreme narration* as an umbrella term for various postanthropomorphic, protean narrators that have been proliferating in narrative fiction across media, especially since the second half of the twentieth century. As Richardson (2006) explains, over the past century we have seen

> a general move away from what was thought to be "omniscient" third person narration to limited third person narration to ever more unreliable first person narrators to new explorations of "you," "we," and mixed forms. There is a similar movement from the psychological novel to more impressionistic renderings of consciousness to the dissolution of consciousness into textuality, and a corresponding move from human-like narrators to quasi-human, non-human, and anti-human speakers, as the figure of the narrator as a recognizable human being recedes into an ever greater eclipse. (13)

To investigate how these posthuman narrators, which Richardson traces so assiduously through the history of late modernist and postmodern print fiction, translate into digital narrativity, in this chapter we look at medium-specific forms of extreme narration in digital fiction. In so doing, we see extreme narration as a key element of antimimetic narrativity, and we explore the extent to which existing concepts of extreme narration might be applicable to or have to be modified and/or extended for medium-specific antimimeticism in digital fiction. In particular, we focus on five subforms of extreme narration as derived from Richardson (2006): in section 4.3, we examine antimimetic unintentional unreliable narrators in digital fiction and how their cognitively compromised minds are represented poignantly by medium-specific digital narrativity. Our second focus, in section 4.4, is on the textual category of the protean interlocutor (Richardson 2006), which is fully conventionalized in digital narratives yet occasionally takes on curiously antimimetic qualities. In 4.5, we demonstrate how digitally enhanced multilinearity and multivariance lend themselves aptly to more and less extreme forms of multiperson and permeable narrators performing different voices or personalities of one and the same character. Finally, in 4.6, we turn to what we define as *machinic narration* and storytelling machines as the perhaps most literally unnatural (in the sense of nonhuman), antimimetic forms of storytelling in digital media, as well as cybernetic narration (Ciccoricco 2015) as a medium-specific form of procedural omniscience.

4.2 EXTREME NARRATION

In his groundbreaking and field-defining book *Unnatural Voices: Extreme Narration in Modern and Contemporary Fiction* (2006), Richardson lays the groundwork for unnatural narratology, focusing specifically on "the creation, fragmentation, and reconstitution of narrative voices" typically found in "late modernist, avant-garde, and postmodern narrative" (ix). His interest lies in instances where "one narration is collapsed into another, and one consciousness bleeds into a second one, or a foreign text inscribes itself on a mind" (12). This tends to lead to a foregrounding of the more or less fragmented, inconsistent or logically impossible subjectivity or ontological composition of the narrator him-/herself, which is foregrounded and thus "becomes itself a miniature drama" (12) or metafictional theme of the text.

In his attempt to do justice to narrative experimentation that does not align with assumptions and concepts of standard narrative theory, Richardson induces what he calls a general "anti-poetics" of narrative, which reflects "a move away from rigid typologies and Chinese box-type models of embedded speakers and toward an alternative figuration that stresses the permeability, instability, and playful mutability of the voices of nonmimetic fictions" (2006, xii). This narrative antipoetics includes investigations of unconventional human and nonhuman speakers, such as animals and fantasy creatures (e.g., Akif Pirinçci's cat-narrated *Felidae* series, 1989–2012, and the Cretan Minotaur in Borges's "The House of Asturion," 1949); demented and mute storytellers (as in Calvino's *The Castle of Crossed Destinies*, 1969); improbably eloquent children (as in John Hawkes's *Virginie: Her Two Lives*, 1981); loquacious corpses (as in Beckett's "The Calmative," 1946); and machines such as the intelligent TV set in Grass's *Local Anaesthetic* (1969) that seems to have access to the protagonist's confused memories. Narrative antipoetics involves studies of narrators that disclose unexpected identities in the course of or towards the end of a narrative. It looks at unusual uses of personal pronouns in second-person ("you"; see chapter 5), first-person plural ("we"), and multiperson narration. It focuses on logically impossible, metaleptic acts of narration (see chapter 2), on distinctly postmodern forms of unreliability, and on what Richardson calls "three curious narrating figures that exist at the limits of the utterable" (2006, xi): the interlocutor, the permeable narrator, and denarration.

In this book, we have chosen to focus on a selection of extreme narrative situations that we consider particularly significant for an understanding of medium-specific antimimetic digital fiction. While we have dedicated full chapters to the key and complex phenomena of metalepsis (chapter 2) and textual "you" (chapter 5), we use this chapter to discuss a number of further, extreme forms of digital narration. We exclude the phenomenon of physically and/or biologically impossible narration, which does occur in digital fiction but—much as in print fiction—does not necessarily contribute to antimimetic effects (such as the ghostly voice of Lana in Pullinger et al.'s *The Breathing Wall*, discussed in chapter 2). As we show below, what is important about narrative voices in digital fictions are their medium-specific encodings, that is, the ways in which they are programmed to respond to the reader/player's interactions with the interface and the hardware, as well as their general embeddedness in the cybernetic feedback loop.

4.3 UNRELIABLE NARRATION AND DIGITAL FICTION

We begin our investigation of medium-specific forms of unreliable narration in digital fiction with Rimmon-Kenan's definition of an unreliable narrator as "one whose rendering of the story and/or commentary on it the reader has reasons to suspect" (1983, 101). Using examples from experimental narrative game design and hypertext fiction, we argue here that digital unreliability that reflects deviant minds can be effectively staged in medium-specific ways to achieve a variety of effects on a continuum between immersive-meditative and permanently defamiliarizing (Iversen 2016).

Since the eighteenth century, unreliability has been as strongly embedded in the evolution of narrative fiction as its growing concern with narrational subjectivity. It is therefore, in its essence, not restricted to modernist or postmodern narratives. However, as Richardson (2006) points out, there are some distinctly postmodern, "extreme kinds of unreliability" that go beyond "the normal abilities and limitations of a human being or humanlike narrating agent" (103) and represent a logical further step in the development "from unreliable narrators to incompetent ones to delusional and then completely insane storytellers" (2)—although it needs to be said that all these attributes can be and have been theorized under the label of unreliability. What Richardson aims to accentuate is the importance of those types of unreliability that do not readily lend themselves to naturalizing readings and are therefore likely to come across as highly antimimetic, or as permanently defamiliarizing.

As Richardson (2006) explains in relation to *extreme* (or what we would term *antimimetic*) unreliability, "we need some new concepts to add to current notions of unreliable and untrustworthy narrators" (103). To him, these new concepts include fraudulent, contradictory, permeable (see section 4.5), incommensurate (see sections 4.4 and 4.5), and disframed narrators. Richardson concedes that there are many varieties of fraudulence and therefore concentrates on its "more interesting" forms (103). By this he means pervasive, "clearly unbelievable" (103) narrators such as the one featuring in Borges's story, "The Immortal" (1949). Here the narrator observes that he is not only unreliable but indeed impossible because his own story has been intermingled with that of another.

In contradictory narratives, such as Coover's "The Babysitter" and Robbe-Grillet's *La Jalousie,* multiple, mutually exclusive versions of an identical framework of events are set forth, with no mechanisms offered (such as different narrators with different memories and agendas) to explain away the resulting, often outrageous contradictions (see chapter 1). Using naturalistic assumptions to comprehend these texts leads directly to interpretive chaos; one must abandon the idea of a self-consistent narrator relating an account of a pre-existing set of events to begin to read these unusual pieces (Richardson 2006, 104). We return to this concept in our reading of *afternoon* in this section.

Disframed narrators, according to Richardson (2006), "move from one level of a text to another in ways that are impossible outside of fiction" (105). For example, "Moran, the narrator of the second part of *Molloy,* claims to have invented characters that appear in other novels by Beckett" (105). Thus, disframed narrators transgress ontological boundaries between different storyworlds or between other, mutually exclusive ontological spheres, such as the fictional world of the characters and that of the author in or outside the text. In this sense, disframed narrators come under the broader label of ontological metalepsis (see chapter 2).

Existing, comprehensive theories of unreliability have offered far more fine-grained psychological typologies than Richardson's rather broad use of the term seems to suggest—especially in relation to his somewhat underspecified category of fraudulent narrators. Indeed, in this section, we begin from a group of theories of unreliability that do not explicitly count themselves under the label of unnatural narratology and, instead, explore unreliability in terms of degrees of intentionality, drawing on pragmatically and sociocognitively grounded typologies. As we will show, they enable us to analyze and understand medium-specific instantiations of deviant and devious storytelling minds, specifically in cases of unintentional, psychopathological unreliability.

In *The Rhetoric of Fiction,* Booth defined the unreliable narrator as a narrator that does not "speak[ ] for or act[ ] in accordance with the norms of the work (which is to say the implied author's norms)" (1967, 158–59). This text-immanent definition was subsequently critiqued by a variety of scholars (e.g., Yacobi 1981; Chatman 1990; Wall 1994; Nünning 1998; Phelan and Martin 1999; Fludernik 1999; Olson 2003). Aiming to "reconceptualize" (Nünning 2005) Booth's concept and informed by various disciplines, including pragmatics and psychology, most of them emphasized the interplay between the reader and textual clues that suggest unreliability and replaced the idea of an "implied author" with that of a text-based, reader-projected authorial voice.

In the analytical part of this section we focus on two cases of antimimetic "unintentional" unreliability, following Heyd's (2006) useful Gricean model. This model understands unreliability in the sense of "violat[ing] the cooperative principle without intending an implicature" (217). In other words, the narrator fails—for a variety of reasons—to apply one of the prime principles of cooperation underlying human communication, that their conversational contribution should be "such as it is required, at the stage at which it occurs, by the accepted purpose or direction of the talk exchange in which [they are] engaged" (Grice 1975, 45). Furthermore, if the Gricean maxim of quality, or truth, is flouted without intending an implicature (e.g., irony), the narrator will be either lying (in cases of intended deception) or showing signs of cognitive impairment (in cases of unintended deception). According to Heyd (2006), intentionality is key to identifying various types of unreliable narration. Based on her proposed axis of intentionality or self-consciousness (227), she distinguishes between three main types of unreliable narration: quiet deception (highly intentional attempts to deceive the reader), self-deception (semiconscious and often grounded in self-denial and self-consciousness), and unintentional unreliability, resulting from a lack of cognitive or intellectual ability. The latter type typically manifests itself in undereducated, naive, and mentally ill narrators, who form some of the most interesting case studies in experimental, medium-specifically antimimetic digital fiction, as we show in the remainder of this section.

With respect to digital narratives more generally, unreliability can be found in more or less antimimetic uses. In mainstream videogames, unreliability in the broadest sense of a narrator turning out to be a different persona from the one assumed to be at the outset of a story arc has been deployed, albeit rarely. This is because mainstream games do not easily lend themselves to ambiguity (Carmichael and Mould 2014, 4). After all, "deliberate frustration of action [in games] seems clearly to be an intolerable option" (Eskelinen 2001), and many players prefer to concentrate on the challenges facing them in terms of mechanics and playable action. Nevertheless, occasionally, unreliable narrators can even be found in commercially driven blockbusters, and yet they tend to be designed in such a way as to not allow immersive gameplay to suffer. A classic example is 2K Boston/Australia's *Bioshock* (2007). It features the narrative voice of Atlas, who tells the reader/player he needs help to save his family from Rapture, an underwater city built by Objectivist business magnate Andrew Ryan, which houses a utopian-elitist yet class-ridden society that has seen an uprising of the lower classes, represented by Atlas. "It turns out Atlas is really a persona fabricated by the person responsible for [the coup that has led to] the city's downfall" (Carmichael and Mould 2014, 4). In this case, we are dealing with a quietly deceptive narrator that strongly intends to mislead the reader/player to the extent that his feigned narrative drives the reader/player's key motivations and actions in the game.[1] The use of unreliable narrator as such, however, in *Bioshock,* is only weakly and temporarily defamiliarizing, and the antimimetic effects are limited to the epiphanic moment when the player realizes they have been deluded into false assumptions for much of the game.

Conversely, more experimental forms of digital fiction offer themselves to staging various forms of unintentional, psycho-pathologically motivated unreliability. They can show us "how manifestations of deviant . . . narration are aesthetically enriched by techniques afforded by the digital medium, such as hypertextual multilinearity, lack of or partial closure, multisensory experi-

---

1. In game studies, this design element has been widely referred to as "ludonarrative dissonance" (Hocking 2007).

ence, fluid transitions and boundaries and, most significantly, the play with reader agency" (Ensslin 2012, 136).

The following two examples of unintentional, pathological unreliability demonstrate very different aesthetic effects. A highly immersive experience is offered by The Chinese Room's 3D walking simulator, *Dear Esther* (2012). The game puts the reader/player in the first-person position of a nameless man who meanders around a deserted island in the Hebrides in Scotland, mourning the death of his eponymous wife and gradually losing his mind over this loss. At key places during his wanderings, the game releases voiced-over chunks of the narrator's interior monologues about his subjective perceptions of and interactions with the island, as well as his monologic dialogues with Esther, which at times show delirious signs of religious self-projection, as well as the very symptoms of his imagined and real insanity:

> I would leave you presents, outside your retreat, in this interim space between cliff and beach. I would leave you loaves and fishes, but the fish stocks have been depleted and I have run out of bread. I would row you back to your homeland in a bottomless boat but I fear we would both be driven mad by the chatter of the sea creatures. (*Dear Esther*)

The protagonist's monologic snippets become more obscure as the narrative proceeds, revealing a deterioration in his cognitive abilities that almost inevitably leads to a tragic closure. The antimimetic effects of this narrative technique likely increase until the player realizes what is likely the cause of the protagonist's increasing opaqueness of thought, at which point naturalization sets in. A subjectifying reading of the game almost forces itself on the reader, corroborated by the main writer and designer's statement that the "landscape is not an island, it's the dream of an island" (Pinchbeck 2017, quoted in O'Sullivan 2017, 319).

A distinctly and deliberately more antimimetic version of unintentional unreliability features in Joyce's *afternoon*, a hypertext fiction that combines the genres of fictional autobiography and psychological novel (Ensslin 2007, 2012; see also chapter 1). One reading that strongly imposes itself suggests that the homodiegetic narrator, Peter, has lost his son in a car accident that he himself caused. Peter comes across as deeply disturbed by his personal bereavement, his feelings of guilt and failed responsibility, and his general inability to come to terms with his existential situation as well as his social environment. His overall confusion, neurosis, and trauma are instantiated by the nonlinear, often looping hypertext structure that keeps forcing the reader back to the narrator's traumatic observation while taking him on various mental trajectories reflecting his need to seek distraction. Furthermore, the degree and intensity of unreliability in the narrator's account changes according to the reader's chosen pathways.

afternoon's default introductory lexia "begin" introduces the homodiegetic narrator who, after a short poetic prelude revolving around the sentence "I try to recall winter," addresses the reader directly, asking "Do you want to hear about it?," whereby the exact reference of the third-person pronoun ("it") is left unclear. Assuming it refers to the "story" in the novel's subtitle, the reader is required to click Y (Yes) or N (No) at the bottom of the Storyspace window. Depending on their decision, their reading experience will be either (partly) revealing (in the case of Y) or deeply frustrating, distorted, and surreal (in the case of N). Clicking Y repeatedly will introduce the reader to the main characters and their relationships: Peter's marriage to and divorce from Lisa, their son Andrew, Peter's friend and employer's Wert's marriage to psychotherapist Lolly, and their jealousies surrounding Nausicaa, another employee of Wert's. The Y trajectory also leads, via Peter's frantic attempts to locate his son, to his visit to the scene of the car crash, which is then followed by a loop of memories of and reflections on the hours leading up to the event. Whereas the Yes trajectory is largely coherent and meaningful up to the point of Peter's looping thoughts surrounding the car accident, the No scenario may be read in terms of a complete mental breakdown. It takes the reader on a journey through entirely disconnected sequences of quasi-feverish ranting, which grotesquely expose Peter's problematic sexual self-image, inferiority complex, and, most importantly, irremediable feelings of guilt and loss (Ensslin 2012, 141).

The experience of reading *afternoon* has been widely claimed (and experimentally corroborated; see Gardner 2004) to be among the most disorienting, defamiliarizing in the history of digital fiction. Despite theories suggesting potential imaginary closure on the reader's part following multiple re-readings (Douglas 1994; Ciccoricco 2007; Ensslin 2007) along the lines of a "do-it-yourself" strategy (Alber 2016), the narrative design is a deliberate attempt to permanently defamiliarize, which is reinforced by the near-impossibility of following the same order and number of lexias twice in any given reading. And yet, in an unnaturalizing reading that accepts the confusing and alienating effects of the text's formal design, a naturalizing thematic parallel can be found (Alber 2016)—that of the true impermeability and aporia of a deeply troubled mind. This acceptance can be further strengthened if readers come to see *afternoon* as a medium-specific unnatural construction that exploits the structural affordances of hypertext to aesthetically reflect psychopathological states of mind.

4.4 THE DIGITAL INTERLOCUTOR

Having discussed some representative cases of psycho-pathologically motivated unreliability in digital fiction, let us now turn to some specific concepts put forward under the theory of antimimetic unnaturalness. In this section, we show how digital fiction almost completely conventionalizes the concept of the interlocutor (Richardson 2006; Ensslin 2018) and yet exhibits some cases in which small degrees of antimimeticism serve to defamiliarize the reading-playing experience, if only temporarily or to small degrees.

Richardson (2006) defines the interlocutor-narrator in print fiction as a "disembodied questioning voice . . . that poses questions which the narrative goes on to answer" (79) and as "an unstable and inherently protean figure (or kind of discourse) that regularly oscillates from one function or status to another as it evokes familiar categories like narrator and narratee in order to blur their edges or transgress them altogether" (85). He thus distinguishes it from voices that can be more clearly identified, such as narrators talking to themselves, or even narrators addressing the reader in cases of rhetorical metalepsis (Ryan 2006a).

Richardson's early example of a questionable interlocutor figure is the narrator in Dostoevsky's 1864 *Notes from the Underground*. Throughout the text, the narrator imagines vocal responses from one or more hypothetical interlocutors "with such precision that they may point to an origin in the narrator's obsessions rather than any mimesis of others' probable speech" (Richardson 2006, 80). Richardson's main case study is, however, the "Ithaca" episode of Joyce's *Ulysses*, which he calls "the source of most modern experiments" (81). The chapter consists of about 2,300 lines of questions and answers, which Joyce himself identifies as "catechism (impersonal)." But it is a "very strange kind of anti-catechism, couched in exaggerated scientific language and containing much more narrative and description than standard doctrine or useful knowledge" (81). It is important to remember here the ultimately monologic nature of projected catechistic dialogicity. The standard, religious genre serves as a pedagogic tool conveying to a congregation or student a catalog of rules and doctrinal thinking patterns that are supposed to be internalized. The respondent "does not respond personally to the question but rather internalizes the answer which the questioner has already supplied" (Hampson 1996, 230). This reduces the respondent's agency to zero, and makes them a discursive tool for the hegemonic voice behind the interlocution.

Joyce, of course, coming from a background steeped in this and other kinds of religious indoctrination, aimed to parody and subvert the orthodox question-and-answer format, thus critiquing "the catechism's inversion of the function of dialogue and problematiz[ing] further the status of the speaking subject" (Richardson 2006, 81). Indeed, throughout the episode readers are left to wonder who the speaker is (or speakers are) of the question or the answer. The catechistic, interlocutory style raises questions about intended levels of perceived orality, of whether we are dealing with one or two speakers, what their status and relationship is vis-à-vis the main characters, and, ultimately, whether the voice asking the questions might even be a projected personification of the implied reader, or that of a fictional "arranger" (Hayman 1982) responsible for the many diverse and often inconclusive voices featuring in the novel.

Richardson (2006) concludes that the elusive form of the interlocutor can be conceptualized in two ways. We might think of it as a kind of "shapeless, contradictory, indeed monstrous [and yet somehow inherently consistent] supernarrator . . . bent on producing irreducible heterogeneity" (86). Alternatively, as he seems to prefer, we might think of it as a more general, fluid concept of textuality that allows for "shifting, depersonalized, multivoiced texts that transcend or traduce the sensibility of a single narrator, a composite figure we may refer to as the 'incommensurate narrator'" (86; see section 4.3). Either way, interlocution is a highly malleable, antimimetic narrative technique that seeks to confuse, bewilder, or at least cause readers to reflect on the communicative situation in print fiction more generally, and their very own role within it.

To begin to explore medium-specific interlocution in digital fiction, let us therefore revisit a well-known and greatly simplified model of narrative communication, developed for print fiction. Fig. 4.1 shows an adaptation of Pfister's (1977) and Jahn's (2017) Chinese box model of the different intra- and extradiegetic layers involved in narrative communication (derived from Chatman's more linear graph in *Story and Discourse* [1978]). In the outer layer (S4/R4), the author addresses a reader at a level of nonfictional communication, in the actual world (see fig. 2.3). This happens indirectly and asynchronously, through a written codex. At the first embedded level (S3/R3), we have an implied reader being addressed by the implied author, who manifests subtextually, in storyworld text-space (fig. 2.3), through inference from textual cues. At the S2/R2 level, an extradiegetic narrator addresses a narratee at the level of fictional mediation in the storyworld world-space (fig. 2.3). Finally, at S1/R1, or diegetic world level (fig. 2.3), character action and (dialogic) interaction happens. The latter is the only bidirectional communication aspect in the traditional print model. Importantly, all other layers involve unidirectional communication. This means that print fiction readers typically receive what they are told rather than being able to talk back, and the same is generally

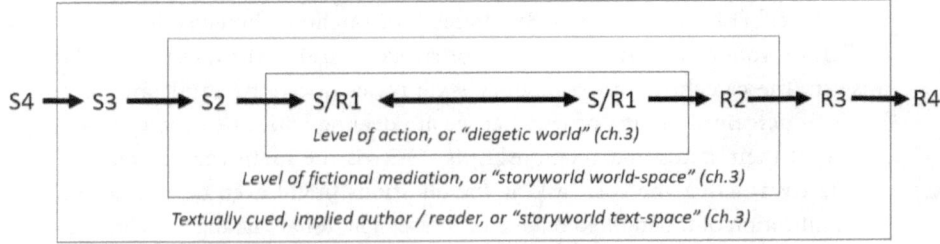

FIGURE 4.1. Chinese box model of narrative communication in print fiction (adapted from Pfister 1977 and Jahn 2017). "S" stands for "sender" and "R" for "recipient."

true at the narrator–narratee level. This unidirectionality does not apply to communication in the fictional world, as characters talk multidirectionally.

The model in fig. 4.1 shows that narrative communication in print assumes a reader-recipient confronted with an essentially monodirectional narrative situation. This situation does not allow any significant agency as far as creative or narrative decision-making is concerned, and the reader's main challenge is to make sense of linguistically represented narrational ambiguities, without, however, actively participating in the construction of the story. In a nutshell, then, we argue that the interlocutor as a form of extreme narration emerges from the unidirectional communication situation we typically find in print, and it is used to signal the monologic, inherently un-"natural" in the sense of anticonversational (following Fludernik 1996) quality of standard, print-based literary communication.

Digital narratives, by contrast, do not face this monodirectional dilemma. They typically put the reader/player in a cybernetic, interactionally metaleptic dialogue (see chapter 2) with various narrative functions, such as characters, narrative voices, or prompts emanating from the storytelling environment. Reader/players typically enact their responses either verbally, through typed keyboard input, or haptically, through various types of physical interactions with the interface (e.g., mouse clicks, controller moves, and fingertip gestures). The sense of agency evoked through these dialogic interactions has been fully conventionalized as part of digital narrativity, from commercial narrative videogames to text adventures and Interactive Fiction. And yet, of course, despite the projection of genuine bilaterality and reader/player agency, we are again dealing with a pre-scripted supernarrative that ultimately delimits the interlocutory options available to the reader/player.

In relation to digital fiction, then, the kind of unidirectionality at the levels of fictional mediation/discourse and nonfictional communication we know from print is lifted and the reader essentially generates the narrative through kinetic interface interaction (rather than mostly cognitive interaction). This is the main reason why an interlocutor figure that speaks to the narratee, or to the reader that impersonates, or enacts, the narratee, is highly conventionalized in digital fiction. That said, there are exceptions where the status of the interlocutor is not all that clear-cut and/or fluid, and where we might therefore locate a certain degree of antimimetic experimentation.

There has been an astonishing range of experimental creativity in relation to human–computer interaction in digital fiction and digital drama, exploring the possibilities of Turing-Test-style communication in particular (Marino 2006a). As explored in chapter 2, *Façade*, for example, stages a conversation between two artificial agents and the player, whose typed conversational turns result in character responses that are possible in a "natural" (Fludernikian) scenario yet not always likely. Still, we are here not really dealing with a situation that Richardson theorizes, where the interlocutor-narrator or narratee is perceived as protean, hybrid, or ontologically elusive.

It is important to recognize that the medium-specific qualities of digital fiction afford specific kinds of antimimetic interlocution, whereby we have to take conventionalized forms of high-agency player involvement into consideration. Hence, we need to adjust Richardson's concept to one of unconventional (antimimetic) digital interlocution, where reader/players encounter unexpected forms of dialogicity that can, for example, put them in a dilemma between expected and constrained agency, or cause them to reflect on the unexpectedly complex personality and potential multivocality of the narrator-interlocutor facing them.

In this context it is worth considering Emily Short's Interactive Fiction, *Galatea* (2000). The text is antimimetic within its own genre, as it takes a psychological, forensic rather than action-oriented approach. The reader/player's aim is to find out as much about the living statue's past and personality as they can, mostly by asking her questions and telling her about aspects of human life. In this process, the narrator-interlocutor assumes the role of a complex, multifaceted stage director. Most of the time she/he provides us an inside view of the reader/player, triggering and responding to Galatea's actions and utterances. But occasionally she/he shape-shifts into a meta-level commentator, transgressing the ontological boundary between fictional and actual world and reprimanding the player, for example, for wanting the reader/player to tell Galatea about sex ("There are some things that fall out of your job description"). Other, more cryptic metacomments advise the player of the logistics and rules of IF software interaction, such as the glossing remark "(General questions: you can almost always find ones that haven't been anticipated)." Here, the passive structure "that haven't been anticipated" augments the remark's disorienting effect, as the reader/player is left in the dark about who might not anticipate certain general questions: Galatea, or the system, or possibly even humankind in general. Admittedly, this metaleptic interlocutor-narrator may not come across as permanently or pervasively alienating as Joyce's anticatechism. However, we may still see it as an example of medium-specific dialogic antimimeticism that may be naturalized partly or fully through satirizing reading strategies (Alber 2016).

Another example of medium-specific antimimetic interlocution is Judi Alston and Andy Campbell's immersive 3D fiction, *WALLPAPER* (see chapter 2). Here the player assumes the perspective of first-person avatar PJ Sanders, who soliloquizes (internally, presumably) about the associations triggered by revisiting the house of his childhood. The language produced by this monologic dialogue therefore seems to have been produced by the reader/player himself, whose personality initially comes across as fairly stable and consistent. However, in the course of the narrative, Sanders becomes gradually dissociated from this assumed stable identity, as well as the reader/player's likely identification with him, as the voices he experiences in the house seem to multiply. He appears to hold uncanny written and spoken conversations with his late mother and father, for example, but the most antimimetic aspect of this protean interlocutor are the passages in which some alter ego seems to be speaking to him. For example, towards the beginning of the narrative, as the reader/player walks towards the entrance door of his mother's house, onscreen text says "Come on, Sanders, just unlock the door, man." This can be seen, initially at least, as an encouraging internal voice to Sanders as well as an instructional hint to the player before entering the house. More poignantly, however, in the latter half of the narrative, the voice seems to disconnect more strongly from the protagonist's intentions: "Upstairs? Are you crazy Sanders?" is displayed onscreen as the player takes the avatar to the doom-inspiring upstairs rooms, thus going against the protagonist's likely intuitions following the traumatic experience in the forbidden room. So, in this example we can see the interlocutor as a medium-specific, protean voice that oscillates between interior character monologue, system feedback, and supernatural character interaction, thus simulating or at least evoking the effects of childhood trauma and psychological repression. To naturalize the plurality of voices projected onscreen, as well as their sources, we may apply a combination of subjectifying and transcendentalizing (Alber 2016) reading strategies. At the same time, however, reader/players are led to read the protean interlocutor as a medium-specific, unnatural construction that achieves its intended, surprising and metamedially consciousness-raising, effects partly or mainly because it violates conventions of system-player dialogue. More specifically, it draws the reader/player's attention to the fact that their entertainment-seeking motivations deviate from those of an emotionally immersed, empathic player that acts in the interests of the reader/player.

4.5 MEDIUM-SPECIFIC POLYVOCALITY

In this section we discuss medium-specific forms of antimimetic narrative polyvocality, where "multiple modes of narration," or "different narrators and modes of narration" (Richardson 2006, 61), are combined to portray an array of voices that either belong to the same individual or reflect a polyphony of different people's voices. Notably, the difference between the two is not always clear-cut, especially in cases where assumed external voices become integrated into the same person (as we shall see in our analyses of *Quadrego* and *Everybody Dies* below). As Richardson explains, "contemporary fiction is replete with a polyphony of competing narrative voices; even where the narrator's speaking situation seems fixed, alternative voices often threaten to destabilize that situation" (63). This trend reflects an expressive need among fiction writers to portray, in innovative and unconventional ways, "dynamic picture[s] of consciousness" (64) and pluralistic, "self-reflexive and unsettling" (65), fluid and often impenetrable epistemologies. In their inductive totality, texts that employ multiperson narration offer

> fresh possibilities for formal literary innovation and they create new methods to reinscribe thematic material at the level of narration, as the text's central concerns are embodied in a correlative formal technique. They can help a writer reproduce more accurately the jagged fissures within a single subjectivity; they can also provide alternative tools to define more sharply or collapse more effectively conventional distinctions between different characters, competing narrative worlds, or tale and frame. Thus, they can cunningly embody contemporary issues in philosophy, cultural studies, and gender theory relating to the reconfiguration of self, mind, and person. Perhaps more importantly, they allow the free play of multiple voices and can be seen as a practice that generates a greater degree of dialogism than more conventional techniques typically allow. (Richardson 2006, 67–68)

In the following two sections, we show how unnatural narratology has explored the various ways in which multiperson narration has been employed in print fiction to reflect such "contemporary issues" in cultural and gender theory in particular, to varying degrees of defamiliarization. We then turn to two examples of multiperson narration in digital fiction and analyze the ways in which its medium-specific affordances lend themselves to representations of polyvocality in hypertext and multimodal hypermedia fiction in particular. We also examine the permeable narrator as a specific subform of polyvocality and analyzes its medium-specific deployment in an example of experimental Interactive Fiction.

4.5.1 Multiperson Narration

In theorizing multiperson narration, Richardson (2006) distinguishes between two major forms: centrifugal and centripetal. In centrifugal texts, different voices "continue to proliferate an irreducible galaxy of different, heterogeneous or antithetical, perspectives" (62). These perspectives typically adopt forms of first-, second-, third-person, and/or other, additional and often language-specific points of view, which "may be presented by the inclusion of more voices and more kinds of voice, or they may take the form of more perspectives that narrate the world of a single figure" (71). The latter variety is exemplified by Carlos Fuentes's novel *The Death of Artemio Cruz* (1962), which portrays the "transformation of its complex protagonist from idealistic revolutionary to oppressive oligarch and, by extension, chronicles the concomitant degeneration of the Mexican revolution" (68). Fuentes deploys "triadic alterations" (Richardson 2006, 68) between first-person present tense, third-person past tense, and second-person future tense, all of which can be applied to the protagonist. However, each pronoun marks a specific type of discourse: the third-person point of view allows insights into thoughts and events that the protagonist cannot be aware of; the first-person passages take the form of a stream-of-consciousness-style interior monologue; and the second-person segments evolve dynamically, fragmenting and coalescing, spanning different time periods and including nonnarrative material (69).

Conversely, centripetal texts, Richardson shows, "begin by producing a number of seemingly disparate voices and stances only to reduce them to a single narrating position at the end" (62). These voices, or registers, may conflate into a single mind, as the alternating third- and second-person sections in Beckett's *Company* (1980) project "a failed attempt to generate 'company'" (Richardson 2006, 95). Alternatively, the voices may collapse into someone else's voice, or a voice that remains inexplicable and evasive, as in the case of Beckett's *The Unnamable* (1958), where an impossible range of inconsistent narrative voices collapse "into an undifferentiated third term, the mediating slash that formerly stood as the sign of demarcation but now disperses itself into an interstitial zone" (Begam 1996, 156). In this extreme case of centripetality, "there is no resolution to the question of the identity of the narrator; he remains to the last a contradictory conflation of self and other, essence and absence" (Richardson 2006, 100–101).

As previously noted, some forms of digital fictions lend themselves particularly well to representations of multivocality. The hypertextual format in particular allows readers to choose, in a nonlinear fashion, between different narrative options. These options can take the form of different characters that readers can follow in any order, as in Deena Larsen's early HyperCard poetry collection, *Marble Springs* (1993); Ruth Nestvold's web-based hypertext fiction, *Cutting Edges, Or: A Web of Women* (1995–2001); or Charles Deemer's one-act online hyperdrama, *The Last Song of Violeta Parra* (1996). In Deemer's case in particular, hypertextual character distribution lies at the center of digital dramatization, thus creating a "dramatic form that would give the individual viewer the choice of following particular characters through the drama, through all their 'exits' and 'entries'" (Ensslin 2007, 81). This effect replaces the materiality of the center stage with a different, computational type of cognitive-haptic interactivity that blends with reading practices associated with closet drama (Schnierer 2001) and aspects of interactive theater.

In the preceding examples, multivocality comes across not as an antimimetic device but rather as a plausible, conventionalized way of harnessing the affordances of multilinear textuality. Indeed, digital portrayals of polyvocality do not necessarily have to be used to represent fragmented identities or impossible narrators. They can follow highly coherent trajectories that enable readers to experience a sense of agency in an experimental form of interactive closet drama and to experience the same storyworld from multiple perspectives. From an unnatural narratological point of view that foregrounds antimimeticism, however, digital fictions that use medium-specific forms of multiperson narration and polyvocality to represent fragmented, problematic, hybrid, fluid, and other types of postmodern identities are of prime interest.

Stefan Maskiewicz's German hypermedia narrative, *Quadrego* (2001), for example, features at its core a female protagonist-narrator, Iris (alias "No"), who suffers from multiple personality disorder—a condition "which splits her perceived personality into four identities ('quadruple ego' > 'quadrego'), whose voices perpetually compete and argue in her consciousness" (Ensslin 2012, 143). The main interface, the "centre of Quadrego," shows pixelated portraits of the narrator-protagonist in the shape of four human faces that strikingly resemble each other yet, simultaneously, exhibit discernible differences. Two of them look more female, the other two more male, yet the seemingly fluid transitions between them suggest an either agendered or transgender scenario. Thus, the visual design of the main interface sets the centripetal scene for the narrative: "a polyphony of competing voices that factually belong to the same character-I yet perform independent personalities on the mental stage of the deranged narrator" (Ensslin 2012, 143). The authorial abstract introduces the protagonist as

> a [nameless] little girl [who] learns to live under the brutality and dominance of her brother. Yet one day she realises that she can free herself. The path to her liberation is determined by her brother's violence, whom she loves. Her conscience starts taking possession of her. (Maskiewicz 2001; translation ours, *et passim*).

Upon mouse-click, reader/players obtain snippets of Iris's interior monologue, depicting the mental torture that her condition causes incessantly to her "harried soul." Verbal descriptions of Iris's internal voices' "continuous fight . . . over power" are complemented with changing images of her competing identities, and depending on the reader/player's choices, the cacophony of multiple personalities, all speaking in the first person, manifests in different ways, suggesting multiple possible causes of Iris's condition. One possible reading assumes that Iris murdered her brother, thus representing a solution to her own trauma. This path is represented textually by a referential shift from the insecure, self-effacing No to the enlightened, proactive Iris, whereby the change in telling names evokes a symbolical shift from self-denial to insight and enlightenment. This kind of subjectifying reading (Alber 2016) might consider the murder as already committed, and her disorder as a symptom of survivor's guilt. The unconventional, medium-specific representation, or rather reader/playerly performance of Iris's psychopathology, is, however, best understood as an unnatural construction that takes advantage of the multilinear, windowed textuality afforded by the digital-interactive screen. This structural affordance of hypertext facilitates antimimetic, unconventional aesthetic practices and allows digital artists to experiment with ways of representing fragmented postmodern identities.

Although the experience of reading *Quadrego*, was, at the time it was first published, and still is surprising and eye-opening to first-time reader/players, it nonetheless yields coherent and meaningful, subjectifying reading strategies. These strategies are facilitated by the fact that the author has provided generous paratextual explanations of the condition portrayed in the narrative, characterizing it as a disease that removes control over the many voices and subjectivities inherent in every human being, often as a result of psychological trauma. Thus, naturalizing reading strategies are explicitly embedded in the text's visual design, and the staged polyvocality serves an immersive-informative rather than alienating purpose.

A very different and distinctly more permanently defamiliarizing reading experience is offered by geniwate and Deena Larsen's ludic, satirical Flash fiction, *The [somewhat disturbing but highly improbable] Princess Murderer* (henceforth *TPM*). The text mixes thematic elements of the Romantic fairy tale, the crime mystery, pornographic magazines, and discursive-interactive elements of digital genres such as hypertext, hypermedia, and videogame (Ensslin and Bell 2012, 50). A digital, feminist, and anti-violent-games remediation of Charles Perrault's "La Barbe bleue" (1697), *TPM* places itself in the mythological canon and transforms elements of Perrault's source text ludically, diegetically, and multimodally. Importantly, it features a curious range of narrative voices and points of view, including first, second, and third person, which are centrifugally arranged and therefore never conflate into the same identity. These perspectives are aligned with different genres and registers: the third person is used to emulate the heterodiegetic, omniscient narrator familiar to us from traditional fairy tales: "There was a bad, bad man. His name was Bluebeard, and he had a penchant for princesses." The first person impersonates the villain, whose perspective the reader is forced to take in their inevitable endeavor to abuse, kill, and breed princesses as the text prescribes them to: "My name is Bluebeard. I sit in my castle like a spider in its lair. The minor female royals are drawn to me, despite their terror." However, it is also used to represent short snippets of character speech portrayed in one particular strand of the narrative, to lend a voice to the victims of Bluebeard's crimes in particular: "His cock is long, thin and sharp. He carves my (cool, layered) flesh with it. Huge flabs flake off before my eyes."

Finally and arguably most importantly, instances of the second-person pronoun are used to orchestrate an ontologically ambiguous interplay between direct apostrophic address to the extratextual reader/player ("As long as you keep clicking the outcome is inevitable") and a hybrid form of second-person narration that is simultaneously a direct form of address to the intradiegetic, impersonated reader/player ("Their disappearance has been noted. You are a suspect. . . . You look at your hands, dripping in blood"). The latter use of "you" in particular has the effect of projecting a sense of immersion and narrative responsibility (see also chapter 5), making the reader feel strangely and helplessly complicit in the abuse and killings of the princesses. This technique serves to instill a sense of self-criticism in the reader/player vis-à-vis the default misogyny characteristically displayed in mainstream videogames.

Throughout the *TPM* reading experience, the narrative stances remain separate, thus evoking the sense of "an irreducible galaxy of different, heterogenous or antithetical, perspectives" (Richardson 2006, 62) and putting the reader/player in the impossible situation of wanting to read/play on and simultaneously abhorring the damage caused by each interactive gesture. This oxymoronic effect, combined with the sheer disgust evoked by the pornographic writing style used throughout, as well as the general lack of agency experienced by readers of hypertext fiction, can also discourage immersion and may lead to an almost visceral sense of alienation. We would thus argue that *TPM* aims to provide an antimimetic reading experience. In terms of naturalizing strategies, it can be partly understood as a cynical satire (Alber 2016) of violent, mainstream game play and partly as a request for the reader to do-it-yourself and interact with the narrative as "free play" (Alber 2016, 53). At the same time, however, it challenges readers to adopt a quasi-Zen approach (Alber 2016, 54). As an unnaturalizing reading strategy (Nielsen 2013), this approach accepts the text as a medium-specific unnatural construction that relies for its effects on the potentially confusing effects of hypertextual multilinearity. This unnaturalizing reading may itself be read as part of the satirizing (Alber 2016) and metaludic critique, thus corroborating the fierceness of the text's intent to subvert the ease with which blockbuster games immerse readers in ethically dubious entertainment.

4.5.2 The Permeable Narrator

Having discussed a range of medium-specific forms of polyvocality in digital fiction, we now turn to a specific form of multiperson narration, which, due to the specific antimimetic grounds on which it operates, merits separate treatment. The permeable narrator can be understood as "the uncanny and inexplicable intrusion of the voice of another within the narrator's consciousness" (Richardson 2006, 95). It occurs when a narrative voice changes spontaneously between (or slips into) different characters, minds, or voices "and speaks what should be impossible for it to know" (xi), thus "threaten[ing] to violate the principle of an autonomous, individual consciousness that is presupposed by all current theories of the narrator" (95). Richardson traces permeable narrators across a range of mostly modernist and postmodern fiction, such as Joyce's *Ulysses,* Borges's "The Circular Ruins," and Beckett's *The Unnamable,* the latter of which he calls the "fountainhead of the most extreme kinds of permeable narrators, as figures on the same ontological level are fused and then separated back out" (102). The most basic riddle evoked by permeability is the complex question of whether we are dealing with external or internal voices, and whether there remains one primary, constant voice that subsumes all others. In extreme cases like *The Unnamable*, Richardson suggests that neither of these questions can be answered adequately, thus negating "the humanistic concept of a narrator who is like a person" and "violat[ing]" what is probably the most important aspect of personhood, which at least since Descartes has been conceived of as a mind. When that mind is contaminated by debris of another, the very possibility of a unitary self is exploded" (102).

A rare digital example of combining multiperson narration and narrative permeability is Jim Munroe's Interactive Fiction (IF) *Everybody Dies* (2008). Unusually for an IF, it uses first- rather than second-person narration, with the perspective switching between different characters. The main protagonist is Graham, "your standard variety skid, rocker, or metalhead depending on which suburb you grew up in." He works at a Cost Cutters grocery store, and his primary task, which the reader has to perform via command-line input, is to collect a sufficient number of shopping carts. However, Graham is prone to slipping into daydreams and consequently experiences a series of fantastic events and deaths, including being eaten by a fish. In the course of the narrative, the first-person perspective changes from Graham's to that of Ranni, a toilet cleaner at Cost Cutters, and then to that of Ranni's supervisor, Lisa.

This more standard form of multiperson narration, which may not necessarily come across as alienating, is interspersed with instances of permeability, as various intrusive voices interfere with the main characters' narratives. As Lisa takes over as first-person narrator, for example, Ranni suddenly breaks into her interior monologue: "Dream? interrupts Ranni from somewhere in the back part of my head. No." In IFs, which are usually consistently narrated by one third-person narrator using the second-person voice, this combination of multiperson and permeable narration is highly unconventional and adds to the defamiliarizing effects of the narrative as a whole. It is thus an example of medium-specific antimimeticism. The antimimetic effects are foregrounded by the fact that reader/players project themselves into the fictional world in their conventional assumption of performing an avatar role and are bound to be surprised by the unexpected cross-infiltration between different, physically separate entities. Thus, the unconventional nature of the IF's narrative design and the frequent switches between focalized characters, their mutually intrusive voices, as well as between storyworld and dream worlds likely defamiliarize the reader throughout. However, we would argue that the permeability of character voices can also be partly naturalized via a subjectifying reading (Alber 2016), which aligns formal idiosyncrasies with the surrealism evoked by the daydreaming theme. Either way, the specific antimimetic effects evoked by employing permeable narration in a medium-specific scenario that has not conventionalized permeability as part of its narrative possibilities have to be seen both as an unnatural construction and as a metamedial allusion to IF as a narrative medium that is still in its experimental infancy.

4.6 MACHINIC NARRATION AND DIGITAL FICTION

Our final focus in this chapter is dedicated to a philosophical idea that has come to the forefront of current debates surrounding robotics and artificial intelligence. When considering forms of unnatural narration in digital media, we cannot and do not wish to forgo the perennial question of what constitutes naturalness in machinic forms of narrative. Digital technologies lend themselves to experimentation not only with the natural in the sense of human verbal expression (as the term *natural language processing* suggests) but also with the artificial languages used to communicate with computers and to cause them to execute a variety of processes. Indeed, the use of source code as a form of verbal art has been studied extensively by scholars of what is known as critical code studies such as John Cayley, Nick Montfort, Rita Raley, and Mark Marino. They begin from the premise that "the computer may be one recipient of the code but there is also the programmer, other programmers, and at times even users who have access to its text" (Marino 2006b) and that code itself, including the algorithmic-generative processes it yields, should be seen as an agent of artistic practice rather than a mere functional-executable device.

This critical code studies proposition is important in that it gives rise to two general assumptions for digital narratology: first, that the machine is part of the creative process and the artwork itself, and, second, that elements of technology, including software code and hardware, should be integrated in analytical processes. For unnatural narratology, the implications of this can be complex. After all, elements of the machinic, which is often seen in opposition to the natural in a more generic, biological sense, are inextricably integrated into human cybernetic interaction and production. Hence, in a posthuman sense, computational production manifests itself in a plethora of cyborgian combinations between human anatomy, physiology, cognition, and creativity, on the one hand, and "artificially" produced, technological substances, platforms and processes, on the other.

That said, considering how human beings today conduct so-called everyday oral storytelling, it becomes clear that even the more narrow meaning of *natural*, per Fludernik's definition, has become deeply entrenched within digital technoculture. Contemporary orality now manifests itself in various types of social media discourses, including the kinds of micronarratives told by journalistic, political, *and* algorithmic, bot-style producers of factual and fictional stories—whereby the boundaries between fact and fiction, and between human and machinic agency and authorship, are increasingly blurring. With this in mind, we argue that elements of the machinic, of the technological underpinnings and affordances that shape contemporary narrative culture, form an intrinsic part of human "natural" (Fludernik) creation and communication.

4.6.1 Storytelling Machines and Generative Literature

Posthuman narrators come in both nonmimetic and antimimetic forms. Nonmimetic narrators that embody cyborgian human-machine fantasies include a curious array of inanimate, procedural, and mediating objects: machines that can tell stories almost as if they were endowed with humanlike intent, and that often possess superhuman powers of psychological insight and/or omniscience. Richardson (2006) shows that Grass's novel *Local Anaesthetic* (1969) features a television set that "appears to display the confused memories of the protagonist" (3), and that in Gibson's *Neuromancer* (1984), there is "a cybernetic device that allows one person to experience virtually the perceptions of another" (3). Stanislav Lem's *The Cyberiad* (1967) even features "prodigious storytelling machines" that "weave intriguing tales that sometimes amuse, other times disturb their listener, but never seem to come to an end. The stories bifurcate continuously, breaking down into subplots and sub-subplots until the Aristotelian linearity of a beginning, middle, and end has been neatly done away with" (Rosenberg 1992, 204).

In many ways, Rosenberg's description of King Trurl's storytelling machines in *The Cyberiad* matches key features of hypertext fiction, especially their disorienting effects on the audience, their inability to reach closure, and their endless bifurcations and the concomitant collapse of Aristotelian unity and linearity. However, in digital fiction scholarship, genuine storytelling machines are generally considered those that are quite literally "generative" in the Oulipian sense of mathematically driven, algorithmically self-generating. In other words, in digital fiction, the underlying software code becomes a storytelling agent that transcends mere representations of narrative machines. Yet computational generation does not necessarily imply complete noninteraction on the part of the reader: indeed, reader input is generally needed to trigger processes within and/or to navigate generative works of literature. Within the discipline of electronic literature, generative digital *poetry* has been a particularly prolific field, exemplified by such important works as Millie Niss and

Martha Deed's text-machine medley, *Oulipoems* (2004); Jim Andrews's rollover randomizing *Stir Fry Texts* (1999); and Stephanie Strickland and Nick Montfort's numerical poetry generator, "Sea and Spar Between" (2011).

Arguably, machine-generated digital *narratives* lend themselves less aptly to experimentation than do more impressionistic and less story-driven works of poetry. Nevertheless, generative works of digital fiction exist that play with concepts of narrative coherence and the prime building blocks of storytelling. Stuart Moulthrop's multimodal fiction *Reagan Library* (1999), for example, features QuickTime movies with random text generation, and Judd Morrissey and Lori Talley's *The Jew's Daughter* (2000) offers readers a single-screen interface of "recombinatory" (Ciccoricco 2007) narrative text "in which some passages are replaced as the reader mouses over them" (Hayles 2007).

Among the most explicit digital experimentations with generative narrativity is Nanette Wylde's combinatorial work, *Storyland* (v. 2, 2004). In a deliberate attempt to create a "popular" generative experience to readers,

> the program generates [micronarratives that] are often quite accessible and amusing. To operate the work, the reader presses a "new story" button. Using a simple "mad-lib" style technique of selecting stock characters, situations and phrases from a database and delivering them into a structured six-paragraph template, *Storyland* delivers its readers a new combinatorial story every time the button is pushed. (Rettberg 2008)

Thus, against the backdrop of the kind of alienation that can be typically expected from machine-generated, combinatorial works, Wylde attempts to help readers naturalize the experience by evoking thematic-metafictional and metamedial readings about key elements of narrative structure (such as stock characters and situations), often to humorous and serendipitously thought-provoking effects. Overall, the antimimetic effects of *Storyland* can be read as a medium-specific unnatural construction that exploits and showcases the affordances of algorithmically generated literature that refigures poetic license and narrative creativity.

4.6.2 Cybernetic Narration and Omniscience

The final section of this chapter focuses on one of the most controversial forms of extreme narration: omniscience. This "most ostentatiously fictional of narrative techniques" (Ryan 2001, 159) has caused lively debate among various postclassical (and particularly unnatural) narratologists because it reflects the superhuman and therefore physically impossible, unnatural ability to have access to and provide insight into characters' internal, psychological processes and the fictional world as a whole.

The fascination associated with the paradoxical, "naturalized unnaturalness of omniscience" (Mäkelä 2013, 160) is reflected in recent fictional creativity across media. Over the centuries, omniscient narration has undergone an ebb-and-flow development in print. It was the standard form of realistic storytelling in nineteenth-century realism, yet subsequently superseded by reflector mode and internal narrative styles in literary modernism (e.g., James Joyce and Virginia Woolf). More recently, in twenty-first-century fiction, omniscient narrators have seen a revival, albeit in more experimental, progressive forms that reflect the impossibility of godlike or representative knowledge or insight. As Paul Dawson (2013) explains, writers such as Zadie Smith, Salman Rushdie, and Martin Amis have been experimenting with more vulnerable, fragmented, confessional forms of authorial narration that reflect both a crisis of fiction writing and the ambition to create new forms of literary authority and thereby to regain cultural capital vis-à-vis other elements of popular culture and narrative media.

Omniscience in digital media has been discussed compellingly by David Ciccoricco (2015), who introduces the role of the "cybernetic narrator" that speaks through either actual or fictional system messages and blurs the boundary between fictional world and the (imagined) actual world of the author-programmer. He explains,

> To account for the . . . recursive exchange between reader and computer in digital fiction and the way in which the machine regulates and contours our reading experience, we can attribute the operational output of digital narratives to a cybernetic narrator or to a process of cybernetic narration. (77)

Drawing on Chatman's (1990) model of cinematic narration and Aarseth's concept of "ergodic intrigue" (1997, 113), Ciccoricco argues that cybernetic narration integrates a composite of semiotic channels that come together as a narrative function. Simultaneously, cybernetic narration involves recursivity between user and machine, as well as the aesthetic effects of the executable source code and its programmable output. In other words, cybernetic narration uses a combination of telling and showing, of diegesis and camera eye (in audiovisual media). Combined with various multimodal resources and algorithm-based procedural mechanics, it thus represents a medium-specific, authorial stance (cf. Stanzel 1984) that combines the developers' intent with the ways in which that intent is ideologically and aesthetically implied in the design of the software in question. This conglomerate perspective resides "outside the storyworld but, at the same time, inside the computer, much like a playful ghost in the machine" (Ciccoricco 2015, 79). Its effects range from the placing of links and other types of choice mechanisms for the projection of player agency to static versus fluid, noninteractive, and interactive interface elements, including, especially in videogames, the strategic placement and navigational functionalization of the player's avatar. But of course it also includes more traditional elements of verbal and visual focalization, including the "who speaks?" as opposed to the "who sees?" This comes to the fore particularly in cases where the reader/player sees a character (impersonated by themselves or not) through the lens of a movable and zoomable (yet nonetheless preprogrammed) camera eye, and where this player-influenced, quasi-cinematic focalization is accompanied by voiced-over or written narrative text.

A particularly compelling example of cybernetic narration and its concomitant subversion in digital fiction is Davey Wreden's experimental indie game, *The Stanley Parable* (2013, *TSP*; see chapter 3). According to its official site, *TSP* is "an exploration of story, games, and choice. Except the story doesn't matter, it might not even be a game, and if you ever actually do have a choice, well let me know how you did it" (Mularcyzk n.d.). Hence, the game foregrounds questions of illusory agency (MacCallum-Stewart and Parsler 2007), of ludonarrative intersections and ruptures, as well as the inevitability of subversive thought and behavior in the player, "which makes cheating not simply a legitimate but indeed a recommended form of player engagement" (Ensslin 2015, 61; see also Thoss et al. 2018).

TSP does not feature any combat situations or indeed any major physical obstacles or materialized enemies. Nor are there any victory or termination conditions. Instead, the invisible narrator turns out to be the player's main antagonist in the game, and the ideological, nonviolent battle between the cybernetic narrator's explicit and implicit voice (whereby the latter is manifested in the choices built into the game) and the player, who strives to undermine the narrator-prescribed behavior of their fictional counterpart (personified by conformist office worker Stanley), is orchestrated in nineteen different paths, or endings.

TSP's perhaps most strikingly antimimetic element is its thematically central relationship between player, reader/player, and quasi-omniscient narrator. It has to be noted here that, in videogames, narration in the sense of a narrative voice telling the story in the past tense (much as if it had already happened as a fixed sequence of events) while the player is enacting emergent narrative gameplay based on a variety of choices is highly unfeasible. After all, past-tense narration assumes that the narrated events cannot be reversed or undone. Clearly, this works well for videogame back stories, which tend to be told by a voiced-over narrator or onscreen text as background information, typically at the beginning of the game or in narrational interludes between gameplay. However, while interacting with the game world, players generate their own emergent narratives in highly personalized ways (Clement 2017). Hence, any additional, pre-scripted narrational voice that dictates a fixed storyline while accompanying emergent gameplay inherently undermines the player's agency and causes antimimetic ruptures.

Unusually for videogame discourse, the narrator's utterances in *TSP* do not appear in the form of directives (telling the player what to do) or present-tense constatives (providing background information, e.g., about context, setting, and gameplay) (Ensslin 2011b). Instead, the narrator recounts a third-person narrative using the past-tense indicative, thereby making propositions about what Stanley did (before he gets a chance to do so) rather than suggestions about where he might go. Whereas, in print narrative, past-tense indicative narration is the accepted, default standard of storytelling, in a game it completely and antimimetically contradicts conventions. It is bound to raise suspicions in the player about the reliability, or trustworthiness, of the narrator from the outset, as well as their curious function in the game and relation to the storyworld per se. As it turns out in the course of gameplay, the more the player alias Stanley attempts to deviate from the narrator's propositions, the more standoffish and annoyed the latter becomes, so much so that, in some extremely deviant endings, his comments, behavior, and visual designs reflect frustration, despair, resignation, or even madness (Ensslin 2015), which ultimately render him unreliable.

Most interestingly perhaps, in the so-called Museum Ending, Stanley meets his intradiegetic death after choosing to take the escape route branching off the "correct" track (according to the cybernetic narrator) to the "Mind Control Facility." He is killed by some kind of machine, yet again the game goes on, and the player (now playing their own diegetic alter ego) finds themselves in a fictional developer's museum, which exhibits all sorts of in-game props and conceptual art. Strikingly, here another narrator emerges, a female voice, which is superordinate to the diegesis of the initial male narrator, who now seems to have disappeared along with Stanley. The female narrator comments on the paradoxical love–hate relationship between reader/player and narrator and advises the player to stop the game to put an end to the endless, meaningless cycle of "walking someone else's path."

Thus, in fig. 4.2 we can see that, in the Museum Ending, another level of diegesis, a metadiegetic level, marked in red, has been added to the ontological universe of the game, and the female narrator, who fulfills the role of

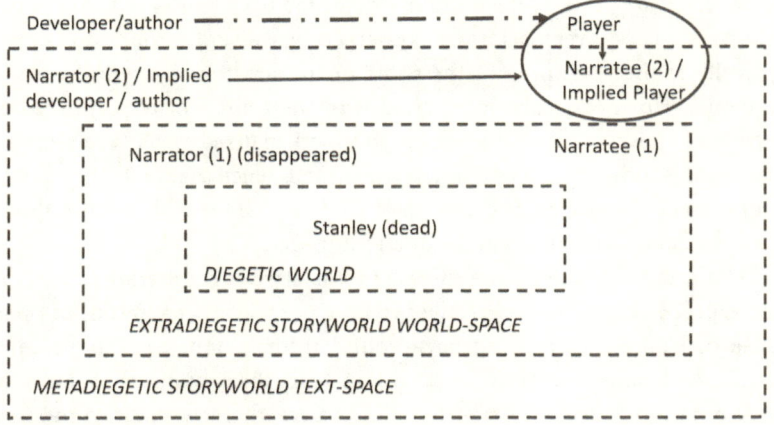

FIGURE 4.2. Diegetic levels as suggested by *The Stanley Parable*'s Museum Ending

an implied developer/author, speaks to the implied player-narratee directly.[2] Interestingly, though, although this supernarrator seems to be more empowered and, because of her metadiegetic insights, endowed with higher-level omniscience than the male narrator dominating the rest of the game, she is equally subject to the player's choices (and of course to the extratextual motivations of the game designers themselves).

Players of *TSP* are likely to apply a variety of cognitive strategies to naturalize the impossibility of the game's narrational constellation. Clearly, the narrative strategies deployed in the game contribute to the overarching allegory (Alber 2016) of the battle between programmer and player, whereby the latter is bound to be defeated and the narrator becomes a functionalized force that serves to distract the player from the programmer's ultimate intentions. That said, an equally valid double-strategy is that of thematic foregrounding and metaludic naturalization. *TSP* can be considered an antiludic game that thematizes and problematizes, through highly diverse and often subversive uses of mechanics, semiotics and/or narrative design, its own gameness and its ideological implications for players entrenched in commercial game culture and the illusion of choice and agency in games (Thoss et al. 2018). Thus *TSP* both foregrounds some key thematic concerns of narrative gameplay and game design and situates itself in an emergent movement of games that seek

---

2. At first glance, it may seem to the actual player that they are also the implied player at Narratee (1) level. Yet in the course of playing the game, it becomes clear that the extradiegetic Narrator (1) cannot be the implied developer, and so Narratee (1) cannot be the implied player either.

to alienate by foregrounding their own very gameness and making players reflect critically on their own habits and expectations. In this way, antimimetic, medium-specific construction serves a reflexive purpose and as a creative response to the perceived lack of innovation in the mainstream game industry.

4.7 CONCLUSION

In this chapter, we have shown how various types of extreme, antimimetic narration operate across digital fiction. We discussed the extent to which medium-specificity shapes the degree to which these "extreme" forms can lead to antimimetic scalable alienating effects, particularly in cases of pathological unreliability, protean interlocutors, multiperson and permeable narration, as well as the play with machinic and cybernetic forms of storytelling and narration. We observed that hypertext fiction lends itself aptly to aesthetic explorations of troubled minds, reflecting trauma in naturalizable ways, for instance through multiperson narration in *Quadrego,* or in permanently defamiliarizing ways, as shown in our discussion of unintentional unreliability in *afternoon*. We also found that the inherent dialogicity of digital media conventionalizes interlocution, as opposed to the unidirectionality assumed by print communication. Nonetheless, there are subtly defamiliarizing ways of deploying the digital interlocutor in medium-specific, unnatural constructions, most powerfully as an ambient conflation of internal monologue, metaleptic, supernatural character speech, and system message, as seen in *WALLPAPER*. We then moved on to instances of machinic narration and explored the role of generative literature and algorithmic authorship in producing what may superficially appear to be unnatural in the sense of non-humanly produced narratives, and yet the ways in which storytelling generators are deployed can help readers develop a sense of coherence and narrative meaning, even from randomly computed digital fiction. Our final discussions then centered around notions of omniscience and cybernetic narration, which are epitomized artistically in the narrator-player battle staged in *The Stanley Parable*.

Focusing on the intersections between human and machine generation and agency in digital fiction, we investigated two narrative phenomena that echo the human fascination with the role of the machinic vis-à-vis assumed "human" roles of programmer, fictional character, avatar, reader, and player. We addressed the question of whether and how computer programs (can) tell stories by focusing on storytelling machines and generative literature. We then dealt with the issue of omniscience in digital narratives. Given that digital works are based in several layers of authorial code, the "author" becomes a composite, cyborgian concept, and narrativity draws on a diverse techniques from verbal diegesis, audiovisual representation, camera work, and player-centered procedurality.

Predictably, the decades to come will revolutionize existing concepts of human–machine interaction, and new concepts will be developed that normalize posthuman, postmedia (Manovich 2014) narrative practices. The examples of generative narrative we have shown in this chapter are only the beginning of a new era of cybernetic narrators and AI-driven storytelling mechanisms that will vastly expand our notion of medium-specific narrative possibility. Thus, many machine-generated narrative forms that may seem antimimetic now will likely enter the mainstream of popular and social media.

5

It's All About "You"

> You is me, but ... it's being suggested that I am a bit like Bluebeard, I've become Bluebeard, uh so you is both, ... it's an amalgamation of me and Bluebeard, I think. ... I've been cheated into being Bluebeard. .... Things are not as simple any more, there's not just that and this, now it's both together, [w]hich is slightly disconcerting. [It] shows how easily the mind can be drawn into a fiction, [how] easily [one] can be made to think in certain ways about oneself.

5.1 INTRODUCTION

The epigraph to this chapter is a reader's oral response to experiencing *The Princess Murderer*, a digital fiction that uses narrative "you" throughout (see chapter 4).[1] As their deliberations suggest, use of the second person can evoke the perception of ontological transgressions, which can puzzle or even upset reader/players. Yet these types of referential ambiguities are only a subset of the manifold cognitive effects that textual "you" can evoke in digital fiction. In this chapter, we focus on the multifarious natural and unnatural uses of "you" in digital fiction. By far the grammatically most malleable pronoun in the English language, "you" gives rise to semantic and referential ambiguity that lends itself to narrative experimentation. It can be used to refer to a protagonist *in lieu* of a first- or third-person reference in what is generally called second-person narration and also to directly address the narratee or the reader/player. This chapter thus necessarily draws on and unites two large thematic areas covered earlier in this book: it extends the discussion of extreme narration from chapter 4 by addressing the full range and complexity of narrative "you," and it shows how "you" can cross the ontological between storyworld

---

1. This data was collected as part of the Reading Digital Fiction project funded by the Arts and Humanities Research Council (Funding Ref: AH/K004174/1). The full data set can be accessed via http://doi.org/10.17032/shu-170009.

and actual world, thus providing an additional, complementary metaleptic strategy to those discussed in chapter 2.

While textual "you" as a narrative device is not as common as first- or third-person narration, as we show in this chapter, the second person is regularly and potently employed in digital fiction. We begin with a survey of existing theories and approaches to textual "you" in narrative theory and present them in the form of a typology that spans print and digital fiction (see also Bell and Ensslin 2011; Ensslin and Bell 2012). We focus in particular on how digital uses of "you" tend to be apostrophic, and how performative uses of "you" are actualized in reader/player input and output. We then move on to an exploration of conventionalized versus antimimetic forms of "you" as they have been theorized in relation to print fiction. In the analytical part of this chapter, we analyze the different thematic concerns that antimimetic "you" can invoke and cause reader/players to critically reflect on, as well as the curiously puzzling phenomenon of digital double deixis as a medium-specific form of ontological transgression via referential ambiguity of "you." Overall, we show that, despite the fact that "you" is ubiquitous and therefore highly conventionalized in digital narratives, its uses can have surprisingly antimimetic effects.

5.2 THEORIZING TEXTUAL "YOU"

"You" is a referentially ambiguous pronoun. In English, it homonymically references female, male, and neutral gender, as well as singular and plural addressees in a stylistically undifferentiating way (as opposed to different polite and casual forms of address in languages such as German and Spanish). It can also be used as a generalized pronoun replacing "one." In a fictional context, it can position the referent of a "you" flexibly between virtual and actual, between intra- and extradiegesis, and between protagonist, characters, narrator, narratee, implied, and actual reader. It represents what Herman (2002) defines as a "special case of person deixis" (332), which, when used intermittently or consistently, produces a "storyworld whose boundaries can be probabilistically but not determinately mapped" (332). That is, because of its flexibility, "you" can refer to individuals whose ontological status is ambiguous and who thus might exist within or outside of a storyworld, or both.

The referential and deictic ambiguity caused by "you" is reflected in narratological typologies and/or terminological distinctions that have been developed to account for the second person in both print and digital fiction (see fig. 5.1).

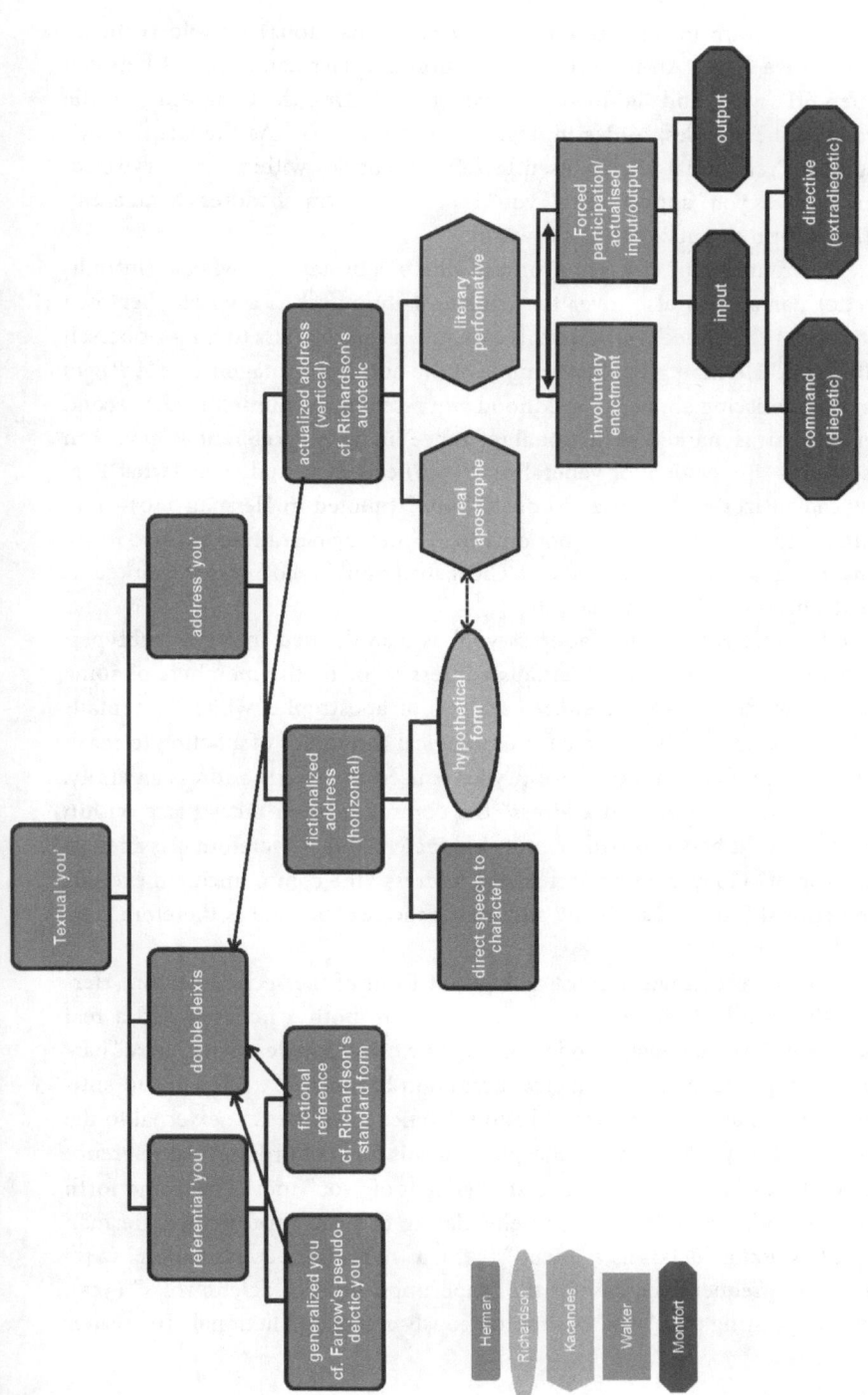

FIGURE 5.1. Functional types of textual "you"

The diagram in fig. 5.1 is topped by Herman's (2002) fivefold typology of narrative "you." An important distinction that Herman makes is between "referential you" and "address you," which, reflecting the complexity of the pronoun, he stresses, "differ in degree, not kind" (341). As the terminology suggests, "referential you" is used to refer to entities within the storyworld, and "address you" applies when "you" is used as a form of address to an entity either within or outside the storyworld.

"Referential you" can take a form in which "a protagonist who, as (intradiegetic) narrator, is also, over the course of the novel as a whole, her own intradiegetic narratee" (340). In this case, the narrator refers to him- or herself with "you." Herman gives the example of the narrator/protagonist of *A Pagan Place* reminiscing about his childhood and referring to himself in the second person. This is marked as "fictional reference" in fig. 5.1. Referential "you" can also be an "impersonal or generalized" (340) collective audience—what Furrow categorizes as "the 'pseudo-deictic' *you*" (quoted in Herman 340)—that "often plays a prominent role not only in . . . literary narratives but also in . . . proverbs, maxims, recipes, [and] VCR instructions" (340); this is marked as "generalized you" on the diagram.

Like "referential you," "address you" is also divided into two subtypes: "*fictionalized* address, which entails address to or by the members of some fictional world . . . and *actualized* address or apostrophe, which . . . entails address that exceeds the frame (or ontological threshold) of a fiction to reach the audience" (341). In both cases, "you" is used to directly address an entity. However, in "fictionalized address" the communication takes place within the storyworld between two or more characters and is therefore classified as "horizontal." Conversely, in "actualized address," the communication exceeds the fictional frame—usually by addressing the reader—and is therefore classified as "vertical."

Last, representing the most ambiguous form of the second person, Herman shows how "you" can be used to refer to both a fictional and a real addressee simultaneously, producing what he calls "double-deixis": here "narrative *you* produces an ontological hesitation between . . . reference to entities . . . internal to the storyworld and reference to entities . . . external to the storyworld" (338). Herman's conception of this form of pronominal reference as "hesitation" might suggest that the referent of "you" moves back and forth between addressees. However, in elucidating this category further, Herman describes double deixis as a "blend" (342), a "hybridized combination," (342) and, more frequently, a case of the "superimposition of deictic roles" (345), terms suggesting that "you" is simultaneously actual and fictional. The reader will thus always feel addressed by "you," but, because "you" also refers to a fictional character, they will not be able to identify with the "you" completely (as our epigraph example shows). Thus, as Herman observes, the reader will find themselves "more or less subject to conflation with the fictional self addressed by you" (345).

Richardson's (2006) typology of second-person narrative is split into three forms: standard, hypothetical, and autotelic. In the "standard" form of second-person narrative, "a story is told, usually in the present tense, about a single protagonist who is referred to in the second person; the 'you' often designates the narrator and narratee as well" (20). It thus correlates with Herman's "fictional reference," in which the narrator addresses themselves in real time. "Hypothetical" forms of second-person narrative, which Richardson (1991) previously termed "subjunctive," are "written in the style of the user's manual or self-help guide . . . [and contain] three features generally absent from standard second person narration: the consistent use of the imperative, the frequent employment of the future tense, and the unambiguous distinction between narrator and narratee. The protagonist is a possible future version of the narratee though it soon takes on an independent, parallel existence" (Richardson 2006, 29). Richardson (2006) cites several short stories from Lorrie Moore's *Self Help* as exemplifying this form because of the user manual or self-help style that they adopt.

The hypothetical form of second-person narration shows how the addressee of "you" can vacillate very subtly in a fictional context. Since the utterances are hypothetical, the imperatives do not have the same illocutionary force they would if they were produced in a nonhypothetical situation. In some ways, therefore, this particular form of second-person narration makes it clear that the address is ultimately made to a supposed version of the narratee and thus it is less likely that the reader will feel directly addressed even though they could partially assume the "you" slot in this case. The hypothetical form of second-person narration still takes place within the fictional world and is therefore "horizontal" according to Herman's taxonomy. In this case the self-help-style imperatives are directed at a hypothetical version of the narratee and are therefore distinct from the standard form of second person that takes place in the present. Importantly, however, because in some cases the imperatives *could* apply to the reader as "you," the hypothetical form of second-person narration can easily slip into an apostrophic form of address to the real reader. The dotted arrow pointing from hypothetical address to real apostrophe on fig. 5.1 indicates that the boundary between fictionalized and actual addressee is fluid.

Richardson's (2006) "autotelic" form of second-person narration is defined as "a direct address to a 'you' that is at times the actual reader of a text and whose story is juxtaposed to and can merge with the characters of the fiction" (30). This form of second-person narration is potentially a form of address, but it is also ontologically flexible insofar as it can switch into a fictional form of reference as the defining attributes of "you" become more specific. It is therefore unlikely to describe the reader entirely, but, at least initially, it can certainly invoke the reader and thus behaves much like Herman's "actualized address" category of "you" before turning into a double-deictic-like form.

As a theory that was chronologically developed before Herman's, Kacandes' (2001, 1993) cannot explicitly engage with Herman's typology. However, drawing on Austin's speech act theory, Kacandes implicitly refines Herman's category of "actualized address" by distinguishing between "apostrophe" and "literary performative." She suggests that readers cannot identify with most cases of fictional apostrophe because the characteristics of the "you" given in the text will rarely match those of the reader completely. However, as a special case of apostrophe, literary performative forms of "you" cause readers to inevitably perform what they are reading and thus become the "you." As an archetype of literary performative, Kacandes gives the example "you are reading this sentence" (2001, 183). That she uses her own example as the archetype is significant. While Kacandes analyzes several examples of "you" that initially fulfill the criteria of literary performative in postmodernist print fiction, she also acknowledges that "literary performatives rarely occur in pure form i.e. as a statement that absolutely any reader can actualize by reading" (1993, 148), simply because the "you" ceases to be the reader as soon as attributes are added to it.

While literary performative *you*s are rare in print fiction, they form an important conceptual basis to digital instantiations of the "you" address. Indeed, in the context of digital narrative, Kacandes's literary performative form of second-person narration offers itself most aptly to a number of interactive texts, the enactment of which relies on the reader/player's response to directives embedded verbally or visually (or both) in the interface. From this point of departure, Jill Walker (2000) subdivides Kacandes's literary performative into two categories: "involuntary enactment," which is typically found in print narrative, and texts that embed "forced participation" by making it impossible for the reader/player to continue in the text without physically performing the actions suggested by the text. As we show in the analysis below, the latter of the two is typically found in interactive, digital narratives. However, even digital narratives encode conceptual and physical interaction to varying degrees. It is thus more useful to think in terms of a continuum rather than a binary division when considering instances of involuntary enactment and forced participation. This relationship is signified on the diagram by the bidirectional arrow between "involuntary enactment" and "forced participation."

Drawing on Montfort (2003), we suggest the term *actualized input/output* as a replacement for the somewhat negatively connoted "forced participation," which Walker characterizes in terms of a "ritual of submission." In his analysis of IF, Montfort adopts computational terminology to conceptualize the reader/player's interaction with the text. According to his model, "anything that the interactor contribute[s], from a press of the space bar to a long typed text, is an *input*" (25), and "whatever texts are produced by the program are *output*" (25). An input and all the outputs that follow until the next input are known as a "*cycle*" (25). Refining input further, Montfort states that "an *input* that refers to an action in the IF world is a *command* [and] is usually in the form of an imperative," and that "all other inputs, such as those that save, restore, quit, restart . . . are *directives*" (26). Since commands affect the contents of the IF's storyworld, they are defined by Montfort as "diegetic," and since directives do not affect the IF's storyworld but instead change circumstances outside the storyworld, they are classified as "extradiegetic." There are obviously similarities here with Aarseth's (1997) concept of the cybernetic feedback loop in which "information flow[s] from text to user" via the modes of representation the text deploys "and back again" (65) via the various interactive functions the reader can perform. However, we use *actualized input/output* to describe a specific kind of cybernetic feedback loop: one in which second-person address is used. It thus emphasizes the interaction that happens between the text-machine and the user when they are addressed as "you."[2]

5.3 UNNATURAL "YOU"

As the preceding theoretical overview suggests, the medium in which textual "you" occurs usually affects how it operates and thereby the extent to which the reader is implicated. Print narratives tend to involve the reader indirectly or ambiguously, whereas reader/players of digital texts can be somewhat obliged to assume the position of "you." The fact that fig. 5.1 exhibits a drift

---

2. In previous work (Bell and Ensslin 2011; Ensslin and Bell 2012), we have refined Montfort's categories further by analyzing "you" in a number of hypertext fictions and suggesting a number of specific functional subtypes of textual "you," a discussion that goes beyond the scope of this book.

towards the bottom-right corner reflects the importance of direct address—or specific forms thereof—to digital narratives.

Importantly, however, while "you" creates ambiguous forms of reference and address, not all uses of the second-person voice in fiction are unnatural. For example, direct speech as "fictionalized address" in which communication occurs between two characters within the same level of a storyworld is not unnatural: neither in a nonmimetic sense, because it does not contravene actual-world logical or physical laws, nor in an antimimetic sense, because it is a fully conventionalized element of fictional dialogue. In fact, fictionalized address closely aligns with the kind of "natural," conversational storytelling discussed by Fludernik (1996).

Similarly, referential forms of "you," such as Herman's example, cited above, of the narrator/protagonist of *A Pagan Place* reminiscing about his childhood and referring to himself in the second person, are not unnatural in a nonmimetic sense. This is because a homodiegetic narrator, using a past tense form of "you," reflects the events from their past that they self-narrate. In such cases, the narrator knows better than anyone else how they behaved and felt; thus, while the narrative style is unusual and hence potentially defamiliarizing, it is not unnatural in the sense of logically or physically impossible.

Below, we suggest that antimimetic forms of "you" manifest in any literary medium according to four devices: omniscience (see also chapter 4); narrative present and/or future tense; the collapse of story and discourse; and the collapse of the actual and the fictional (see also chapter 2). We address these forms of "you" separately, but we maintain that the ontological ambiguity of "you" necessarily means that some *you*s are inevitably unnatural in more than one way at the same time.

5.3.1 Omniscience

Some forms of "you" are unnatural because they indicate knowledge by an extradiegetic narrator of and about a fictional character to the extent that they exhibit impossible levels of omniscience (see chapter 4). Alber (2016) refers to such "you"-narratives as exhibiting "impossible mind-reading abilities" (84) because "in nonfictional discourse we cannot tell our addressees in great detail what they experience, think, and feel" (84). Like third-person omniscience, second-person narration provides access to and insight into characters' internal, psychological processes. However, the difference between the two voices is that while third-person omniscience tells an extradiegetic addressee what the characters are experiencing, second-person omniscience tells the character what they are experiencing. This latter strategy adds an antimimetic element to the otherwise conventionalized strategy of third-person omniscient narration in general.

Indeed, Fludernik (1996) determines that "second-person fiction [is] 'impossible' in the sense of narrating to the reader or an addressee what that addressee qua story protagonist must know much better" (262). She quotes a passage from John Updike's short story "How to Love America and Leave It at the Same Time" in which the narrator tells "you" what happens as he arrives at a motel after a long journey (e.g., "your legs unbend weirdly after all that sitting behind the wheel"). In a digital context, Bell (2013) has shown how this form of "you" works in Stuart Moulthrop's hypertext fiction *Victory Garden*. Introducing a new scene, the narrator proclaims "*you always knew it would look like this*" (Moulthrop, quoted in Bell 2013, 193; italics in original), thus exhibiting an even greater level of omniscience than in the Updike example insofar as they exhibit knowledge about the "you" character's mental state. Irrespective of medium, "you" narratives often display omniscience because the second-person pronoun often refers to a fictional entity that is not always just the narrator themselves. "You" thus points away from itself, and, when used to describe internal mind states in particular, it results in an antimimetic physical impossibility.

5.3.2 Present and/or Future Tense

While "you" narratives can be narrated in the past tense, the use of present or future tense intensifies their antimimeticism because it represents narratives which unfold as they are told and/or predict the future—both of which are impossible. As Fludernik (1996) notes, present-tense "you" is impossible because "one cannot realistically 'live' the story and narrate it at the same time or tell what one is currently experiencing *as a story*" (252). Both the Updike and the Moulthrop examples above represent this form of second person. Similarly, a narrator cannot know what is going to happen to the "you" in the future, much as a narrator in a game like *The Stanley Parable* cannot know what the reader/player did before they get an opportunity to decide what they are going to do (see chapter 4). Indeed, "you" narratives that use present and future tense are always antimimetic in ways that past-tense "you" narratives are not; it is impossible for someone to know what is happening or will happen to someone else (or indeed themselves) in the future, but it is possible for a narrator to know what did happen to someone else or to themselves at a point in the past. Both present and future tense thus work in conjunction with omniscient narrative strategies and result in antimimetic storytelling scenarios.

5.3.3 Story/Discourse Collapse (Metaleptic "You" Type I)

Since some forms of second-person narrative involve an address from a narrator to an intradiegetic narratee, "you" can break the boundary between the world of the storyteller and the world of the story (see chapter 2). Indeed, Fludernik (1994) suggests that the unnaturalness of second-person texts comes precisely from their ability to "frequently undermine th[e] story-discourse dichotomy by the very nonnaturalness of their design, telling the narratee's or addressee's story" (457). She thus associates the unnaturalness of "you" with the impossibility of breaking the standard fictional communicative model (e.g., Genette 1982) that keeps the story and discourse levels discrete; it is not possible in the actual world for narrators to be located at the same ontological levels as the characters they are narrating, as the collapse of the boundary between the world of the teller and the world of the telling in the Updike and Moulthrop examples above show. "You" narratives are thus antimimetic given that such forms of communication are not possible in natural narrative and the ontological maneuver that they imply is permanently defamiliarizing (Iversen 2016).

5.3.4 Actual/Fictional Collapse (Metaleptic "You" Type II)

Richardson's, Alber's and Fludernik's accounts of the second person in fiction largely focus on forms of "you" that construct a fictional character referred to by "you." While they each recognize that "you" can also extend to incorporate the reader, they do not focus on apostrophic forms of "you" to the same level of detail. However, as we have suggested above, apostrophic forms of "you" are a prevalent and thus important feature in a digital context. While largely neglected in narrative theory so far (but see, for example, McHale 1992, 93–95; Wolf 2005, 93–94), we argue that address "you" is also unnatural in the sense of being physically and logically impossible and defamiliarizing because it can reach out of the storyworld to address the reader directly. Margaret Atwood's (1983) short story "Happy Endings" begins "John and Mary meet. What happens next? If you want a happy ending, try A" with two sections of text, A and B, below. The narrator thus uses the second person to address the reader, playfully asking them to make a choice about which part of the text they would like to read. A similar use of the second person can be found at the beginning of Michael Joyce's hypertext fiction, *afternoon, a story*, which invokes the reader by asking "Do you want to hear about it?" and requiring them to respond in order to progress through the text (see Bell 2007; see chapter 4).

Either in a pure form such as literary performative or as part of some forms of doubly deictic "you," apostrophic forms of address "you" breach the boundary between the actual and fictional worlds and therefore constitute a form of metalepsis. Of course, when a second-person address is used in fiction, readers are not really addressed by a fictional narrator or character; this is impossible because they do not belong to the same ontological domain. However, as Hanebeck (2017) puts it, this "radical game" (100) is precisely what readers are asked to imagine happens in some cases of second-person address. He continues:

> I propose to confine the term second-person (or lectorial) metalepsis to those transgressions in which the individual . . . *addressed* moves across the boundary between the domains of the signified and the domain of the signifier. The "ontological hesitation" potentially induced by the use of narrative *you* often suggests more than one context in which the "you" being addressed is located (or perhaps, more accurately, in which reader, listeners, or viewers locate the addressed entity/being; a constructive effort which may imply the "real" world). (98)[3]

While Hanebeck recognizes that the ambiguity of "you" can lead to the invocation of more than one addressee, he also maintains that the addressee of a "you" can be located in the real world. "You" therefore becomes metaleptic. Wolf (2005) also suggests that doubly deictic "you" can also be classified as metaleptic because the "use of the pronoun 'you' with this double reference could here already be classified as a tendential metalepsis: for it positions an addressee who exists outside a fictional world simultaneously (as the employment of the present tense suggests) inside it" (94).

As we showed in chapter 2, some metalepses are physically impossible on the basis that, in the actual world, entities from two different ontological domains cannot interact. Hanebeck's account of metalepses shows how fictional apostrophes are impossible because such forms of "you" suggest that communication can take place across the actual-to-storyworld boundary. As we also showed in chapter 2, some metalepses are logically impossible because they suggest that an individual exists in two domains at the same time. In

---

3. Hanebeck's (2017) example of second-person metalepsis is taken from the comic book *Animal Man*, in which a second-person address is used in direct speech and accompanied by an image of a character looking out of the panel, potentially at the reader. Importantly, then, Hanebeck's example shows how direct speech can be metaleptic.

Hanebeck's account, a second-person address can imply that the speaker is, like the addressee, also located in the actual world as opposed to holding a conversation across an ontological boundary between fictional and actual. However, whichever way we conceptualize it, a second-person metalepsis creates an impossible state of affairs because it is not possible for fictional characters to interact with readers in the actual world, and the impossibility of this communication is defamiliarizing.

While pure forms of metaleptic "you" are rare in print, as we show in the proceeding analyses, second-person metalepses are highly likely to occur in digital fictions in which readers are involved in an actualized input/output cycle. Initially at least, the reader of any narrative media can be seen as the intended recipient of any second-person address because they are the person receiving the communication (cf. Fludernik 1995, 106). In digital fiction, however, second-person address is even more likely to implicate the reader because they are physically involved in the construction of the text. They must, for example, use a mouse to select a link and thus make a decision about their experience of the text. Consequently, they are likely more to feel addressed by a "you" especially when the "you" is used in conjunction with a metafictional comment about the digital reading context (cf. Bell 2007, 2010, 2011). Moreover, Fludernik (1996) suggests that the second person is one of a set of "pronouns, which require considerable effort on the reader's part to be narrativized within the fictional context" (236). However, as we show below, direct address is not necessarily hard to naturalize in digital fiction because it is used so ubiquitously in digital media and thus is a relatively conventional feature of many digital texts. In the analysis below, we show how "you" has become more or less conventionalized and thus more or less defamiliarizing in a digital context specifically. Of particular importance in the discussion of antimimetic forms of "you" are cases in which the text draws attention to the impossibility of the communication between textual entity and reader, and also examples in which the referent of "you" is ambiguous and which thus cause doubly deictic forms of unnaturalness.

5.4 CONVENTIONALIZED "YOU" IN DIGITAL FICTION

As indicated above, "you," specifically in its autotelic form, is a common feature of digital narratives such as Interactive Fictions (Montfort 2003, 2007), videogames, hypertext and hypermedia fictions, and app-fictions. This is because digital, interactive texts implement various manifestations of the cybernetic feedback loop between reader/players and the text/game, thus allowing "you" to bring about a species of ontological violation that is not possible in printed texts. Reader/players are involved in the ongoing, material construction of the text as they traverse the story or game world, and the use of "you" in this context is not particularly unusual. Hence, reader/players have naturalized the logical aporia of being addressed by fictional discourse that breaks the ontological boundary between diegesis and extradiegesis and, likewise, of being able to impact the storyworld directly through verbal and kinetic input. Similarly, readers addressed by "you" in digital fictions are, unlike print readers, led to enact their responses to apostrophic interpellations directly and materially, for instance by clicking on action buttons or by keying text into onscreen lines or boxes (Ensslin and Bell 2012, 56).

Interactive Fiction is the mode of digital fiction that employs "you" in perhaps the most explicit and sustained way. As shown in chapter 1, IFs use present tense and the imperative "you" to create the illusion of being present in a storyworld that is constructed by the reader in creative interaction with the programmed text. In IFs, "you" is the main character, role-played by the reader (Douglass 2007, 129). As Ryan (2005) puts it, "IF is one of the rare narrative forms where the use of 'you' enters into a truly dialogical rather than merely rhetorical relation with an Other, and where 'present' denotes narrow coincidence between the time of the narrated events and the time of the narration" (519).

The vertical form of apostrophic "you" is also used extensively in videogame discourse and the paratexts surrounding the games themselves (such as manuals, discussion fora, blogs, and magazines). For their part, Harrigan and Wardrip-Fruin (2007) define the "you" used in videogames in terms of player choice and responsibility, with the player considered a singular entity rather than a collective audience: "you are the person for whom the story is being told" (xiv), and the "you" fills the role(s) enabled by any chosen game's avatar selection or customization mechanism. Players see their *alter egos* embodied in the shape of an avatar, an object, vehicle, or simply a cursor, which may be compared to *I-cum-you* internal dialogues or self-communication (Margolin 1990, 428). However, in the case of the avatar as embodied *alter ego*, "you" in a game does not tend to be indicative of self-alienation, in contrast with some of the postmodern print narratives discussed by Margolin (1990). On the contrary: the fact that players tend to narrate their own past gaming experiences in the first person suggests that they identify with the reader/player or avatar representing them in the game world.

"You" is embedded multimodally and verbally in most videogame interfaces (Ensslin 2011b). The variety of elements sensitive to player input can be seen as directive prompts for player action and interaction. Many narrative games make indexical use of strong colors to signal that an object or non-player character will, when activated, convey important ludic and/or diegetic information. This information is then usually conveyed dialogically, using "you" as a combination of apostrophic address to the player, to trigger action, yet in a fictionalized form, directed to their in-world avatar. This usually happens either by means of character voice-over or through the display of written text. Tutorials and instruction manuals, on the other hand, encode the reader/player verbally in terms of a strongly apostrophic and directive "you." In English-language manuals, such modes of address typically occur in the syntactic form of imperatives ("To view what your Creature has learned, select the Creature Learning icon on the Toolbar [. . .]"; *Black and White 2* Manual [Lionhead Studios 2005]: 16), conditionals using modal verbs ("If you have enough Tribute, you can buy toys for your Creature to play with"; *Black and White 2*, 17), and explanatory indicatives in the present and future tense, pertaining to the overarching storyworld ("Although your Creature is intelligent, he will only learn your will if he's nudged in the right direction"; *Black and White 2*, 17).[4]

5.5 ANTIMIMETIC "YOU" IN DIGITAL FICTION

In the previous section we showcased how apostrophic "you" in digital, interactive narratives can operate in ways that, despite breaking the boundary between fictional and actual worlds and therefore staging ontologically impossible scenarios, do not necessarily have any (pronounced) antimimetic effects on the reader/player. In fact, "you" is ubiquitous in digital narrative (and particularly videogame) discourse and therefore highly conventionalized. Conversely, when employed in more literary digital contexts, "you" invites very different and often antimimetic types of reader engagement. Many hypertext fictions employ second-person narration as a means of drawing attention to and harnessing the reader's unique function in the text (Bell 2007, 2010; Bell and Ensslin 2011). That said, unlike IF, hypertext fiction foregrounds the importance of the authored text and limits reader agency to varying degrees of navigational freedom rather than allowing readers to enter into co-productive, dialogic text construction characteristic of IF. In Shelley Jackson's (1995) *Patch-*

---

4. At the time of writing, videogame instruction manuals, which tended to come as part of the DVD box, have become a historical genre. In contemporary games, instructions tend to be built implicitly into the mechanics of tutorial levels, and explicit instructions are communicated to the reader/player by in-world coaches, or masters, and to the player by onscreen GUI prompts.

work Girl, for example, the protagonist tells the reader "I am buried here. You can resurrect me, but only piecemeal," with readers then required to choose links which provide information about the Patchwork Girl. The reader must move a mouse and click a button or type a response on a keyboard in order to learn more about the fictional world and its inhabitants. This aligns with Montfort's (2003) diegetic command input, albeit in a syntactically reduced, non-linguistically creative form. The second person here draws medium-conscious attention to the corporeal role that readers play in hypertext fiction.

In the case of hypertext fiction, we are thus dealing with a less conventionalized and therefore potentially more defamiliarizing form of apostrophic "you" than in most videogames. After all, hypertext readers interact with the textual and diegetic world in a far less ontological and more exploratory manner (Ryan 2006a) than if they are represented in-world by a verbally or visually rendered avatar in an IF or audiovisual game world. As Ryan (2006a) notes, hypertext readers remain "external to both the time and space of the virtual world . . . ; [their] actions do not simulate the behavior of a member of the virtual world; and interactivity is limited to the freedom to choose routes in a textual space that has nothing to do with the physical space of a narrative setting" (108). Thus, they are bound to notice the violation of the ontological boundary between actual and fictional worlds far more strongly than while conceptualizing and seeing themselves embodied in the fictional world of a 3D role-playing game, for example. The metaleptic second person in *Patchwork Girl* is therefore more antimimetic than in a standard role-playing videogame or IF scenario.

The following subsections focus on a variety of unconventional uses of "you" in digital fiction, which draw attention to the form itself and the ease with which it not only breaks the fourth wall and lulls players into an immersive state but also can perform a range of secondary, thematic and critical functions. Our analysis thus expands Alber's (2016) thematizing reading strategy by showcasing how medium-specific antimimeticism can have strongly empathic and/or didactic effects on immersed reader/players (see also chapter 1).

5.5.1 "Players just like you"—Comic Antimimetic Effects in *EarthBound*

Given that apostrophic, or autotelic "you" is ubiquitous in videogame metadiscourse, players are used to being addressed directly by videogame interfaces. This is particularly prevalent in paratextual segments such as customization menus and configuration screens. Players of role-playing games (RPGs), for example, are used to spending significant time personalizing their interface and avatar before they embark on gameplay proper and follow autotelic instructions by the system in doing so.

A game that makes antimimetic subversion of such default settings and expectations part of its satirical-humoristic intent is Earthbound Ape Inc. and HAL Laboratory's RPG, *EarthBound* (1994). Originally published by Nintendo under the title *Mother 2* for the Super Nintendo Entertainment System, the game features a party of four companion characters, whose names can be customized, and one of whom is the player's avatar. The game is set in an everyday, Western environment, and the player's main goal is to free the world from an alien force named Giygas, which has spread hatred around the world and transformed humans, animals, and objects into malicious beings.

Prima facie, *EarthBound* follows many of the design standards of contemporaneous two-dimensional RPGs: the player's team of characters have to navigate a range of cities, villages, dungeons, and caves, fighting numerous enemies on their way, to gain XP (experience points). However, *EarthBound* was designed from the outset to parody its own genre. It was meant to come across as "quirky and goofy" (Schreier 2016) and was deliberately written in Japanese kana script to lend the dialogues a conversational, witty tone.[5] The English/American localization emulates this colloquial, slangy register, and players are met with menu and customization design that is meant to defamiliarize and amuse right from the outset. While the game uses conventional character design, for the design of the player interfaces it offers a range of ludically irrelevant, quasi-baroque color choices, or "flavors," such as "Plain," "Mint," Strawberry," and "Banana."

The game pokes intertextual fun at mainstream RPG design throughout, and while the autotelic instructions in the customization part of the game or the intermittent, formulaic player feedback ("You won") do not deviate greatly from what players of this game genre would expect, after several hours of immersive gameplay, an antimimetic, vertical apostrophic address suddenly breaks the player's illusion: in the Summer (a seaside town) level, just after beating a "Crazed Sign" on the main road in team combat and having entered the building housing the Stoic Club, a telephone ringtone occurs that seemingly calls the reader/player. In the ensuing dialogue, however, it turns out that the caller is the protagonist's best friend and roommate, Tony, who wants to talk to the player themselves on what turns out to be an instant messaging system. Tony explains that he is "collecting players' names for a school project. You know, players just like you. That's right, you, holding the controller.

---

5. Kana is the most conceptually oral script system in Japanese.

Would you register your name, please? Don't spell your name wrong." Subsequently, the player is shown the same alphabetic choice menu as at the beginning of the game, when they first customized and named their avatar, except that now the expectation is—for the sake of Tony's fictional survey—that the player enter their actual name. Having done so, the interlocutor thanks the player and asks them to check their name again on the same alphabetic menu, after which Tony continues by apologizing "for any trouble this may have caused you." The previously and ordinarily extradiegetic customization window thus undergoes an ontological shift into the diegetic world of the game, where the player's assumed actual name becomes part of a fictional research project. Tony closes the conversation by advising the player not to "put my friend [protagonist's name] in any dangerous situations, okay? I worry about him. I really do . . . Well, talk to you later. . . . I hope that I can see you again when you are feeling up to it. From T-O-N-Y . . . You got that? Well, I've been on the phone too long . . . Gotta go . . . Good luck . . . Take care . . . So long . . . This time, I'm really gonna hang up. Goodbye. *Beeeep*." The transliterated beep tone signals the end of Tony's socially hesitant end monologue, which conveys nuances of his personality that link him emotionally to the player ("I hope I can see you again"), who is thus further drawn into the diegetic world of the game's characters and their peculiar mindsets—a further antimimetic feature in an otherwise genre-typically action-oriented 2D RPG.

The metaleptic "you" in *EarthBound* marks a collapse between actual and fictional worlds (type II; see section 5.3.4.) that is perceived as antimimetic because it breaches the convention of keeping the interlocutor-feedback mechanism anonymized, or embedded in the software system. What happens in the Tony scene above, when a diegetic character addresses the extradiegetic player in an ascending ontological metalepsis, is unexpected in the sense of unprecedented in the game's established communication pattern, thus having an estranging, antimimetic effect on the player. What adds to this effect is the unexpected behavior of the interviewer, who comes across as somewhat unprofessional in his struggle to finish the conversation and is thus reminiscent of an unintentional unreliable narrator—again an unconventional element in RPGs. Overall, the antimimeticism of the interaction adds to the comic-satirical atmosphere of the game as a whole and can therefore be naturalized by the player as a parody of other games of the same genre.

5.5.2 "You will control nothing"—Abuse as Antimimetic in *Loved*

As we have shown throughout this chapter so far, apostrophic "you" in digital fiction and commercial videogames commonly occurs to give reader/players different options, or choices for shaping the narrative in a personalized, emergent way (Clement 2017; Jenkins 2004). This medium-specific convention lends reader/players a sense of agency that, albeit always restricted by and to the conditional logic of algorithmic code, reader/players expect.

Loved: A Short Story, by Alexander Ocias (2010), is a Flash-based browser game that reduces player control psychologically, through forms of verbal and mechanics-induced physical abuse, and thus procedurally and verbally stages the traumatic experience of being in an abusive relationship. Represented mostly in black-and-white, with colors deployed selectively to display hyperlinks and/or to symbolize challenges and adversary elements, the game uses a simplistic, schematic visual-level design, thus directing player attention to meanings beyond conventional 2D platform gameplay. The voice of the abusive narrator manifests itself in the form of written onscreen dialogue directed at the player and their avatar. "Are you a man, or a woman?" it asks at the very beginning, a question that is problematic not only because of its underlying binary gender bias but because it turns out to be manipulative. Whichever gender the player chooses, the narrator will subvert it immediately afterwards by bluntly objecting "No, you're a boy" (if the player chooses to play as a woman, and vice versa if they choose to play as a man). The narrator thus renders themselves a bully by way of their disrespectful neglect of the player's personal choices and, even more so, by reducing the player's identity to that of an immature child that arguably needs guidance and control. Indeed, in their next utterance, the narrator makes it clear that "you will control nothing," thus subverting the player's expectations regarding choice and agency and reminding them of their inferior position vis-à-vis the omnipotent authorial narrator. The player's belittled identity in the game is further augmented by the fact that their avatar appears in the shape of a cuddly teddy bear.

Through intermittent feedback, the narrator patronizes the player, praising them in their enforced minor role ("Good boy/girl!"). They also give the reader/player abusive tasks to perform ("Throw yourself into the barbs"), offend them verbally ("Ugly creature!"), and ask the reader/player leading questions forcing them to confirm the narrator's self-imposed, dominant, and possessive role ("Do I own your body or your mind?"). The repetitive verbal abuse is combined with occasional physical abuse. If the player fails to make their avatar jump successfully across the "pit of barbs" at the beginning of the game, for example, they will see their avatar thrown back to the start position so forcefully that the teddy's body bounces back from a wall, and the visual impact made by its body is accompanied by a reverberant background noise.

The game's procedural rhetoric, augmented by abusive forms of player address, creates an intense, affective experience for the player, which allows them to empathize with victims of abuse. By the same token, the game's mechanics allows if not requires the player to adopt a subversive strategy in the course of the game, developing the skills that will help them master each level despite the odds. The resilience developed by the player, which enables them to complete the game, ultimately exposes the narrator's psychological weakness and dependency on the reader/player. Just before the avatar enters the exit level of the game, the abuser's surrendering voice appears onscreen ("Why do you hate me? I loved you. Where will you go? Will you be close to me?"), seeking forgiveness from their victim as they finally manage to leave the world that kept them in emotional fetters.

This procedural rhetoric creates an empathic, educational experience for the player that causes them, via a thematic-didactic reading strategy (Alber 2016), to reflect on the self-empowering options that victims of abuse often have in real life yet cannot always implement, for complex psychological and social reasons. The unconventional use of "you" to represent an abused yet self-liberating reader/player thus instrumentalizes antimimeticism as a learning and potentially even a therapy tool that allows players to experience—through unconventional play, trial, and error—potential strategies of overcoming unbalanced power relationships.

5.5.3 "Why should you care?"—Unethical Warfare as Antimimetic in *Spec Ops: The Line*

Most conflict-oriented videogames are grounded in a fairly clear-cut moral dichotomy of good versus evil, and players tend to be aware of how (at least vaguely) the decisions they make may have an impact on the game world, its inhabitants, and their own persona in the game. Players stereotypically embody a heroic figure whose task it is to save a nation or population invaded by an enemy force. Hence, the default expectation for the player is to follow an ultimately altruistic goal, although the path to that goal tends to be riddled with enemies that they have to eradicate—typically by violent means.

Exceptions to this trajectory in genres that are unmistakably marked as violence- and action-driven (such as first-person shooters, action adventures, and RPGs) usually come across as unconventional and thus conceptually, medium-, and/or text-specifically antimimetic, where the degree of defamiliarization, as always, depends on both the player's personal frame of reference and experiential background, as well as on the actual game and how it implements the deviation procedurally and representationally. A war game that deviates from the altruistic-heroic pattern with the intent to demonstrate the impossibility of moral integrity in warfare is Yager Development's *Spec Ops: The Line* (2012, *SOTL*).

Drawing on literary sources like *Heart of Darkness*, *SOTL* focuses on the psychological repercussions of experiencing the horrors of war and bearing responsibility for them. While the game exhibits the typical mechanics and graphical user interface (GUI) items of a third-person shooter, it carries an unconventional focus on the gruesome reality of facing death, mutilation, torture, and decomposition directly and graphically. The protagonist and reader/player, Captain Martin Walker, is tasked with locating survivors in a postapocalyptic version of Dubai. Throughout the game, he and his Delta Force team increasingly show the symptoms of posttraumatic stress disorder and related psychotic conditions vis-à-vis the impossibility of maintaining their ethical standards towards civilians and unarmed military personnel. Overwhelmed by conflicting feelings and the impossibility of performing his mission according to his own standards, Walker loses emotional control over his initially professional conduct. Significantly, the deteriorating psychosis he and his team experience is represented metaleptically by direct loading-screen system messages to the player. These messages refer to a mixture of metacognitive, pathological conditions associated with the impossibility of making the right moral decision (e.g., "Cognitive dissonance is an uncomfortable feeling caused by holding two conflicting ideas simultaneously"). They also contain apostrophic questions that cannot be read other than as a cynical critique of the player's assumed uncritical stance towards fictionalized yet highly realistic violence and unethical military conduct: "The US military does not condone the killing of unarmed combatants. But this isn't real, so why should you care?"

The fact that *SOTL* cannot be played without making impossible, amoral decisions puts the player in a similar psychological dilemma as the characters. Unlike most shooters, the game thus makes a statement about the moral implications of its own genre, and the antimimetic-metaleptic second person serves as an ethical reminder to the player that there is no such thing as ethical warfare, and that by engaging in belligerent entertainment they become spiritually complicit in the horrors of war. Thus, antimimetic use of apostrophic "you" contributes to the player's thematic reading (Alber 2016) of the game and, at the same time, their heuristic process of learning and internalizing the antiwar message the game seeks to deliver.

5.6 DIGITAL DOUBLE DEIXIS

The previous sections showcased how antimimetic "you" in digital fictions and narrative videogames in particular can evoke specific comic and thematic-didactic effects in the player. For the final analytical section of this chapter, let us now return to the empirical reader quoted in the epigraph. The passage is a spontaneously generated response to a special case of "you" (in this case, a passage from geniwate and Deena Larsen's *The Princess Murderer*; see below), which typically puzzles reader/players because the evoked referent mentally oscillates between a character in the text (and particularly the protagonist) and the actual reader/player themselves. As explored in section 5.2, instances of "you" that create this kind of ontological hesitation between fictional and actual referent are "doubly deictic" (Herman 2002). In digital fiction, this hesitation can be particularly powerful in its antimimetic effects because reader/players physically interact with onscreen material, thus executing narrative processes.

In the following analyses, we show how the digital fiction reader's dual embodiment can be exploited to achieve diverse antimimetic effects. Medium-specific double deixis may induce feelings of guilt resulting from unintentional yet inevitable complicity in violent acts onscreen, or it may serve to generate empathy and imaginary dialogue with a protagonist that seeks to overcome conflicting desires of pervasive knowledge and respectful mystery.

5.6.1 Complicit Clicking and Double Deixis in *The Princess Murderer*

As introduced in chapter 4, *TPM* is a metaludic digital fiction that takes aim at violent, misogynist gamer culture. Not only does it feature multiperson narration, it also uses second-person pronouns to blend the identities of the fictional villain, Bluebeard, and the doubly embodied player, who either kills or "breeds" a princess with every mouse-click they activate (see Picot 2003). *TPM* relies on drawing the reader into the storyworld. It also acts interdiscursively, in a way designed to criticize other forms of digital narrative and their accompanying critical theories, many of which have overemphasized the degree of freedom and agency possessed by users in their interactions with digital works (see Ensslin and Bell 2012, 60).

To augment the impression of the victims' eroticized suffering, each click triggers a high-pitched, voiced-over sigh that can only be evaded by turning off the computer's sound. This sound effect inevitably puts the reader in an uneasy position, linking their actual-world actions to fictional abuse. *TPM* makes ample use of second-person involuntary enactment (Walker 2000) throughout, questioning simultaneously these same (brutal) instances of enactment. Similarly, the reader's increasing guilt is reflected in the text at a moral or ethical level. For example, in passaged like "the conjunction between you and Bluebeard grows stronger. / Your innocence drifts away with each sign you select and starting again won't change that," the "you"-as-reader is forced into a position in which they become a permanent ally to the villain. The growing harm induced by the reader/player' clicking action is reinforced by increasing perspectival multivocality. The dying princesses' first-person metaleptic cries of suffering ("I beg you, no more clicks. U-gggghhh! I'm dying, you sadomasochistic torturer!") seem to be directed at the reader. Conversely, second-person fictional references such as "You look at your hands, dripping in blood" can—at least on a literal level—only refer to entities located within the fictional world.

On the whole, readers experiencing *TPM* are inadvertently confronted with the oscillating tension between fictionalized and apostrophic address. This leaves them wavering between different readings of "you" and anchoring events, by turns, in contexts associated both with the virtual and with the actual world. This effect is most strongly generated by instances of doubly deictic "you." For example, a quasi-apostrophic address resembling penal discourse ("Don't you believe in their pain? That is the only interpretation that saves you from being a psychopath") simultaneously implicates the actual reader and a fictional addressee producing "hesitation between reference to entities, situations, and events internal to the storyworld and . . . external to the storyworld" (Herman 2002, 338). Clearly, the reader/player knows that they are not actually involved in a legal trial and that the "you" must therefore refer to a fictional or hypothetical addressee. However, they will have inevitably killed and/or raped several princesses within the fictional world to get to this point. The referential dexterity of the second-person pronoun thus forces readers to assume a level of responsibility and induces sensations of unavoidable complicity and associated guilt.

5.6.2 Character Empathy and Double Deixis in *Opacité/Opacity*

As opposed to causing feelings of guilt vis-à-vis the reader/player's onscreen misdoings, doubly deictic referential ambiguity of "you" in digital fiction may also evoke empathic effects. Serge Bouchardon et al.'s hypermedia short story,

Opacité/Opacity (2012, *Opacity*), uses instances of "you" to stage an interlocution between its two main characters while, at the same time, drawing the reader into its philosophical deliberations. Coded in HTML5, the text uses visuals as well as text and poetically implements the protagonist's musings about the oxymoronic desire for simultaneous transparency and opacity in romantic relationships. Its four sections move from a study of the interior of a computer to an examination of the speaker's wife's body, then to an investigation of language used to convey intimacy and mutual knowledge, and finally to the material opacity of a frosted-glass shower door. As Flores (2012) reflects,

> Each part leads readers to reflect on what lies beneath the surface of something or someone and whether having that knowledge leads to a [deeper] understanding or a better relationship. The final part leads us to think about how opacity, a little mystery even, is good for marriage, and enhances desire. (n. pag.)

Flores's reading is prompted by the naked female body depicted behind a semitransparent shower door and the sound of running water suggesting that the viewer is metaleptically situated in a voyeuristic scenario of observing another person's showering (an act of cleansing that may be considered an attempt at increasing corporeal transparency).

Opacity features three main narrative voices: that of a first-person homodiegetic narrator and male-identified protagonist who seeks to gain greater transparency of life, technology, himself and others—and particularly of his wife's innermost thoughts and feelings; a female voice-over that appears at the end of each section—possibly the protagonist's wife but potentially an inanimate, computer-generated voice directed at the reader; and an anonymous voice representing the system, which has been programmed to communicate with the reader about extradiegetic, metafictional, and technical matters.

The text begins with a system message asking the reader whether their "computer's sound is on." This represents a clear apostrophic function of "you," asking readers to carry out a physical, extradiegetic action. The first part then introduces the narrator as he "dream[s] about transparency" against an audiovisual background that evokes machinic associations: as the reader repeatedly mouses over the blackened image of a computer's motherboard, the photograph gradually reveals itself, square by square. This clearing action is accompanied by repetitive metallic noises, thus evoking the desire to look into and understand the black box of a computer, which is notoriously concealed by contemporary (and particularly touchscreen) technologies. The impenetrable computer stands in a cyborgian-synecdochic relationship to the protagonist's identity, and that of other people. This relationship is also expressed by the protagonist's desire to "have a clear understanding of [him]self. / And of others." The section closes with the female voice-over asking "where are you?" Since, at this stage, the reader has met the protagonist only, the referent of "you" is ambiguous. It could be the reader themselves, the protagonist, or indeed yet another fictional character whom the reader is yet to meet. The ontological ambiguity is reinforced by the fact that the reader does not yet know who is represented by the female voice, and whether it is located intra- or extradiegetically.

The second part of the story shows an interactive image of a female body, over which the reader has to rub the mouse to trigger written text chunks—similar to the quasi-pixelated revelation of the showering figure in the first part. As the reader progresses, they are shown increasing levels of internal anatomic detail, which are accompanied by the following, consecutively released thoughts: "My wife. / What could she be hiding from me? / I want to see through her. / Deep down beneath the surface." Thus, although the narrator is trying to broaden his understanding by seeking to permeate symbolic and iconic female corporeality, represented by the motherboard metaphor and the actual physical body depicted onscreen, he fails to gain the kind of cognitive, metaphysical clarity and understanding he is aiming for. Indeed, the second part ends with another female voice-over—"what are you looking for?"—which is likely attributable to his wife trying to instill a sense of reason in him. So, here the "you" is used as a fictional reference to the protagonist.

In terms of textual "you," part 3 is the most interesting, as it introduces a polyphony of dialogic utterances containing forms of apostrophic "you." Prima facie, they seem to revolve around the relationship between the protagonist and his wife ("our relationship is still to be built," "I am nothing without you," "you are less opaque"). This reading suggests that, in dialogue with his wife, he comes to understand that the kind of absolute, corporeal transparency he has been looking for is not actually desirable, and that he has developed a preference for certain degrees of mystery and opacity with regard to his understanding of self and others. A close analysis of the typography and orthography used in the above dialogic utterances, however, reveals that certain words in the dynamically rendered utterances are highlighted. Most notably, "you" (and, by opposition, "I" and "me," in some instances at least) appears bolded in the following passages: "**You** do **nothing** with **me**," "**You** do **nothing** without **me**," "**You** make **nothing** of **me**," "What do **you** make of us?," "For **you** I would like to build everything," "**You** know so little about me," "**You** hardly reveal **yourself**," "I discover **you** progressively," "I think of **you**," "**You** are less opaque," and, finally, "I enlighten **You**." Examining the highlighted words only, we can see a change from lack of insight, represented by "nothing" in between the interlocutors, to increased respect for the interests of the other person, conveyed by the fronting of "You" in the penultimate and the uppercase "Y" in the final sentence, "I enlighten You." Furthermore, the unconventional uppercase initial in the final phrase lends itself to being read as an address to the reader themselves, along the lines of seeing the protagonist's transformation as reader "enlighten"-ment.

For the investigation of antimimetic "you" in digital fiction, it is important to reiterate that reader address itself is ontologically impossible, as discussed in chapter 2 on interactional metalepsis. Whereas the apostrophic function of "you," however, is fully conventionalized in digital media, its doubly deictic uses in *Opacity* are not. Ontological oscillation is caused by medium-specific unnatural constructions of "you," from the ambiguous, doubly deictic voice-over at the end of part 1, to the orthographic and typographic anomalies and fluidity experienced linguistically in part 3. Reader/players are led to naturalize these defamiliarizing features in terms of a thematic reading that evokes empathy with the protagonist and ultimately has a didactic effect on the reader/player.

5.7 CONCLUSION

In this chapter, we focused on uses of the second person as a particularly pertinent and effective tool for engaging readers in experimental digital fictions. Fictional play with second-person narration and other forms of textual "you" have proliferated since the second half of the twentieth century, as have theoretical treatises by leading narratologists. In the case of digital narratives, "you" becomes ubiquitous as a form of drawing reader/players into fictional worlds, as well as serving as a system-operational linguistic marker of interactivity. The ubiquity of "you" in digital media means that players of games and readers of digital narratives will be very familiar with apostrophic "you" as a fully naturalized, medium-specific way of instructing users how to navigate and play an interactive text. They will also likely assume that "you" by default refers to themselves as doubly embodied in the fictional world of the game and the extradiegetic world of the technology operator. Against this backdrop, we discussed how this default and widely naturalized use of "you" is implemented in diverse works of digital fiction, to more or less defamiliarizing effects. We found, for example, that the hypertext fiction *Patchwork Girl* is generally understood as an unnatural narrative in that it presents reader/players with a variety of contradictory, multilinear pathways (see chapter

1). Yet the way in which it invites reader/players to build the protagonist, via direct apostrophic address, does not come across as antimimetic, or as defamiliarizing as such, because the interactional metalepsis, in the sense of transgressing ontological boundaries, is fully naturalized as a medium-specific convention.

Although our analyses in this chapter have shown that "you" can operate as a fully conventionalized feature of digital media discourse, the conventionalization of "you" can be subverted to cause antimimetic effects. Our investigation of antimimetic uses of "you" demonstrates that unconventional, medium-specific uses of "you" are often put to unique and powerful affective uses, such as comic effect in *EarthBound*. Indeed, the overall framing of the game affords a satirizing and therefore naturalizing reading strategy. We have also shown that the antimimetic effects created by games such as *EarthBound* can only be temporarily rather than permanently defamiliarizing because players are likely to integrate the unconventionalities of the game into its overall satirical agenda.

Through our analyses of *Loved* and *Spec Ops: The Line*, conversely, we showed how antimimetic apostrophic "you" can be implemented in a more pervasive way, to enhance a game's critical undertones. Player expectations are subverted throughout in games like *Loved* and *SOTL* as players receive unconventional forms of feedback that go beyond comments on and responses to their performance and that use apostrophic "you" to raise awareness of critical aspects of the games. Since players are used to mostly ludic feedback and merit-related progress in games, this treatment is bound and intended to alienate. Apostrophic "you" is thus embedded in a thematically framed yet far more consistent and therefore more permanently defamiliarizing (Iversen 2016) ludonarratological conceit. Although players can naturalize the unconventional by deploying a thematic reading strategy, the unique narrative game design nonetheless follows a highly surprising, antimimetic agenda that contributes to didactic or even therapeutic effects for the resilient and resilience-enacting player.

In our final analyses, we showed that specific, carefully designed uses of digital, doubly deictic "you" can cause poignant antimimetic effects. These effects can make reader/players feel unwittingly complicit, as in the case of *The Princess Murderer*, which tends to have highly alienating effects on its readers. Alternatively, antimimesis might place the reader/player in a heuristic dialogue with a socially challenged protagonist that makes them part of a gradual, personal learning process by employing the referential ambiguity of doubly deictic "you" in medium-specific ways (as in the case of *Opacity*). We have shown that digital double deixis can be used to engage with medium-specific interactive *and* cognitive processes and assumptions, thus exceeding the limitations of Walker's (2000) "forced participation" and Montfort's (2003) "actualized input/output." Both Walker's and Montfort's concepts foreground the kinetic, physically and verbally interactive idiosyncrasies of medium-specific autotelic reader/player involvement without, however, paying attention to the nuanced psychological effects that can be evoked by metaleptic and ontological vacillation.

In short, our exploration of medium-specific unnatural forms of "you" in digital fiction has shown that the second-person pronoun can be put to poignant affective, metacognitive, educational *and* critical effects, causing reader/players to question their own extradiegetic role and ethical responsibility vis-à-vis the lives and feelings of fictional characters, which are metaleptically affected by reader interactions with the software. Thus, "you" can be considered one of, if not the most powerful, linguistic-rhetorical device for digital fiction writers and developers, especially if combined with consistent multimodal and procedural rhetoric.

CONCLUSION

In this book, we have provided an unnatural narratology of digital fiction and thus offered the first comprehensive and systematic theoretical, methodological, and analytical examination of unnatural narratives as they occur in computer-based literary and ludic narrative media. We have adapted key tenets and analytical principles of unnatural narratology to the distinctive, medium-specific affordances of digital-born fiction and introduced new approaches, concepts, and tools required by the medial and procedural affordances of digital-interactive narratives. We have thus made significant contributions to unnatural narratology by expanding its remit to include digital fictions, to transmedial narratology by adapting narrative theory for its application to digital narrative media, and to cognitive narratology by investigating the medium-specific ways that unnatural digital narratives are processed by reader/players. In this chapter, we highlight the original methodological, theoretical, and analytical contributions we have made throughout this book and propose ways in which our findings can be used in the future to support the analysis of other digital fiction texts and other unnatural narratives across media, as well as in empirical research that aims to investigate the responses of reader/players and other users of unnatural narratives.

6.1 METHOD

In terms of methodological approach, we have developed a new framework that can be used to theorize and analyze: unnatural narrative devices at work in digital fiction, the effect of those devices on reader/players, and the strategies that reader/players adopt to make sense of them. More specifically, we have adopted Richardson's "intrinsic" approach to the unnatural which determines that unnatural narratives have to contain devices that are noticeably impossible in the real world and that thus cause at least some degree of defamiliarization. We have also used Alber's (2016) "extrinsic" readerly strategies, which seek to understand how readers make sense of unnatural elements in a text. Developing a medium-conscious approach to the unnatural, we have expanded Alber's reading strategies to address the way that unnatural narratives are cognitively processed by reader/players of digital fiction specifically.

As we have noted throughout this book, defining the unnatural on the basis of what is defamiliarizing has consequences for both the diachronic and the medium-specific analysis of unnatural texts because the relative conventionality of unnatural devices can change over time and/or across media. In recognizing the medium-specific context in which texts are produced and received, we have distinguished between unnatural devices that have become conventionalized in digital narrative media and those that are more permanently defamiliarizing (Iversen 2016). However, we have also been explicit that this distinction in our work is contingent on current practices and conventions, in a particular medium, and from a Western Anglophone perspective. It is important, therefore, to emphasize that while our definition of the unnatural is fixed, our methodological approach consciously determines that what constitutes the "unnatural" is necessarily and, at times, unavoidably relative. Thus, while we maintain that some narrative devices are more likely to be permanently defamiliarizing (Iversen 2016) than others, we also acknowledge that a text's ability to defamiliarize is subjective and culturally determined.

6.2 MODELS

While unnatural narratology necessarily informs the theoretical contributions of this book, we have also used tools, approaches, and models from narrative theory and digital media theory more widely. We have therefore developed both medium-specific and transmedial theoretical models for analyzing reader/players' cognitive and material interactions with digital storyworlds. In chapters 1 and 3, we showed that videogames and other types of 3D immersive narratives are more strongly anchored in spatial exploration than in any other narrative medium. As we argued in chapter 1, reader experiences of multilinearity in digital media can have a distinctly spatial quality because the same storyworld is often visually experienced multiple times. In plotting the medium-specific spatial configurations that digital fictions of all kinds create, we have modeled the way that readers move across and within digital storyworlds. This has included developing a cognitive approach to interactional metalepsis in chapter 2 which represents the ontological transgressions that occur between the reader/player in the actual world and what we have defined as the "text-space" and "world-space" (cf. Juul 2005) within digital fiction storyworlds. In focusing specifically on impossible spaces in chapter 3, we also developed a model that draws on Punday's (2017) division between "orienting space" and "primary storytelling space" and explored how medium-specific antimimeticism experienced in a digital fiction's "text-space" might turn "orienting space" into "disorienting space."

In chapter 4, we showed that some forms of medium-specific narration (such as multiperson and cybernetic narration) can problematize the distinction between character and narrator, between player and narratee vis-à-vis the medium-specific, ambivalent interlocutor, as well as between machine and human. We proposed a modification to the traditional Chinese box model of narrative communication by highlighting the medium-specific, bidirectionality between (implied) authorial and diegetic voices, and the voice and interactions of the reader/player. Finally, in chapter 5, we theorized the way that some forms of digital "you" create input/output cycles that implicate the reader/player within the storyworld—either individually or simultaneously with a character—and thus complicate the ontological divide between actual world and storyworld. Chapters 4 and 5 thus both explore devices that undermine the ontological distinction between the actual world and the storyworld and emphasize that the potential for and reader/player expectations about interactivity are key ways in which the digital medium departs from other nonergodic media such as print.

6.3 ANALYSIS

Throughout the analyses we showed how a diversity of narrative forms that are antimimetic in print and other types of more sequential and less interactive media are fully conventionalized in digital fictions but also that digital fictions ubiquitously experiment with antimimetic devices causing defamiliarization, surprise, critical and metamedial stances, educational insights, and often fun for reader/players.

In chapter 1, we focused on the narrative contradictions resulting from multilinear narrative constructions. We showed that while logical contradictions in Storyspace hypertext fictions like *Victory Garden* likely prevent readers from forming satisfactory naturalizing strategies, other hypertext fictions, such as *Lucy Hardin's Missing Period,* use what we call "transparent multilinearity" for navigational clarity, which can lead to immersion within a multilinear storyworld. Reader/players of Interactive Fiction and videogames expect that they will read/play the text multiple times, but we have shown that particular texts play with this convention either to humorously draw attention to the form itself (in *Zork*) or to self-reflexively use multilinearity to create a thematic message (*The Novelist*). We concluded that logical contradictions in some forms of digital fiction are fully accepted if not expected by reader/players and can thus be seen as a medium-specific form of conventionalization because multilinearity and mutually contradictory storylines are inextricably built into digital, interactive narratives and therefore are part of reader/players' horizon of expectation. At the same time, those horizons of expectation can be subverted as writers of digital narrative media play with the structural conventions on which they are self-consciously drawing.

Our exploration of interactional metalepsis as an inevitable, medium-specific convention in chapter 2 also showed ways in which antimimetic devices can be used to immerse or estrange the reader to varying degrees. We showed that ontological leaps between actual world and storyworld are so common and multifarious that they necessitate the new narratological concept of interactional metalepsis that goes far beyond existing theoretical approaches to metalepsis in print and applies more specifically to digital-born narratives. Interactional metalepsis exploits the interactive nature of digital technology via medium-specific, ergodic modes of expression and foregrounds reader/player embodiment in the actual world and simultaneously, via interface representation, in the storyworld. In offering a multipronged, conceptually open-ended typology of interactional metalepsis, induced from readings of select digital fictions, we introduced the idea of a cline between weak and strong forms of interactional metalepsis, depending on the relative, ontological intrusion of the reader/player's representation into the storyworld and the degree to which attention is drawn to it. We showed that some forms of ontological metalepsis are very much conventionalized; the player's manifestation in a videogame world as an avatar is completely normalized, for example. Likewise, there are even cases where the intended effect of the metalepsis is to merge worlds and thus deeply immerse the reader/player within the text. This includes what we call "convergent metalepsis," which appears to blend the actual world and storyworld, and instances in which reader/players experience what we call "emotionally metaleptic" romantic relationships between real and fictional people in online worlds. Yet while interactional metalepses can immerse the reader/player, we showed that numerous texts work antimimetically. This includes the strange case of the reader/player's image being placed in the text in *Loss of Grasp*, the way in which the reader/player's breath advances the story in *The Breathing Wall*, and texts, such as *Disappearing Rain*, that use hyperlinks metaleptically. Interactional metalepsis is thus a malleable device that can be used to immerse and/or defamiliarize.

In our analyses of unnatural spatiality in chapter 3, we arrived at a seemingly paradoxical conclusion: on the one hand, highly logically impossible spaces such as the Escher-esque, non-Euclidean game spaces featured in puzzle games like *Monument Valley* and *Back to Bed* are likely naturalized with great efficiency and functionalized for fast leveling-up and progress. On the other hand, worlds such as the one featured in *Everybody's Gone to the Rapture* can have curiously defamiliarizing, or what we have called "environmentally antimimetic," effects because of the cognitive clash caused by the juxtaposition of extreme 3D panoramic photorealism—what we define as *hypermimetic space*—and the eerie atmosphere evoked by a mysteriously abandoned and haunted village. Within that chapter, we also compared different corporeal game spaces and concluded that having one's avatar navigate and interact with internal bodily environments like symbolical brains and animated blood vessels can be either more illusion-enhancing, as in the case of the ludically driven *Psychonauts*, or more antimimetic, as in the case of the more experimental and decisively sociocritical *Inkubus*.

Our examination of unnatural time in chapter 3 showed that existing investigations of antimimetic temporality needed to be expanded to do justice to the experimentation apparent in digital fiction. While we showed how medium-specific forms of existing categories of unnatural temporarily—and particularly antinomic temporality, temporal loops, and anticausality—can work in digital fiction, we also added two categories that are needed to explain the way in which some ergodic, ludic digital fictions play with temporality. First, we explored what we define as *multivariant chronology*, which is the phenomenon of fragmentation and rearrangement at story level in digital fiction that occurs when reader/players are required to create their own pathways through the storyworld, thereby experiencing different degrees and varieties of temporal rearrangement that affect their understanding of what happened in the story, who experienced these events, and in what order. Our example of multivariant chronology in the detective fiction *Her Story* showed how this form of "agglutinative" (Hussey 2017) temporal structuring can lead to highly antimimetic effects. Second, we added the term *cybertextual velocity* to describe cases in which the time given to readers to peruse discourse-level textual material is manipulated by the text-machine, thereby diminishing their agency and ability to read at their own pace. Examining this phenomenon in *Hegirascope* and *Dakota*, we showed that it generates a highly antimimetic experience is that near-impossible to naturalize and requires a Zen approach that accepts and unnaturalizes the kind of experimental, avant-garde defamiliarization that is characteristic of verbal art and electronic literature.

Our focus on extreme forms of narration in chapter 4 demonstrates how the medium-specific combination of multilinearity and unreliability lends itself aptly to variably defamiliarizing representations of characters' confusion, trauma, and psychosis. We showed how unreliable narrators can appear in conjunction with medium-specific structures—such as hypertextual multilinearity—to create a confused, traumatized, or schizophrenic protagonist's storyworld, or, in more antimimetic cases, such as *afternoon*, multiple versions of a storyworld whose ontological status is hard to discern. In our discussion of medium-specific interlocution, we analyzed the narrator-interlocutor in the Interactive Fiction *Galatea* to show how, in an impossible ontological transgression, the otherwise unmarked voice of a second-person narrator-interlocutor can become a critical stage director for the player's textual performance, thus creating an antimimetic-satirical effect. We used the example of *WALLPAPER* to show how, in an otherwise highly immersive 3D fiction, an array of different interlocuting voices can evoke an ambient, spooky, and ultimately defamiliarizing atmosphere, and we showed how multiperson narration works alongside visual elements in the text in *Quadrego* to represent multiple personality disorder. Using the videogame *The Stanley Parable* as a case study, we demonstrated how omniscience can be generated via cybernetic and machinic forms of narration and thus how medium-specific narrational impossibilities can manifest in digital narrative media.

Finally, in examining the ubiquitous and narrationally powerful role of "you" in digital fiction, we combined and extended the focus on interactional metalepsis and extreme narration from previous chapters and emphasized the importance of the cybernetic, embodied, and dialogic nature of the second-person pronoun in digital narratives. We showed that the distinctly malleable and ambiguous nature of "you" can have deeply immersive effects, such as in standard videogames and the metatexts surrounding them. We also showed how "you" can trigger distinctly reflexive, critical, and metamedial stances in curiously antimimetic artifacts such as humor in the parodical role-playing game *EarthBound*, empathetic shock in relation to emotional abuse in *Loved*, or guilt resulting from unethical warfare in *Spec Ops: The Line*. We also investigated the ontological oscillations caused by doubly deictic "you" in digital fiction which can cause reader/players to feel disconcerted and confused about their ontological status in the actual versus the fictional world, as in the case of the experimental hypermedia fictions *The Princess Murderer* and *Opacity*.

6.4 THEORY

Our analyses show how unnatural devices work in individual digital fictions, but they also show ways in which unnatural narratology needs to be developed to become more transmedially applicable. Throughout our analyses, we have shown that some digital fictions are antimimetic precisely because the devices they use defy the conventions of the digital medium. In chapter 1, for example, we showed that some videogames subvert the convention of multiple play-throughs to deliver their overall thematic message, and in chapter 2 we analyzed the way that hyperlinks—a highly conventionalized form of navigational interactivity—can be used self-reflexively. In chapter 3, we showed, for example, how 3D videogame photorealism can become antimimetic when combining hypermimetic and nonmimetic features, and in multiple chapters we analyzed how apostrophic "you" and other medium-specific stylistic and design elements can be deployed to subvert the convention of player immersion via interactional metalepsis. To account for these forms of antimimeticism which play with established conventions of a particular medium, we created the term *medium-specific antimimeticism*. Richardson's (2016, 3) definition of the unnatural shows that some texts are antimimetic because they defy the conventions of existing, established genres; until now, however, the role of the medium-specific conventions has not been taken into account in unnatural narratology.

Overall, our analyses have demonstrated that unnatural narratives in digital fiction can have various degrees of antimimetic effects but that specific unnatural forms and conceits are not intrinsically defamiliarizing. The effect of antimimetic devices depends on the way they are used, the attention that is drawn to them, and the relative conventionality of the device in the respective medial context. Importantly, from a theoretical point of view, our analyses have led to the observation that defamiliarization can be felt by readers to greater or lesser degrees depending on contextual parameters and on their relative experience with and exposure to different types of digital narratives. Thus, defamiliarization is a gradable phenomenon—it can either endure or dissipate—and thus its effects can be more permanent or more temporary. Antimimetic devices such as illogical narrative contradictions, visual interactional metalepses caused by webcams, and cybertextual velocity are strikingly and permanently defamiliarizing (Iversen 2011) because they create narrative and/or reading situations that radically depart from our experience of the actual world. They can potentially be naturalized by seeing them as thematic devices, for example, but their estranging effect remains strong. On the other hand, some forms of antimimeticism may initially feel defamiliarizing for the reader/player, but this effect may fade or disappear as they move through the text and discover information that resolves their potential impossibility. Finally, with unnatural features such as omniscient narration in print texts, a device that was once defamiliarizing in digital fiction can potentially become conventionalized over time. It might be, for example, that interactionally metaleptic hyperlinks or unreliable cybernetic narrators become less and less unusual so that they gradually lose their defamiliarizing effect.

In accounting for the way that readers make sense of antimimetic narratives, we have applied insights from existing cognitive unnatural narratology to show that all the naturalizing reading strategies proposed by Alber (2016) for print narratives apply equally to digital fictions. However, while we have drawn on other existing frameworks that theorize the reader/player's interaction with particular unnatural devices (e.g., Ryan 2006b), the range and types of antimimeticism as found in digital fiction have necessitated the expansion of Alber's framework.

First, drawing on Richardson's (2016) concept of *unnatural construction*, which he uses to "designate texts constructed to be processed in surprising and unexpected ways, particularly those that invert or defy conventional reading practices" (391), we have shown that reader/players of digital fiction can simply accept some unnatural narrative devices as an inevitable part of digital media. This includes some forms of narrative contradiction and interactional metalepsis in which the materiality of the reading experience can be used to account for the unnaturalness of a narrative. Representing a subcategory of Alber's "Zen way of reading," this new strategy, which we call *accepted as an unnatural construction*, is employed by reader/players who apply a medium-specific evaluative frame to the text in question in order to explain the antimimetic device. Importantly, the application of this new reading strategy does not mean that particular texts are not antimimetic. However, it allows the reader to see the unnaturalness of the text's structure or composition as an inevitable part of the reading experience.

Representing a second medium-specific addition to Alber's framework, we have proposed a "metamedial" reading strategy, which reader/players must deploy in order to activate internalized medium-specific conventions used in a text and to widen the scope of what they consider possible in a digital storyworld, especially when facing cases of medium-specific antimimeticism. This includes accepting the ways in which a digital fiction might foreground and subvert players' medium-specific expectations, such as when videogame mechanics stretch and rewire human imagination and logic reasoning and thus ask players to internalize and master seemingly counterintuitive concepts and/or mechanics of time, space, and narrative voice (including digital forms of permeable narration and second-person address).

Finally, we have created a subcategory of Alber's (2016) thematizing reading strategy by showcasing how some antimimetic texts can have strongly pedagogical or even therapeutic effects on immersed reader/players. This applies to texts in which players enact or feel the effect of some form of abuse and thus are taught to be wary of, for example, insidious forms of violence or control. This particular reading strategy is not specific to digital fiction and, in fact, could be applied to narratives across media.

6.5 FUTURE DIRECTIONS

The theoretical contributions and analytical findings presented in this book have shown the effectiveness of our new methodology, which combines and extends both intrinsic and extrinsic methods. Adopting an intrinsic stance towards the unnatural—as exemplified by Richardson (2006, 2011)—allowed us to focus our analyses on the narrative strategies at work in antimimetic narratives and, specifically, on whether they are permanently or temporarily defamiliarizing. Our analyses also showed that an extrinsic approach to unnatural narratology, and specifically the cognitive reading strategies proposed by Alber (2016) and extended by us, can serve as useful transmedial toolkits for naturalizing *and* unnaturalizing readings of narrative impossibilities. Important to both parts of our method, however, is the attention we have paid to the digital medium both in terms of the devices that it makes possible and the relative conventionality of those devices. Yet, while we have focused on digital fiction in particular, the methodological approach that we have developed in this book can be applied to unnatural narratives across media. In synthesizing intrinsic and extrinsic perspectives, we have shown that the relative conventionality of antimimetic devices—in terms of how physical and logical impossibilities are processed by readers or players in a medium-specific context—must always be taken into account. This applies to narratives across all media—including those produced in print—and we suggest that all narrative theories, methods, and analyses—whether cognitive, structuralist, unnatural, or transmedial—should be medium-conscious.

We have demonstrated that highly idiosyncratic, antimimetic narratives proliferate in digital fiction. This has included relatively niche types of narrative media such as experimental electronic literature, but it has also included very popular videogames that currently have a much wider appeal. The diversity of our corpora shows that unnatural forms of narrative can be found across digital narrative media and, further, that audiences are not necessarily averse to antimimetic devices. As the recent popularity of the interactive Netflix film *Bandersnatch* has shown, hypertextual structures are no longer particularly unusual. Rather, they are converging with other forms of (interactive) narrative media—such as television or film—that audiences are perhaps more familiar with.

While antimimetic devices may well continue to appear within and outside of digital media, the wider effect of those devices on internationally networked and thus diverse audiences will need to be addressed. Our work has shown that the overall theoretical framework of unnatural narratology is grounded in Western understandings of what is possible or impossible. Whether or not one manages to avoid the cultural pitfalls evoked by unnatural narratology as a theoretical-terminological apparatus, one of the major challenges to be tackled is the need for more diverse and specialized analytical tools that give rise to a conceptual repository that does justice to the range of experimental narrativity and the sheer variety of effects that it can have on its varied audiences. What we have observed throughout this book is that *antimimetic* as a catch-all term for defamiliarization can only ever serve as a starting point for more nuanced studies into medium- and culturally specific, unconventional forms and techniques of storytelling.

Finally, in closing, we call for further research that picks up where we have left off and that develops the growing repository of analytical forms and concepts further, in line with proliferating new technologies and digital fiction experimentation. We also recommend empirical reader/player response research that puts the models, analyses, and theories developed in this book in dialogue with data about what actual readers do. This aligns with our recent scholarly endeavors in the Reading Digital Fiction project,[1] which has produced empirical research on various formal aspects of digital fiction, including doubly deictic "you" (Bell et al. 2019), levels and dynamics of immersion in digital fiction (Bell et al. 2018; Ensslin et al. 2019), and reader perceptions

---

1. The Reading Digital Fiction project (https://www.readingdigitalfiction.com) developed empirical methods for and insights into digital fiction. It was funded by the UK's Arts and Humanities Research Council (Funding Reference: AH/K004174/1).

of hyperlinks (van der Bom et al., 2021). We regard this book as a stepping stone to developing multiple areas of narratological investigation—unnatural, structuralist, cognitivist, transmedial, and empirical—and it is with great anticipation that we look forward to seeing them thrive, proliferate, and continuously defamiliarize the creative and critical spheres of unnatural narrative and digital fiction.

BIBLIOGRAPHY

PRIMARY REFERENCES

2K Boston and 2K Australia. 2007. *Bioshock*. Novato, CA: 2K Games.

Alderman, Naomi, and Rebecca Levene. 2012. *Zombies, Run!* London: Six to Start.

Allen, Woody. 1980. "The Kugelmass Episode." In *Side Effects*, 41–55. New York: Random House.

Amis, Martin. 1992 [1991]. *Time's Arrow or the Nature of the Offence*. New York: Vintage.

Anthropy, Anna. 2013. *Queers in Love at the End of the World*. http://auntiepixelante.com/endoftheworld/.

Atwood, Margaret. 1983. "Happy Endings." In *Murder in the Dark*, 37–40. Toronto: Coach House.

Barlow, Sam. 2015. *Her Story*. https://store.steampowered.com/app/368370/Her_Story/.

Beckett, Samuel. 1963. *Play*. In *Samuel Beckett: The Complete Dramatic Works*. London: Faber & Faber.

Bedtime Digital Games. 2014. *Back to Bed*. Aalborg: Bedtime Digital Games.

BioWare. 2017. *Mass Effect: Andromeda*. Redwood City, CA: Electronic Arts.

———. 2009. *Dragon Age: Origins*. Redwood City, CA: Electronic Arts.

Bithell, Mike. 2012. *Thomas Was Alone*. UK: Bithell Games.

Blast Theory. 2015. *Karen*. UK: Blast Theory.

Blow, Jonathan. 2009. *Braid*. US: Number None, Inc.

Boluk, Stephanie, Leonardo Flores, Jacob Garbe, and Anastasia Salter, eds. 2016. *Electronic Literature Collection 3*. http://collection.eliterature.org/3/.

Bouchardon, Serge, Léonard Dumas, Vincent Volckaert, and Herve Zénouda. 2012. *Opacity: A 4-Part Interactive Story*. http://i-trace.fr/opacity/.

Bouchardon, Serge, and Vincent Volckaert. 2010. *Loss of Grasp.* http://lossofgrasp.com/.

Breeze, Mez, and Andy Campbell. 2017. *All the Delicate Duplicates.* https://allthedelicateduplicat.es/.

Bruce, Alexander. 2013. *Antichamber.* Melbourne: Demruth.

Campbell, Andy, and Judi Alston. 2015. *WALLPAPER.* Dreaming Methods. http://WALLPAPER.dreamingmethods.com/.

Campbell, Andy, and Judy Alston. 2010. *Consensus Trance II.* https://digitalfiction.dreamingmethods.com/nightingalesplayground/.

Campbell, Andy, Judi Alston, and Billy Johnson. 2008. *Clearance.* Dreaming Methods. http://dreamingmethods.com/clearance/.

Campbell, Andy, and Christine Wilks. 2014. *Inkubus.* http://dreamingmethods.com/inkubus.

The Chinese Room. 2016. *Everybody's Gone to the Rapture* (for PC). Microsoft Windows, The Chinese Room, and SCE Santa Monica Studio.

———. 2012. *Dear Esther.* http://dear-esther.com.

Chyr, William. 2017. *Manifold Garden.* http://manifold.garden/.

Coover, Robert. 1969. "The Babysitter." In *Pricksongs & Descants.* New York: New American Library.

Cortázar, Julio. 1967. "The Continuity of Parks." In *Blow-Up and Other Stories,* translated by Paul Blackburn, 63–65. New York: Pantheon.

Danielewski, Mark Z. 2000. *House of Leaves.* New York: Pantheon.

Deemer, Charles. 1996. *The Last Song of Violeta Parra.* http://www.uv.es/~fores/programa/deemer_violeta.html.

Dena, Christy. 2015. *Magister Ludi.* Universe Creation 101 Pty Ltd. https://apps.apple.com/au/app/magister-ludi-game/id1031562918.

Dontnod Entertainment. 2015. *Life Is Strange.* Square Enix Feral Interactive.

Earthbound Ape Inc. and HAL Laboratory. 1994. *EarthBound.* Kyoto: Nintendo.

Fincher, David. 2008. *The Curious Case of Benjamin Button.* Hollywood, CA: Paramount Pictures.

Fisher, Caitlin. 2001. *These Waves of Girls.* http://www.yorku.ca/caitlin/waves/.

Fitzgerald, F. Scott. 2008 [1922]. *The Curious Case of Benjamin Button and Other Jazz Age Stories.* London: Penguin.

Fowles, John. 2004 [1969]. *The French Lieutenant's Woman.* London: Vintage.

Freebird Games. 2011. *To the Moon.* Canada: Freebird Games.

Giant Sparrow. 2017. *What Remains of Edith Finch.* West Hollywood, CA: Annapurna Interactive.

Gilliam, Terry. 1981. *Time Bandits.* UK: HandMade Films.

Hight, Jeremy, Jeff Knowlton, and Naomi Spellman. 2002. *34 North 118 West.* http://34n118w.net/.

Holeton, Richard. 2001. *Figurski at Findhorn on Acid* [CD-ROM]. Watertown, MA: Eastgate Systems.

Howarth, Brian. 1981. *Arrow of Death Part 1.* http://bbcmicro.co.uk/game.php?id=1675.

Infocom. 1980. *Zork 1.* Cambridge, MA: Personal Software and Infocom. Accessed via the Interactive Fiction Database. https://ifdb.tads.org/viewgame?id=0dbnusxunq7fw5ro.

Inglis, Gavin. 2002. *Same Day Test.* http://www.bareword.com/sdt/.

Inkle. 2012. *Future Voices.* Inkle Studios.

Jackson, Shelley. 1997. *my body—a Wunderkammer*. https://collection.eliterature.org/1/works/jackson__my_body_a_wunderkammer.html.

———. 1995. *Patchwork Girl; Or, a Modern Monster by Mary/Shelley, & herself*. CD-ROM, Massachusetts, USA: Eastgate Systems.

Jackson, Steve. 2014. *Sorcery!* Inkle Studios.

Johnson, B. S. 1999 [1969]. *The Unfortunates*. Basingstoke: Picador.

Joyce, Michael. 1987. *afternoon, a story*. Watertown, MA: Eastgate Systems.

Larsen, Deena. 2000. *Disappearing Rain*. http://www.deenalarsen.net/rain/.

Linden Lab. 2003. *Second Life*. http://secondlife.com/.

Lionhead Studios. 2005. *Black and White 2*. Redwood City, CA: Electronic Arts.

Marche, Stephen. 2010. *Lucy Hardin's Missing Period*. http://walrusmagazine.com/lucyhardin/.

Maskiewicz, Stefan. 2001. *Quadrego*. http://www.quadrego.de/start.htm.

Mateas, Michael, and Andrew Stern. 2005. *Façade: A One Act Interactive Drama*. http://www.interactivestory.net/.

Milk, Chris. 2012. *The Treachery of Sanctuary*. http://milk.co/treachery at *Digital Revolution*, Barbican Gallery, London, UK, 3 July–14 September 2014.

Montfort, Nick. 2000. *Ad Verbum*. http://nickm.com/if/adverbum.html.

Moriarty, Brian. 1986. *Trinity*. Cambridge, MA: Infocom.

Moulthrop, Stuart. 1995/1997. *Hegirascope*. http://www.cddc.vt.edu/journals/newriver/moulthrop/HGS2/HGS121.html.

———. 1991a. *Victory Garden*. Watertown, MA: Eastgate Systems.

Munroe, Jim. 2008. *Everybody Dies*. https://nomediakings.org/games/everybody_dies_takes_bronze_at_ifcomp.html.

Nelson, Jason. 2003. *Dreamaphage*. http://adelta.westernsydney.edu.au/items/show/137.

Nestvold, Ruth. 1995–2001. *Cutting Edges, Or: A Web of Women*. http://www.lit-arts.net/Cutting_Edges/1stpage.htm.

Niantic, Inc. 2013. *Ingress*. https://www.ingress.com/.

Niss, Millie, and Martha Deed. 2004. *Oulipoems*. http://collection.eliterature.org/1/works/niss__oulipoems.html.

Nolan, Christopher. 2000. *Memento*. Santa Monica, CA: Summit Entertainment.

O'Brien, Flann. 2001 [1967]. *The Third Policeman*. London: Flamingo.

———. 1967 [1939]. *At Swim-Two-Birds*. London: Penguin Books.

Ocias, Alexander. 2010. *Loved: A Short Story*. https://ocias.com/loved.php.

Olsen, Lance, and Tim Guthrie. 2005. *10:01*. http://www.lanceolsen.com/1001.html.

Orthogonal Games. 2013. *The Novelist*. Orthogonal Games, LLC 2013–2015.

Poundstone, William. 2002. *3 Proposals for Bottle Imps*. http://www.williampoundstone.net/Bottle.html.

Prickitt, Lyndee. 2014. *We Are Angry*. Digital Fables. http://www.weareangry.net/.

Pullinger, Kate, Chris Joseph, and Participants. 2007. *Flight Paths: A Networked Novel*. https://www.flightpaths.net.

Pullinger, Kate, Stefan Schemat, and Babel. 2004. *The Breathing Wall* [CD-ROM]. UK: self-published.

Ramis, Harold. 1993. *Groundhog Day*. Culver City, CA: Columbia Pictures.

Reed, Ishmael. 1976. *Flight to Canada*. New York: Random House.

Schafer, Tim. 2011. *Psychonauts*. San Francisco, CA: Double Fine Productions.

Short, Emily. 2000. *Galatea*. https://emshort.blog/my-work/.

Story City. 2016. *Story City*. http://www.storycity.com.au/.

Strickland, Stephanie, and Nick Montfort. 2011. "Sea and Spar Between." https://nickm.com/montfort_strickland/sea_and_spar_between/.

Tale of Tales. 2009. *The Path*. Tale of Tales.

Tender Claws. 2015. *Pry*. https://prynovella.com.

Thomas, M. D. 1981. *The White Hotel*. London: Victor Gollancz Ltd.

Tykwer, Tom. 1998. Dir. *Lola rennt* [*Run, Lola Run*]. X-Filme Creative Pool.

Ustwo Games. 2017. *Monument Valley 2*. London: Ustwo.

———. 2014. *Monument Valley*. London: Ustwo.

Valve Software. 2011. *Portal 2*. Bellevue, WA: Valve Corporation.

———. 2007. *Portal*. Bellevue, WA: Valve Corporation.

Wiesner, David. 2015. *Spot*. Chicago, IL: Houghton Mifflin Harcourt.

Wilson, John. 1988. *Behind Closed Doors*. https://www.worldofspectrum.org/infoseekid.cgi?id=0005998.

Woolf, Virginia. 1928. *Orlando: A Biography*. London: Hogarth.

Wreden, Davey. 2013. *The Stanley Parable*. USA: Galactic Café.

Wylde, Nanette. 2004. *Storyland*. http://collection.eliterature.org/1/works/wylde__storyland.html.

Yager Development. 2012. *Spec Ops: The Line*. Novato, CA: 2K Games.

Young Hae Chang Heavy Industries. 2001. *Dakota*. https://www.yhchang.com/DAKOTA.html.

Zhang, Jin, Thomas Loh, Nicola Harwood, Bessie Wapp, and Fred Wah. 2016. *High Muck a Muck: Playing Chinese*, by the High Muck a Muck Collective. http://www.highmuckamuck.ca.

SECONDARY REFERENCES

Aarseth, Espen. 1997. *Cybertext: Perspectives on Ergodic Literature*. Baltimore: Johns Hopkins University Press.

Alber, Jan. 2016. *Unnatural Narrative: Impossible Worlds in Fiction and Drama*. Lincoln: University of Nebraska Press.

———. 2013a. "Unnatural Spaces and Narrative Worlds." In Alber, Nielsen, and Richardson 2013, 45–66.

———. 2013b. "Unnatural Narrative." In *The Living Handbook of Narratology*, edited by Peter Hühn et al. Hamburg: Hamburg University. http://www.lhn.uni-hamburg.de/article/unnatural-narrative.

———. 2012. "Unnatural Temporalities: Interfaces between Postmodernism, Science Fiction, and the Fantastic." In *Narrative Interrupted: The Plotless, the Disturbing and the Trivial in Literature*, edited by Markku Lehtimäki, Laura Kartunen, and Maria Mäkelä, 174–91. Berlin: Walter de Gruyter.

———. 2011. "The Diachronic Development of Unnaturalness: A New View on Genre." In Alber and Heinze 2011, 41–67.

———. 2009. "Impossible Storyworlds—and What to Do with Them." *Storyworlds: A Journal of Narrative Studies* 1, no. 1: 79–96.

Alber, Jan, and Rüdiger Heinze, eds. 2011. *Unnatural Narratives, Unnatural Narratology*. Berlin: Walter de Gruyter.

Alber, Jan, Stefan Iversen, Henrik Skov Nielsen, and Brian Richardson. 2013. "What Really Is Unnatural Narratology?" *Storyworlds* 5: 101–18.

———. 2012. "What Is Unnatural about Unnatural Narratology? A Response to Monika Fludernik." *Narrative* 20, no. 3: 371–82.

———. 2010. "Unnatural Narratives, Unnatural Narratology: Beyond Mimetic Models." *Narrative* 18, no. 2: 113–36.

Alber, Jan, Henrik Skov Nielsen, and Brian Richardson, eds. 2013. *A Poetics of Unnatural Narrative*. Columbus: The Ohio State University Press

Albin, Frankie J. 2016. "Life Is Strange." *Electronic Literature Directory*. http://directory.eliterature.org/individual-work/4679.

Allison, Fraser, Marcus Carter, and Martin Gibbs. 2015. "Good Frustrations: The Paradoxical Pleasure of Fearing Death in DayZ." In *OzCHI '15 Proceedings of the Annual Meeting of the Australian Special Interest Group for Computer Human Interaction*, 119–23.

Barron, Natania. 2011. "An Ode to Alistair: Love, Lust, and Loss in Fereldan." *Wired.com*, April 15, 2011. https://www.wired.com/2011/04/an-ode-to-alistair-love-lust-and-loss-in-fereldan/.

Barthes, Roland. 1990 [1974]. *S/Z*. Translated by Richard Miller. Oxford: Blackwell.

Begam, Richard. 1996. *Samuel Beckett and the End of Modernity*. Stanford: Stanford University Press.

Bell, Alice. 2021. "'It all feels too real': Digital Storyworlds and 'Ontological Resonance.'" In "Uncertain Ontologies in 21st-Century Storyworlds," edited by Lieven Ameel and Marco Caracciolo, special issue, *Style*.

———. 2018. "Digital Fictionality: Possible Worlds Theory, Ontology, and Hyperlinks." In *Possible Worlds Theory and Contemporary Narratology*, edited by Alice Bell and Marie-Laure Ryan, 249–71. Lincoln: University of Nebraska Press.

———. 2016a. "Interactional Metalepsis and Unnatural Narratology." *Narrative* 24, no. 3: 294–310.

———. 2016b. "'I felt like I'd stepped out of a different reality': Possible Worlds Theory, Metalepsis and Digital Fiction." In *World Building: Discourse in the Mind*, edited by Joanna Gavins and Ernestine Lahey, 15–32. London: Bloomsbury.

———. 2014a. "Media-Specific Metalepsis in *10:01*." In *Analyzing Digital Fiction*, edited by Alice Bell, Astrid Ensslin, and Hans K. Rustad, 21–38. New York: Routledge.

———. 2014b. "Schema Theory, Hypertext Fiction and Links." *Style* 48, no. 2: 140–61.

———. 2013. "Unnatural Narration in Hypertext Fiction." In Alber, Nielsen, and Richardson 2013, 185–98.

———. 2011. "Ontological Boundaries and Conceptual Leaps: The Significance of Possible Worlds for Hypertext Fiction (and Beyond)." In *New Narratives: Stories and Storytelling in the Digital Age*, edited by Ruth Page and Bronwen Thomas, 63–82. Frontiers of Narrative Series. Lincoln: University of Nebraska Press.

———. 2010. *The Possible Worlds of Hypertext Fiction*. Basingstoke: Palgrave Macmillan.

———. 2007. "'Do you want to hear about it?' Exploring Possible Worlds in Michael Joyce's Hyperfiction, *afternoon, a story*." In *Contemporary Stylistics*, edited by Peter Stockwell and Marina Lambrou, 43–55. London: Continuum.

Bell, Alice, and Jan Alber. 2012. "Ontological Metalepsis and Unnatural Narratology." *Journal of Narrative Theory* 42, no. 2: 166–92.

Bell, Alice, and Astrid Ensslin. 2018. "Unnatural Narrative in Digital Fiction." In *The Edinburgh Companion to Contemporary Narrative Theories*, edited by Zara Dinnen and Robyn Warhol, 291–304. Edinburgh: Edinburgh University Press.

———. 2011. "'I know what it was. You know what it was': Second-Person Narration in Hypertext Fiction." *Narrative* 19, no. 3: 311–29.

Bell, Alice, Astrid Ensslin, and Hans K. Rustad, eds. 2014. *Analyzing Digital Fiction*. New York: Routledge.

Bell, Alice, Astrid Ensslin, Dave Ciccoricco, Jess Laccetti, Jessica Pressman, and Hans Rustad. 2010. "A [S]creed for Digital Fiction." *Electronic Book Review*, March 7, 2010. http://www.electronicbookreview.com/thread/electropoetics/DFINative.

Bell, Alice, Astrid Ensslin, Isabelle van der Bom, and Jen Smith. 2019. "A Reader Response Method Not Just for 'You.'" *Language and Literature* 28, no. 2: 241–62.

———. 2018. "Immersion in Digital Fiction." *International Journal of Literary Linguistics* 7, no. 1. https://journals.linguistik.de/ijll/index.php/ijll/article/view/105.

Bentley, Matthew. 2012. "Braid Deconstructed—A Retrospective." *Gamasutra*, January 11, 2012. https://www.gamasutra.com/blogs/MatthewBentley/20121101/180779/Braid_Deconstructed__A_Retrospective.php.

Bizzocchi, Jim, and Robert F. Woodbury. 2003. "A Case Study in the Design of Interactive Narrative: The Subversion of the Interface." *Simulation Gaming* 34: 550–68.

Bogost, Ian. 2007. *Persuasive Games: The Expressive Power of Videogames*. Cambridge, MA: MIT Press.

Bolter, J. David. 2001. *Writing Space: Computers, Hypertext, and the Remediation of Print*, second edition. New York: Routledge.

———. 1991. *Writing Space: The Computer, Hypertext, and the History of Writing*. Hillsdale, NJ: Lawrence Erlbaum.

Booth, Wayne. C. 1967. *The Rhetoric of Fiction*. Chicago: University of Chicago Press.

Bouchardon, Serge. 2014. "Figures of Gestural Manipulation in Digital Fictions." In *Analyzing Digital Fiction*, edited by Alice Bell, Astrid Ensslin, and Hans K. Rustad, 159–75. New York: Routledge.

Burnett, Kathleen. 1993. "Toward a Theory of Hypertextual Design." *Postmodern Culture* 3, no. 2: n. pag.

Carmichael, Gail, and David Mould. 2014. "Chronologically Nonlinear Techniques in Traditional Media and Games." In *Proceedings of the 9th International Conference on the Foundations of Digital Games*, edited by Tiffany Barnes and Ian Bogost. Liberty of the Seas, Caribbean, April 3–7, 2014. http://www.fdg2014.org/proceedings.html.

Chatman, Seymour. 1990. *Coming to Terms: The Rhetoric of Narrative in Fiction and Film*. Ithaca, NY: Cornell University Press.

———. 1978. *Story and Discourse: Narrative Structure in Fiction and Film*. Ithaca, NY: Cornell University Press.

Ciccoricco, David. 2015. *Refiguring Minds in Narrative Media*. Lincoln: University of Nebraska Press.

———. 2010. "About Time." *Electronic Literature Directory*, http://directory.eliterature.org/individual-work/375.

———. 2007. *Reading Network Fiction*. Tuscaloosa: University of Alabama Press.

Cixous, Hélène. 1991. *Coming to Writing and Other Essays*. Edited by Deborah Jenson. Translated by Sarah Cornell, Ann Liddle, and Susan Sellers. Cambridge, MA: Harvard University Press.

Clement, Ryan. 2017. "Playing the Story: The Emergence of Narrative through the Interaction between Players, Game Mechanics, and Participatory Fan Communities." PhD thesis, University of Waterloo (CA).

Coover, Robert. 1992. "The End of Books." *New York Times,* June 21, 1992. https://www.nytimes.com/books/98/09/27/specials/coover-end.html.

Culler, Jonathan. 1975. *Structuralist Poetics: Structuralism, Linguistics and the Study of Literature.* New York: Routledge and Kegan Paul.

Dawson, Paul. 2013. *The Return of the Omniscient Narrator: Authorship and Authority in Twenty-First Century Fiction.* Columbus, OH: The Ohio State University Press.

Delany, Paul, and George, P. Landow. 1991. *Hypermedia and Literary Studies.* Cambridge, MA: MIT Press.

Deleuze, Gilles, and Felix Guattari. 1988. *A Thousand Plateaus: Capitalism and Schizophrenia.* Translated by Brian Massumi. London: Athlone.

Derrida, Jacques. 1981. *Dissemination.* Translated by Barbara Johnson. Chicago: University of Chicago Press.

Douglas, Jane Yellowees. 1994. "'How Do I Stop This Thing?' Closure and Indeterminacy in Interactive Narratives." In *Hyper/Text/Theory,* edited by George P. Landow, 159–88. Baltimore, MD: Johns Hopkins University Press.

Douglass, Jeremy. 2007. "Enlightening Interactive Fiction: Andrew Plotkins's *Shade.*" In *Second Person: Role-Playing and Story in Games and Playable Media,* edited by Pat Harrigan and Noah Wardrip-Fruin, 129–36. Cambridge, MA: MIT Press.

Duus, Rikke, and Mike Cooray. 2015. "How We Discovered the Dark Side of Wearable Fitness Trackers." *The Conversation,* June 19, 2015. https://theconversation.com/how-we-discovered-the-dark-side-of-wearable-fitness-trackers-43363.

Ensslin, Astrid. 2018. "The Interlocutor in Print and Digital Fiction: Dialogicity, Agency, (De-)Conventionalization." *MATLIT: Materialities of Literature* 6, no. 3: 21–34. https://impactumjournals.uc.pt/matlit/article/view/5288/4818.

———. 2017. "'Electronic Fictions: Television, the Internet, and the Future of Digital Fiction." In *The Cambridge Companion to Postmodern American Fiction,* edited by Paula E. Geyh, 181–97. Cambridge: Cambridge University Press.

———. 2015. "Video Games as Unnatural Narratives." In *Diversity of Play,* edited by Mathias Fuchs, 41–72. Lueneburg, Germany: Meson.

———. 2014a. *Literary Gaming.* Cambridge, MA: MIT Press.

———. 2014b. "Toward Functional Ludo-Narrativism: Metaludicity, Allusive Fallacy and Illusory Agency in *The Path.*" In *Analyzing Digital Fiction,* edited by Alice Bell, Astrid Ensslin, and Hans K. Rustad, 75–93. New York: Routledge.

———. 2012. "'I Want to Say I May Have Seen My Son Die This Morning': Unintentional Unreliable Narration in Digital Fiction." *Language and Literature* 21, no. 2: 136–49.

———. 2011a. "Diegetic Exposure and Cybernetic Performance: Towards Interactional Metalepsis." Plenary Presentation at Staging Illusion conference, University of Sussex, December 8–9, 2011. https://www.academia.edu/1157402/Diegetic_Exposure_and_Cybernetic_Performance_Towards_Interactional_Metalepsis.

———. 2011b. *The Language of Gaming.* Basingstoke: Palgrave Macmillan.

———. 2010. "From Revisi(tati)on to Retro-intentionalisation: Hermeneutics, Multimodality and Corporeality in Hypertext, Hypermedia and Cybertext." In *Reading Moving Letters: Digital Literature in Research and Teaching,* edited by Roberto Simanowski, Peter Gendolla, and Joergen Schaefer, 145–62. Bielefeld, Germany: transcript.

———. 2009. "Respiratory Narrative: Multimodality and Cybernetic Corporeality in 'Physiocybertext.'" In *New Perspectives on Narrative and Multimodality,* edited by Ruth Page, 155–65, London: Routledge.

———. 2007. *Canonizing Hypertext: Explorations and Constructions.* London: Continuum.

———. 2005. "Women in Wasteland—Gendered Deserts in T. S. Eliot and Shelley Jackson." *Journal of Gender Studies* 14, no. 3: 205–16.

Ensslin, Astrid, and Alice Bell. 2012. "'Click = Kill': Textual *You* in Ludic Digital Fiction." *Storyworlds* 4: 49–74.

———. 2007. *New Perspectives on Digital Literature: Criticism and Analysis,* special issue, *dichtung-digital.* http://www.dichtung-digital/Newsletter/aktuell.

Ensslin, Astrid, Alice Bell, Isabelle van der Bom, Jen Smith, and Lyle Skains. 2019. "Immersion, Digital Fiction, and the Switchboard Metaphor." *Participations: Journal of Audience and Reception Studies* 16, no. 1: 320–42.

Ensslin, Astrid, and Eben Muse, eds. 2011. *Creating Second Lives: Community, Identity and Spatiality as Constructions of the Virtual.* New York: Routledge.

Ensslin, Astrid, and Lyle Skains. 2017. "Hypertext: Storyspace to Twine." In *The Bloomsbury Handbook of Electronic Literature,* edited by Joseph Tabbi, 293–307. London: Bloomsbury.

Ensslin, Astrid, Lisa Swanstrom, and Pawel Frelik, eds. 2017. "Small Screen Fictions." Special issue, *Paradoxa* 29. http://smallscreenfictions.net/.

Eskelinen, Markku. 2001. "The Gaming Situation." *Game Studies* 1, no. 1. http://gamestudies.org/0101/eskelinen.

Falkenstern, Max. 2013. "Einmal tot, immer tot: Permadeath in Videospielen." *PCGames.de,* January 18, 2013. https://www.pcgames.de/Spiele-Thema-239104/Specials/Einmal-tot-immer-tot-Permadeath-in-Videospielen-1044001/.

Fletcher, Robert. 2015. "3 Proposals for Bottle Imps." *Electronic Literature Directory,* http://directory.eliterature.org/individual-work/4608.

Flores, Leonardo. 2012. "'Opacity' by Serge Bouchardon, i-Trace Collective, and Léonard Dumas." *Iloveepoetry.com,* http://iloveepoetry.com/?p=369.

Fludernik, Monika. 2012. "How Natural Is 'Unnatural Narratology'; or, What Is Unnatural about Unnatural Narratology?" *Narrative* 20, no. 3: 357–70.

———. 2003. "Scene Shift, Metalepsis, and the Metaleptic Mode." *Style* 37, no. 4: 382–400.

———. 1999 "Defining (In)sanity: The Narrator of *The Yellow Wallpaper* and the Question of Unreliability." In *Grenzüberschreitungen: Narratologie im Kontext / Transcending Boundaries: Narratology in Context,* edited by Walter Grünzweig and Andreas Solbach, 75–95. Tübingen, Germany: Gunter Narr Verlag.

———. 1996. *Towards a 'Natural' Narratology.* London: Routledge.

———. 1995. "Pronouns of Address and 'Odd' Third Person Forms: The Mechanics of Involvement in Fiction." In *New Essays in Deixis,* edited by Keith Green, 99–129. Amsterdam: Rodopi.

———. 1994. "Second-Person Narrative as a Test Case for Narratology: The Limits of Realism." *Style* 28, no. 3: 445–79.

Gaggi, Silvio. 1998. *From Text to Hypertext: Decentering the Subject in Fiction, Film, the Visual Arts, and Electronic Media.* Philadelphia: University of Pennsylvania Press.

Gardner, Colin. 2004. "Meta-Interpretation and Hypertext Fiction: A Critical Response." *Computers and the Humanities* 37: 33–56.

Genette, Gérard. 1980. *Narrative Discourse: An Essay in Method.* Translated by Jane E. Lewin. Ithaca, NY: Cornell University Press.

Geyh, Paula, Fred G. Leebron, and Andrew Levy, eds. 1997. *Postmodern American Fiction: A Norton Anthology*. New York: Norton.

Grice, John. 1975. "Logic and Conversation." In *Syntax and Semantics. 3: Speech Acts*, edited by Peter Cole and Jerry L. Morgan, 41–58. New York: Academic Press.

Guyer, Carolyn. 1992. "Something about *Quibbling*, a Hyperfiction." *Leonardo Electronic News* 3, no. 1: 258.

Hampson, Robert. 1996. "'Allowing for Possible Error': Education and Catechism in 'Ithaca.'" In *Joyce's "Ithaca,"* edited by Andrew Gibson, 229–67. European Joyce Studies 6. Amsterdam: Rodopi.

Hanebeck, Julian. 2017. *Understanding Metalepsis: The Hermeneutics of Narrative Transgression*. Narratologia 56. Berlin: Walter de Gruyter.

Harrigan, Pat, and Noah Wardrip-Fruin. 2007. *Second Person: Role-Playing and Story in Games and Playable Media*. Cambridge, MA: MIT Press.

Hawking, Stephen W. 1988. *A Brief History of Time: From the Big Bang to Black Holes*. Toronto: Bantam Books.

Hayles, N. Katherine. 2007. "Electronic Literature: What Is It?" *The Electronic Literature Organization*. http://eliterature.org/pad/elp.html#sec2.

———. 2004. "Print Is Flat, Code Is Deep: The Importance of Media-Specific Analysis." *Poetics Today* 25, no. 1: 67–90.

———. 2000. "Flickering Connectivities in Shelley Jackson's *Patchwork Girl*: The Importance of Media-Specific Analysis." *Postmodern Culture* 10, no. 2: n. pag. http://www.iath.virginia.edu/pmc/text-only/issue.100/10.2hayles.txt.

Hayman, David. 1982. *Ulysses: The Mechanics of Meaning*, rev. ed. Madison: University of Wisconsin Press.

Heinze, Rüdiger. 2013. "The Whirligig of Time: Towards a Poetics of Unnatural Temporality." In Alber, Nielsen, and Richardson 2013, 31–44.

Herman, David. 2002. *Story Logic: Problems and Possibilities of Narrative*. Lincoln: University of Nebraska Press.

———. 1994. "Textual 'You' and Double Deixis in Edna O'Brien's *A Pagan Place*." *Style* 28, no. 3: 378–411.

Heyd, Theresa. 2006. "Understanding and Handling Unreliable Narratives: A Pragmatic Model and Method." *Semiotica* 162: 217–43.

Hocking, Clint. 2007. "Ludonarrative Dissonance in *Bioshock*." *Click Nothing*, October 7, 2007. https://www.clicknothing.com/click_nothing/2007/10/ludonarrative-d.html.

Hussey, Joshua. 2017. "The Image of Agglutination, or Many Small Screens Chained Together: Narrative Assembly in Merritt Kopas's *Obéissance* and Sam Barlow's *Her Story*." In "Small Screen Fictions," edited by Astrid Ensslin, Lisa Swanstrom, and Pawel Frelik, special issue, *Paradoxa* 29: 169–98.

Ingress. 2016a. "Ingress Portals." *Ingress Manual*. http://decodeingress.me/ingress-manual/ingress-portals/.

———. 2016b. "Candidate Portal Criteria." *Ingress Help*. https://support.ingress.com/hc/en-us/articles/207343987-Candidate-Portal-criteria.

Iversen, Stefan. 2016. "Permanent Defamiliarization as Rhetorical Device; or, How to Let Puppymonkeybaby into Unnatural Narratology." *Style* 50, no. 4: 455–61.

Jahn, Manfred. 2017. "Narratology: A Guide to the Theory of Narrative," v. 2.0. English Department, University of Cologne. http://www.uni-koeln.de/~ame02/pppn.htm.

Jenkins, Henry. 2004. "Game Design as Narrative Architecture." In *First Person: New Media as Story, Performance, and Game*, edited by Noah Wardrip-Fruin and Pat Harrigan, 118–30. Cambridge, MA: MIT Press.

Jones, Steven. 2002. *Antonymy: A Corpus-Based Perspective*. London: Routledge.

Juul, Jesper. 2005. *Half-Real: Video Games between Real Rules and Fictional Worlds*. Cambridge, MA: MIT Press.

———. 2001. "Games Telling Stories?—A Brief Note on Games and Narratives." *Game Studies* 1, no. 1. http://www.gamestudies.org/0101/juul-gts.

Kacandes, Irene. 2001. *Talk Fiction*. Lincoln: University of Nebraska Press.

———. 1993. "Are You in the Text?: The 'Literary Performative' in Postmodernist Fiction." *Text and Performance Quarterly* 13, no. 2: 139–53.

Karmali, Luke. 2014. "The Stanley Parable Sales Pass 1 Million Mark." *IGN*, October 21, 2014. https://ca.ign.com/articles/2014/10/21/the-stanley-parable-sales-pass-1-million-mark.

Klevjer, Rune. 2012. "Enter the Avatar. The Phenomenology of Prosthetic Telepresence in Computer Games." In *The Philosophy of Computer Games*, edited by John Richard Sageng, Hallvard J. Fossheim, and Tarjei Mandt Larsen, 17–38. London & New York: Springer.

Klimek, Sonja. 2011. "Metalepsis in Fantasy Fiction." In Kukkonen and Klimek 2011, 20–44.

Kukkonen, Karin. 2011a. "Metalepsis in Popular Culture: An Introduction." In Kukkonen and Klimek 2011, 1–21.

———. 2011b. "Metalepsis in Comics and Graphic Novels." In Kukkonen and Klimek 2011, 213–31.

Kukkonen, Karin, and Sonja Klimek, eds. 2011. *Metalepsis in Popular Culture*. Berlin: Walter de Gruyter.

Landow, George P. 2006. *Hypertext 3.0: Critical Theory and New Media in an Era of Globalization*. Baltimore, MD: Johns Hopkins University Press.

———. 1997. *Hypertext 2.0: The Convergence of Contemporary Critical Theory and Technology*. Baltimore, MD: Johns Hopkins University Press.

———. 1994. "What's a Critic to Do? Critical Theory in the Age of Hypertext." In *Hyper/Text/Theory*, edited by George, P. Landow, 1–48. Baltimore, MD: Johns Hopkins University Press.

Lee, Kwan Min. 2004. "Presence, Explicated." *Communication Theory* 14, no. 1: 27–50.

Limoges, Jean-Marc. 2011. "Metalepsis in Animation Film." In Kukkonen and Klimek 2011, 196–212.

Linderoth, Jonas. 2011. "Beyond the Digital Divide: An Ecological Approach to Gameplay." *Proceedings of DiGRA 2011*, September 14–17, 2011, Utrecht, Netherlands. http://www.digra.org/wp-content/uploads/digital-library/11307.03263.pdf.

MacCallum-Stewart, Esther, and Justin Parsler. 2007. "Illusory Agency in *Vampire: The Masquerade—Bloodlines*." *dichtung-digital* 37. http://dichtung-digital.de/2007/maccallumstewart_parsler.htm.

Maher, Jimmy. 2015. "Trinity." *The Digital Antiquarian: A History of Computer Entertainment*. https://www.filfre.net/2015/01/trinity/.

Mäkelä, Maria. 2013. "Realism and the Unnatural." in Alber, Nielsen, and Richardson 2013, 142–66.

Manovich, Lev. 2014. "Postmedia Aesthetics." in *Transmedia Frictions: The Digital, the Arts, and the Humanities*, edited by Marsha Kinder and Tara McPherson, 34–44. Oakland: University of California Press.

Margolin, Uri. 1990. "Narrative 'You' Revisited." *Language and Style* 23, no. 4: 425–46.

Marino, Mark C. 2006a. "I, Chatbot: The Gender and Race Performativity of Conversational Agents." PhD diss., University of California, Riverside.

———. 2006b. "Critical Code Studies." *Electronic Book Review*, December 4, 2006. http://www.electronicbookreview.com/thread/electropoetics/codology.

McHale, Brian. 1992. *Constructing Postmodernism*. London: Routledge.

———. 1987. *Postmodernist Fiction*. New York: Routledge.

Miles, Adrian. 2003. "There's No Need to Bite the Breast." *Journal of Digital Information* 3, no. 3: n. pag. https://www.academia.edu/7292260/Theres_No_Need_to_Bite_the_Breast.

Montfort, Nick. 2007. "Narrative and Digital Media." In *The Cambridge Companion to Narrative*, edited by David Herman, 172–86. Cambridge: Cambridge University Press.

———. 2003. *Twisty Little Passages: An Approach to Interactive Fiction*. Cambridge, MA: MIT Press.

Morris, Steven. 2008. "Real and Virtual Chase for Second Life Divorce Couple." *Guardian*, November 15, 2008. https://www.theguardian.com/technology/2008/nov/15/secondlife-digitalmedia.

Moulthrop, Stuart. 2017. "Deep Time in Play." In "Small Screen Fictions," edited by Astrid Ensslin, Lisa Swanstrom, and Pawel Frelik, special issue, *Paradoxa* 29: 123–44.

———. 1991b. "Reading from the Map: Metonymy and Metaphor in the Fiction of Forking Paths." In *Hypermedia and Literary Studies*, edited by Paul Delany and George P. Landow, 119–32. Cambridge, MA: MIT Press.

Mularcyzk, Sam. n.d. *The Stanley Parable: A Galactic Café Game*. http://www.stanleyparable.com.

Murray, Janet. 2017. *Hamlet on the Holodeck: The Future of Narrative in Cyberspace*, 2nd ed. Cambridge, MA: MIT Press.

Nelson, Jason. 2006. "Dreamaphage (Versions 1 and 2)." In *Electronic Literature Collection, Volume 1*, edited by N. Katherine Hayles, Nick Montfort, Scott Rettberg, and Stephanie Strickland. College Park, MD: Electronic Literature Organization. http://collection.eliterature.org/1/works/nelson__dreamaphage.html

Nielsen, Henrik, Skov. 2013. "Naturalizing and Unnaturalizing Reading Strategies: Focalization Revisited." In Alber, Nielsen, and Richardson 2013, 67–93.

———. 2011. "Unnatural Narratology, Impersonal Voices, Real Authors, and Non-Communicative Narration." In Alber and Heinze 2011, 71–88.

Nieuwland, Mante S., and Jos J. A. van Berkum. 2006. "When Peanuts Fall in Love: N400 Evidence for the Power of Discourse." *Journal of Cognitive Neuroscience* 18, no. 7: 1098–1111.

Nitsche, Michael. 2008. *Video Game Spaces: Image, Play, and Structure in 3D Worlds*. Cambridge, MA: MIT Press.

Nünning, Ansgar. 2005. "Reconceptualizing Unreliable Narration: Synthesizing Cognitive and Rhetorical Approaches." In *A Companion to Narrative Theory*, edited by James Phelan and Peter, J. Rabinowitz, 89–107. Malden, MA: Blackwell.

———, ed. 1998. *Unreliable Narration: Studien zur Theorie und Praxis unglaubwürdigen Erzählens in der englischsprachigen Erzählliteratur*. Trier, Germany: Wissenschaftlicher Verlag Trier.

Olson, Greta. 2003. "Reconsidering Unreliability: Fallible and Untrustworthy Narrators." *Narrative* 11, no. 1: 93–109.

O'Sullivan, James. 2017. "'The Dream of an Island': *Dear Esther* and the Digital Sublime." In "Small Screen Fictions," edited by Astrid Ensslin, Lisa Swanstrom, and Pawel Frelik, special issue, *Paradoxa* 29: 313–26.

Parker, Joshua. 2001. "A Poetics of the Link." *Electronic Book Review* 12. http://www.altx.com/ebr/ebr12/park/park.htm.

Parkin, Simon. 2012. "Shigeru Miyamoto: A Rushed Game Is Forever Bad." *Guardian*, April 27, 2012. https://www.theguardian.com/technology/gamesblog/2012/apr/27/shigeru-miyamoto-rushed-game-forever-bad.

Peterson, Jean Sunde, and Karen E. Ray. 2006. "Bullying and the Gifted: Victims, Perpetrators, Prevalence, and Effects." *Gifted Child Quarterly* 50: 148–68.

Pfister, Manfred. 1977. *Das Drama*. Munich: Wilhelm Fink.

Phelan, James. 2009. "The Beginning of *Beloved*: A Rhetorical Approach." In *Narrative Beginnings*, edited by Brian Richardson, 195–212. Lincoln: University of Nebraska Press.

———. 1996. *Narrative as Rhetoric: Technique, Audiences, Ethics, Ideology*. Columbus: The Ohio State University Press.

Phelan, James, and Mary Patricia Martin. 1999. "The Lessons of Weymouth: Homodiegesis, Unreliability, Ethics and *The Remains of the Day*." In *Narratologies: New Perspectives on Narrative Analysis*, edited by David Herman, 88–109. Columbus: The Ohio State University Press.

Picot, Edward. 2003. "What Makes Them Click?" *Archive of the trAce Online Writing Centre 1995–2005*. http://tracearchive.ntu.ac.uk/review/index.cfm?article=76.

Pier, John. 2011. "Afterword." In Kukkonen and Klimek 2011, 268–76.

———. 2005. "Metalepsis." In *The Routledge Encyclopedia of Narrative Theory*, edited by David Herman, Manfred Jahn, and Marie-Laure Ryan, 303–4. London: Routledge.

Pike, Chris, and Zillah Watson. 2016. "Virtual Reality Sound in *The Turning Forest*." *BBC Online*, May 10, 2016. https://www.bbc.co.uk/rd/blog/2016-05-virtual-reality-sound-in-the-turning-forest.

Pope, James. 2010. "Where Do We Go from Here? Readers' Responses to Interactive Fiction: Narrative Structures, Reading Pleasure and the Impact of Interface Design." *Convergence* 6, no. 1: 75–94.

———. 2006. "A Future for Hypertext Fiction." *Convergence* 12, no. 4: 447–65.

Punday, Daniel. 2017. "Space across Narrative Media: Towards an Archeology of Narratology." *Narrative* 25, no. 1: 92–112.

Reed, Ashley. 2015. "Relativity Is the Mind-Bending Cousin of Portal and Echochrome." *gamesradar*, June 17, 2015. https://www.gamesradar.com/relativity-mind-bending-cousin-portal-and-echochrome.

Rettberg, Scott. 2008. "Dada Redux: Elements of Dadaist Practice in Contemporary Electronic Literature." *The Fibreculture Journal* 11. http://eleven.fibreculturejournal.org/fcj-071-dada-redux-elements-of-dadaist-practice-in-contemporary-electronic-literature/.

Richardson, Brian. 2016. "Unnatural Narrative Theory." *Style* 50, no. 4: 385–405.

———. 2015. *Unnatural Narrative: Theory, History, and Practice*. Columbus: The Ohio State University Press.

———. 2011. "What Is Unnatural Narrative Theory?" In Alber and Heinze 2011, 23–40.

———. 2006. *Unnatural Voices: Extreme Narration in Modern and Contemporary Fiction*. Columbus: The Ohio State University Press.

———. 2002. "Beyond Story and Discourse: Narrative Time in Postmodern and Nonmimetic Fiction." In *Narrative Dynamics: Essays on Time, Plot, Closure, and Frames*, edited by Brian Richardson, 47–63. Columbus: The Ohio State University Press.

———. 1991. "The Poetics and Politics of Second Person." *Genre* 24, no. 3: 309–30.

Rimmon-Kenan, Shlomith. 1983. *Narrative Fiction: Contemporary Poetics*. London: Routledge.

Rosenberg, John R. 1992. "The Clock and the Cloud: Chaos and Order in *El diablo mundo.*" *Revista de Estudios Hispánicos* 26: 203–25.

Ryan, Marie-Laure. 2016. "Response to Brian Richardson's Target Essay 'Unnatural Narrative Theory.'" *Style* 50, no. 4: 478–83.

———. 2015. *Narrative as Virtual Reality 2: Revisiting Immersion and Interactivity in Literature and Electronic Media*. Baltimore, MD: Johns Hopkins University Press.

———. 2012. "Impossible Worlds." In *The Routledge Companion to Experimental Literature*, edited by Joe Bray, Alison Gibbons, and Brian McHale, 368–79. London: Routledge.

———. 2009. "Temporal Paradoxes in Narrative." *Style* 43, no. 2: 142–64.

———. 2006a. *Avatars of Story*. Minneapolis: University of Minnesota Press.

———. 2006b. "From Parallel Universes to Possible Worlds: Ontological Pluralism in Physics, Narratology, and Narrative." *Poetics Today* 27, no. 4: 633–74.

———. 2005. "Narrative and Digitality: Learning to Think with the Medium." In *A Companion to Narrative Theory*, edited by James Phelan and Peter J. Rabinowitz, 515–28. Malden, MA: Blackwell.

———. 2004a. "Metaleptic Machines." *Semiotica* 150, no. 1: 439–69.

———. 2004b. *Narrative across Media*. Lincoln: University of Nebraska Press.

———. 2001. *Narrative as Virtual Reality: Immersion and Interactivity in Literature and Electronic Media*. Baltimore: Johns Hopkins University Press.

———. 1991. *Possible Worlds, Artificial Intelligence and Narrative Theory*. Bloomington: Indiana University Press.

Ryan, Marie-Laure, and Jan-Noël Thon, eds. 2014. *Storyworlds across Media: Toward a Media-Conscious Narratology*. Lincoln: University of Nebraska Press.

Salt, Barry. 1983. *Film Style and Technology: History and Analysis*. London: Starword.

Schank, Roger C., and Robert P. Abelson. 1977. *Scripts, Plans, Goals and Understanding: An Inquiry into Human Knowledge*. Artificial Intelligence Series. Hillsdale, NJ: Erlbaum.

Schnierer, Peter Paul. 2001. "Hyperdrama: Prototypes, Current Practice, Problems." In *What Revels Are in Hand? Assessments of Contemporary Drama in English in Honour of Wolfgang Lippke*, edited by Bernhard Reitz and Heiko Stahl, 139–52. Trier: Wissenschaftlicher Verlag.

Schreier, Jason. 2016. "The Man Who Wrote *EarthBound*." *Kotaku*, March 24, 2016. https://kotaku.com/the-man-who-wrote-earthbound-1188669175.

Simanowski, Roberto. 2011. *Digital Art and Meaning: Reading Kinetic Poetry, Text Machines, Mapping Art, and Interactive Installations*. Minneapolis: University of Minnesota Press.

Stanzel, Franz. 1984. *A Theory of Narrative*. Cambridge: Cambridge University Press.

Steuer, Jonathan. 1992. "Defining Virtual Reality: Dimensions Determining Telepresence." *Journal of Communication* 42, no. 4: 73–93.

Thomas, Bronwen. 2007. "Stuck in a Loop? Dialogue in Hypertext Fiction." *Narrative* 15, no. 3: 358–72.

Thon, Jan-Noël. 2016. *Transmedial Narratology and Contemporary Media Culture*. Lincoln: University of Nebraska Press.

———. 2009. "Perspective in Contemporary Computer Games." In *Point of View, Perspective, and Focalization. Modeling Mediation in Narrative*, edited by Peter Hühn, Wolf Schmid, and Jörg Schönert, 279–99. Berlin; New York: Walter de Gruyter.

———. 2008. "Immersion Revisited. On the Value of a Contested Concept." In *Extending Experiences: Structure, Analysis, and Design of Computer Game Player Experience*, edited by Amyris Fernandez, Olli Leino, and Hanna Wirman, 29–43. Rovaniemi: Lapland University Press.

Thoss, Jeff. 2011a. "'Some Weird Kind of Video Feedback Time Warp Zapping Thing': Television, Remote Controls, and Metalepsis." In Kukkonen and Klimek 2011, 158–70.

———. 2011b. "Unnatural Narrative and Metalepsis: Grant Morrison's *Animal Man*." In *Unnatural Narratives—Unnatural Narratology*, edited by Jan Alber and Rüdiger Heinze, 189–209. Berlin: Walter de Gruyter.

Thoss, Jeff, Astrid Ensslin, and David Ciccoricco. 2018. "Narrative Media: The Impossibilities of Digital Storytelling." *Poetics Today* 39, no. 3: 623–43.

Turk, Tisha. 2011. "Metalepsis in Fan Vids and Fan Fiction." In Kukkonen and Klimek 2011, 83–103.

Turner, Mark. 1996. *The Literary Mind*. New York: Oxford University Press.

van der Bom, Isabelle, Lyle Skains, Alice Bell, and Astrid Ensslin. 2021. "Reading Hyperlinks in Hypertext Fiction: An Empirical Approach." In *Style and Reader Response: Minds, Media, Methods*, edited by Alice Bell, Sam Browse, Alison Gibbons, and David Peplow. Amsterdam: John Benjamins.

Vial, Stéphane, and Neal Stimler. 2014. "Digital Monism: Our Mode of Being at the Nexus of Life, Digital Media and Art." *Theorizing the Web 2014*, April 26, 2014, New York, United States. https://www.slideshare.net/nealstimler/tt-w14-c4vialstimler-1.

Waern, Annika. 2011. "'I'm in Love with Someone That Doesn't Exist!': Bleed in the Context of a Computer Game." *Journal of Gaming and Virtual Worlds* 3, no. 3: 239–58.

Walker, Jill. 2000. "Do You Think You're Part of This? Digital Texts and the Second Person Address." In *Cybertext Yearbook 2000*, edited by Markku Eskelinen and Raine Koskimaa. University of Jyväskylä, Finland: Research Centre for Contemporary Culture. http://jilltxt.net/txt/do_you_think.pdf.

———. 1999. "Piecing Together and Tearing Apart: Finding the Story in *Afternoon*." In *Proceedings of the Tenth ACM Conference on Hypertext and Hypermedia*, February 21–25, 1999, Darmstadt, Germany, ACM Press, 111–17.

Wall, Kathleen. 1994. "*The Remains of the Day* and Its Challenges to Theories of Unreliable Narration." *Journal of Narrative Technique* 24, no. 1: 18–42.

Waugh, Patricia. 2003 [1984]. *Metafiction: The Theory and Practice of Self-Conscious Fiction*. London: Routledge.

Welbourn, David. 2015a. "Key & Compass Presents: Trinity by Brian Moriarty." http://www.plover.net/~davidw/sol/t/trini86.html.

———. 2015b. "Trinity, by Brian Moriarty." *The Interactive Fiction Database*, v. 10. https://ifdb.tads.org/viewgame?id=j18kjz8ohxjtyayw.

Wertheim, Eleanor H., and Susan J. Paxton. 2011. "Body Image Development in Adolescent Girls." In *Body Image: A Handbook of Science, Practices and Prevention*, edited by Thomas F. Cash and Linda Smolak, 76–84. New York: Guilford.

Wolf, Werner. 2013. "'Unnatural Metalepsis' and 'Immersion.'" In Alber, Nielsen, and Richardson 2013, 113–41.

———. 2005. "Metalepsis as a Transgeneric and Transmedial Phenomenon: A Case Study of the Possibilities of 'Exporting' Narratological Concepts." In *Narratology Beyond Literary Criticism: Mediality, Disciplinarity*, edited by Jan Christoph Meister, 83–107. Berlin, Germany: Walter de Gruyter.

Yacobi, Tamar. 1988. "Time Denatured into Meaning: New Worlds and Renewed Themes in the Poetry of Dan Pagis." *Style* 22, no. 1: 93–115.

———. 1981. "Fictional Reliability as a Communicative Problem." *Poetics Today* 2, no. 2: 113–26.

INDEX

3 Proposals for Bottle Imps (Poundstone), 117

34 North 118 West (Hight, Knowlton, and Spellman), 76, 78

10:01 (Olsen and Guthrie), 69n4

Aarseth, Espen, 52, 85, 114, 145, 157

About Time (Swigart), 113–14, 119

actualized input/output, 156–57, 162

afternoon, a story (Joyce), 23, 24, 30, 31n2, 34, 35, 117, 125, 128–29, 149, 161, 184

Alber, Jan, 4–6, 7–13, 16, 20–21, 22–24, 25, 26, 28, 33, 34, 35, 40, 41, 46, 47, 51, 56–57, 68, 72, 75, 79, 81, 83, 84, 88–90, 93, 95, 96, 99, 101, 103, 105, 106, 107–8, 110, 111, 114, 117, 118, 129, 134, 138, 140, 141, 148, 158, 160, 165, 169, 170, 180, 186–87

All the Delicate Duplicates (Breeze and Campbell), 103–6, 110

Alston, Judi, 49, 69n4, 80, 103–4, 134. See also *Clearance* (Campbell, Alston, and Johnson); *Consensus Trance II* (Campbell and Alston); *WALLPAPER* (Campbell and Alston)

Animal Man (DC Comics), 53, 161n3

Antichamber (Bruce), 99–100

antimimetic, 9, 14, 15, 181–8; narration, 4–6, 7, 9, 17, 25, 29, 33, 36, 38, 42, 43, 46, 47, 75, 79, 80, 88, 93, 159–60, 186, 187. *See also* extreme narration

antimimeticism: environmental, 15, 93, 118, 183; medium-specific, 4, 9, 14, 15, 16, 19–20, 25, 33–34, 44, 47, 57, 65–66, 68, 71, 72, 94, 99, 100–102, 103, 105, 106, 109, 111, 112–13, 114, 115, 116–17, 118, 119–20, 122–23, 124, 127, 134–35, 137, 141–42, 164–70, 181, 185, 187

app-fiction, 2, 15–16, 21, 59–60, 73–78, 85, 101, 102–3, 118, 162

Arrow of Death Part 1 (Howarth), 26

At Swim-Two-Birds (O'Brien), 51

Back to Bed (Bedtime Digital Games), 99–100, 183

Bandersnatch (Brooker), 188

"Barbe bleue, La" (Perrault), 139

Barthes, Roland, 13, 31

Bartlett, Marigold, 60 fig. 2.2

BBC (British Broadcasting Corporation), 80

Behind Closed Doors (Wilson), 26

Bell, Alice, 2, 5n4, 20, 31, 36n3, 37, 39, 50, 51, 53, 56–57, 69n4, 71, 74, 117, 139, 152, 157n2, 159, 161, 162–63, 164, 171, 188

Bentley, Matthew, 111

Beyond Two Souls (Quantic Dream), 112

Bioshock (2K Boston/Australia), 127

Bizzocchi, Jim, 63

Bolter, J. David, 9–10, 31–32, 71, 85, 87, 102; *Writing Space*, 85–86

Braid (Blow), 110–12, 119

Breast, The (Roth), 12

Breathing Wall, The (Pullinger, Schemat, and Babel), 64–67, 80, 81, 124, 183

Breeze, Mez, 103–4. See also *All the Delicate Duplicates* (Breeze and Campbell)

Cadre, Adam, 26

"Calmative, The" (Beckett), 124

Campbell, Andy, 49, 69n4, 96, 99, 103–4, 134. See also *All the Delicate Duplicates* (Breeze and Campbell); *Clearance* (Campbell, Alston, and Johnson); *Consensus Trance II* (Campbell and Alston); *Inkubus* (Campbell and Wilks); *WALLPAPER* (Campbell and Alston)

Castle of Crossed Destinies, The (Calvino), 124

Cayley, John, 142

Chatman, Seymour, 114, 126, 131–32, 145; *Story and Discourse*, 131–32

Ciccoricco, David, 17, 52, 87, 113, 123, 129, 144, 145–46

"Circular Ruins, The" (Borges), 140

Cixous, Hélène, 31

Cleansed (Kane), 12

Clearance (Campbell, Alston, and Johnson), 69n4

cognitive narratology, 4, 11–13, 14, 15, 16, 20, 25, 56, 61–62, 80–81, 84–85, 179, 186, 188–89

Company (Beckett), 136

Composition No. 1 (Saporta), 4

Consensus Trance II (Campbell and Alston), 103

conventionalization, 7–8, 9–10, 11, 14, 25, 47, 50, 65, 68, 71, 72, 75, 80, 81–82, 88, 90, 92, 101–2, 105, 107, 109, 112, 114, 115–16, 118, 123, 130, 132–33, 137, 142, 149, 152, 158–59, 162–65, 175, 176, 180, 181–82, 185, 186. See also unconventionalization

Coover, Robert, 9, 13, 19, 20, 23, 31 108, 125; "The Babysitter," 9, 13, 20, 23, 108–9, 125; "The End of Books," 19

Culler, Jonathan, 1n1, 5, 8. See also naturalize

Curious Case of Benjamin Button, The (film, Fincher), 11

"Curious Case of Benjamin Button, The" (Fitzgerald), 109

Cutting Edges, Or: A Web of Women (Nestvold), 137

Cyberiad, The (Lem), 143

cybertextual velocity, 16, 85, 109, 114–17, 119, 184, 186

Dakota (Young Hae Chang Heavy Industry), 114, 115, 120, 184

Dawson, Paul, 145

Dear Esther (The Chinese Room), 93, 128

Death of Artemio Cruz, The (Fuentes), 136

Delany, Paul, 31, 32

Deleuze, Gilles, 31

denaturalize, 88, 100–101

Derrida, Jacques, 31

Descartes, René, 141

diegetic: information, 164; levels, 50–52, 55–56, 59, 131–32, 132 fig. 4.1, 147–48, 148 fig. 4.2; opacity, 105; time, 114; voices, 181; worlds, 62, 131, 157, 165, 167

"Digital Monism", 78–79

Disappearing Rain (Larsen), 70–72, 81, 183

discourse (syuzhet), 5, 10, 16, 19, 21, 25, 38, 39, 40, 45, 46, 105, 106–7, 112, 114, 119, 160

double deixis, 152–56, 153 fig. 5.1, 161–62, 171–75, 176–77, 185, 188

Douglas, Jane Yellowees, 34, 35

Dreamaphage (Nelson), 103, 119

EarthBound (Earthbound Ape Inc. and HAL Laboratory), 165–67, 176, 184

Eastgate Systems, 21

Electronic Literature as a Model of Creativity and Innovation in Practice Knowledge Database (ELMCIP), 5

Electronic Literature Collections, 1–3, 5, 76

Electronic Literature Directory, 5
empirical research, 17, 179, 188
Ensslin, Astrid, 2n3, 5n4, 9, 39n4, 40–41, 52–53, 64, 65, 69, 74, 82, 89, 91, 100, 110, 111, 114–15, 117, 128, 129, 130, 137–38, 139, 146–47, 152, 157n2, 163, 164, 171, 188
environmental storytelling, 86, 93, 122
ergodic, 2, 46, 52–55, 57, 58, 81, 118, 145, 181, 182, 183
Everybody Dies (Munroe), 26, 135, 141–42
Everybody's Gone to the Rapture (The Chinese Room), 42–43, 45, 93–94, 183

Façade (Mateas and Stern), 73, 133
Felidae (Pirinçci), 124
Figurski at Findhorn on Acid (Holeton), 54n2
Finnegans Wake (Joyce), 38
Flash fiction, 2, 114, 115, 120, 139–40, 168–69, 184
Flight Paths (Pullinger and Joseph), 59
Flight to Canada (Reed), 108
Flores, Leonardo, 173
Fludernik, Monika, 1, 1n1, 3, 5, 8, 33, 50–52, 55, 63, 126, 132–33, 142–43, 158, 159, 160, 162; *Towards a Natural Narratology*, 3. *See also* narrativizing; natural narrative; unnatural narrative; unnatural narratology
French Lieutenant's Woman, The (Fowles), 20, 23
Future Voices (Inkle), 59

Galatea (Short), 133–34, 184
Genette, Gérard, 50–51, 55, 63, 112, 114, 160; anachrony, 112
graphical user interface (GUI), 87, 122, 170
Groundhog Day (Ramis), 108
Guardian, The, 90
Guattari, Felix, 31

Hanebeck, Julian, 50–51, 161–62, 161n3
"Happy Endings" (Atwood), 160
Harrigan, Pat, 163
Harry Potter series (Rowling), 12–13
Heart of Darkness (Conrad), 170

Heinze, Rüdiger, 7, 16, 106. *See also* discourse (syuzhet); story (fabula)
Herman, David, 2, 152, 153 fig. 5.1, 154–56, 158, 171, 172
Her Story (Barlow), 112–13, 119, 183–84
Heyd, Theresa, 126–27
High Muck a Muck: Playing Chinese (High Muck a Muck Collective), 59
"House of Asturion, The" (Borges), 124
House of Cards (Netflix), 54
House of Leaves (Danielewski), 8
Howl (Ginsberg), 38
"How to Love America and Leave It at the Same Time" (Updike), 159
Hussey, Joshua, 113, 184
hypermedia fiction, 136, 137–39, 162, 172–75, 185
hypermimetic game worlds, 15, 84, 90, 93–94, 104, 118, 183, 185
hypertext fiction, 2, 3, 5n4, 14–15, 19, 20, 21–22, 23, 24–25, 29–42, 43, 46, 47–48, 52, 54n2, 58–59, 69–72, 81, 85, 113–14, 116–17, 124–25, 127–29, 136, 137, 138, 139, 140, 143, 149, 157n2, 159, 161–62, 164–65, 175–76, 182; Storyspace hypertext, 20, 21, 25, 30, 31n2, 33–34, 36, 36n3, 39, 41–42, 58–59, 182; Twine, 3, 40–41, 114
hypertext theory, 16, 29–42, 46, 69–72, 127, 140, 184, 188

"Immortal, The" (Borges), 125
Ingress (Niantic, Inc.), 77–78
Inkubus (Campbell and Wilks), 96–99, 97 figs. 3.1, 3.2, 98 figs. 3.3, 3.4, 118, 183
interactive drama, 15
Interactive Fiction (IF), 2–3, 10, 14, 19–20, 24, 26–29, 44, 47, 91–93, 111, 132, 133–34, 136, 141–42, 157, 162–63, 164, 182, 184; Interactive Fiction Database, 26n1
Iversen, Stefan, 4, 8, 9, 32, 46, 85, 90, 103, 125, 160, 176, 180, 186. *See also* permanently defamiliarizing

"Jabberwocky" (Carroll), 92
Jacques the Fataliste (Diderot), 50
Jahn, Manfred, 131–32, 132 fig. 4.1
Jalousie, La (Robbe-Grillet), 125

Jenkins, Henry, 86, 122, 168
Jew's Daughter, The (Morrissey and Talley), 144
Juul, Jesper, 10, 42, 44, 58, 87–88, 119

Kacandes, Irene, 153 fig. 5.1, 156
Karen (Blast Theory), 73–75, 73 fig. 2.4, 78, 81
Klevjer, Rune, 61
Klimek, Sonja, 53, 55–56, 55 fig. 2.1, 61–62
"Kugelmass Episode, The" (Allen), 5–52
Kukkonen, Karin, 52, 56

Landow, George P., 9, 30–32, 34, 69
Last Song of Violeta Parra, The (Deemer), 137
laws of excluded middle, 89
laws of non-contradiction, 89
Life Is Strange (Dontnod Entertainment), 45, 46, 110
Limoges, Jean-Marc, 54, 73
Local Anaesthetic (Grass), 124, 143
location-based mobile narratives, 15, 78
Locus Solus (Roussel), 117
Lola rennt [Run, Lola, Run] (Tykwer), 20, 23
Loss of Grasp (Bouchardon and Volckaert), 67–69, 183
Loved: A Short Story (Ocias), 168–69, 176, 184
Lucy Hardin's Missing Period (Marche), 39–40, 41, 46, 182

Madame Bovary (Flaubert), 51
Magister Ludi (Dena), 59–60, 60 fig. 2.2, 62, 64
Manifold Garden (Chyr), 83
Marble Springs (Larsen), 137
Margolin, Uri, 163
Marino, Mark, 133, 142
McHale, Brian, 25, 35–36, 38, 45, 56, 63, 73, 160
Memento (Nolan), 107, 112
metafiction, 13, 29, 34, 38, 51, 66, 72, 123, 144, 162, 173
metalepsis, 4, 5, 10, 15, 16, 49–54, 56, 58, 63, 88, 124, 130, 152, 161–62, 161n3, 165, 167, 170, 172, 173, 177, 182–83; emotional, 79, 183; interactional, 5n4, 15, 49–82, 62 fig. 2.3, 78 fig. 2.5, 104, 132, 175, 176, 181, 182–83, 184, 185, 186; ontological, 51, 56, 79, 126, 167, 182
metamedial readings, 16, 94–95, 101, 103, 105, 111, 117, 118–20, 122, 144, 186–87
Midsummer Night's Dream, A (Shakespeare), 109
Miles, Adrian, 35, 36
Miyamoto, Shigeru, 90
modernism, 108, 145
Molloy (Beckett), 125
Money (Amis), 57
Montfort, Nick, 26, 28, 142, 144, 153 fig. 5.1, 157, 157n2, 162, 165, 177
Monument Valley (Ustwo Games), 99, 100, 183
Moulthrop, Stuart, 31, 36; *Hegirascope*, 114, 115, 184; *Reagan Library*, 144; *Victory Garden*, 30, 34, 36–39, 41, 46, 69, 100, 159, 160, 182
moustache, La (Carrère), 23
multilinearity, 4, 14, 16, 19–48, 81, 86, 105, 108, 119, 123, 127, 137, 138, 140, 175, 181, 182, 184
multivariant chronology, 16, 85, 109, 112–14, 119, 183–84
my body—a Wunderkammer (Jackson), 30

narration: extreme, 4, 5n4, 16, 122–50, 151, 184; cybernetic, 17, 122–23, 144–50, 181, 184, 186; machinic, 17, 123, 142–43, 149, 184; second-person, 2, 4, 17, 26, 37, 38, 51, 54, 74, 83, 122, 124, 141, 151–77, 153 fig. 5.1, 157n2, 161n3, 181, 184–85, 187. *See also* antimimetic narration
narrator: extradiegetic, 37, 50, 55, 59, 62 fig. 2.3, 131, 148n2, 152, 153 fig. 5.1, 158, 173; heterodiegetic, 37, 56, 121, 139; homodiegetic, 1, 117, 128, 129, 158, 173; metadiegetic, 147–48, 148 fig. 4.2; multiperson and permeable, 16–17, 123, 124, 125, 135–42, 149, 171, 181, 184, 187; narrator, 152, 154, 160; omniscience, 144–50, 158–60, 184, 186; protean interlocutors, 123, 124, 130–35, 149; unintentional unreliable narrators, 123, 126–29, 149, 167, 184
narrative contradiction, 9, 13, 14, 19–48
narrative levels: extradiegetic, 37, 50, 51, 55, 59, 131, 148n2, 157, 158–59, 167, 173–74, 175,

177; hypodiegetic, 55; intradiegetic, 8, 55, 107, 139, 147, 154, 160

narrativizing, 1, 1n1, 5, 24–25, 33, 34–35, 85, 105, 109, 112, 118, 162

National Theatre Wales, 73 fig. 2.4

natural narrative, 3–5, 7–8, 14, 15. *See also* unnatural narrative

naturalize, 5, 8, 10–11, 13–16, 20, 22–25, 28, 31, 32, 33, 34, 35–36, 40, 42, 44, 45, 47, 58, 60, 64, 66, 71, 79, 83–85, 88–90, 92–93, 103, 106, 109, 110, 115, 118, 125, 128, 129, 134, 139, 140, 141, 144, 145, 148, 149, 162, 163, 167, 175–76, 182, 183–84, 186, 187. *See also* denaturalize

Neuromancer (Gibson), 143

New York Times, 19

Nielsen, Henrik Skov, 4, 7, 9–10, 13, 46, 140

Nintendo, 90, 91, 166

Nitsche, Michael, 16, 86–87, 89, 94, 102, 119

nonmimetic, 4, 6, 9, 11, 15, 64, 89–91, 93, 95, 101, 111, 112, 118, 123, 143, 158, 185

Notes from the Underground (Dostoevsky), 130

Novelist, The (Orthogonal Games), 43–45, 46, 182

Opacité/Opacity (Bouchardon, Dumas, Volckaert, and Zénouda), 172–75, 176, 185

Oppenheimer, Julius Robert, 111

Orlando (Woolf), 109

Oulipoems (Niss and Deed), 143–44

Pagan Place, A (O'Brien), 154, 158

palimpsestic spaces, 16, 85, 102–4, 118–19

Parker, Joshua, 39, 70

Patchwork Girl (Jackson), 30–31, 34, 58, 62, 164–65, 175–76

Path, The (Tale of Tales), 100–101, 104

permanently defamiliarizing, 4, 8, 9, 17, 32, 85, 90, 96, 103, 112, 119, 125, 129, 139, 149, 160, 176, 180, 186, 187

Pfister, Manfred, 131–32, 132 fig. 4.1

physio-cybertext, 15, 64–67

Picot, Edward, 65

Pier, John, 50, 51, 52, 56, 63

Play (Beckett), 107

Plotkins, Andrew, 26

Pokémon Go, 77

polyvocality. *See* extreme narration

Portal (Valve Software), 99, 100

possible worlds theory, 5n4, 33, 57, 84, 89

postmodern, 4, 7, 25, 31n2, 38–39, 122–25, 137, 138, 140, 156, 163

poststructuralism, 31–32

Prince of Persia, 91

Princess Murderer, The (Larsen), 139–40, 151, 171–72, 176, 185

Pry (Gorman and Cannizzaro), 102–3

Psychonauts (Schafer), 95–96, 99, 104, 118, 183

Punday, Daniel, 16, 87, 91, 92, 95, 102, 103–4, 111, 119, 181

Quadrego (Maskiewicz), 135, 137–38, 149, 184

Queers in Love at the End of the World (Anthropy), 39, 40–41, 46, 114

Raley, Rita, 142

Reading Digital Fiction project, 49n1, 151n1, 188–89, 188n1

reading strategies: accepted as an unnatural construction, 20, 25, 34, 47, 66, 186; allegorical (Alber), 12, 13, 23, 41, 47, 66, 111; blending of frames (Alber), 11, 13, 66, 90, 101–2, 106; didactic, 12, 17, 45, 99, 114, 119, 165, 169, 171, 175, 176, 187; do it yourself (Alber), 13, 22, 23, 28, 66, 140; external, 13, 24; generification (Alber), 11, 13, 66, 101, 110; hermeneutic, 23, 35, 64; internal, 11, 13, 24; metamedial, 16, 94, 103, 105, 111, 117, 118, 120, 144, 186–87; satirization and parody (Alber), 12, 13, 23, 66, 93, 134, 140, 176; subjectification (Alber), 11, 13, 22, 23, 66, 96, 101, 106, 113, 134; thematic (Alber), 12, 13, 23–24, 26, 35, 39, 40–41, 47–48, 66, 68, 72, 75, 96, 99, 103, 111, 114, 116, 117, 129, 144, 148, 169, 170–71, 175, 176, 187; therapeutic, 169, 176, 187; transcendental (Alber), 12–13, 66, 88–89, 101, 134; Zen (Alber) 13, 22, 28, 33, 34, 47, 66, 103, 115, 140, 184, 186

Reed, Ashley, 83

Rhetoric of Fiction, The (Booth), 126

Richardson, Brian, 4, 6–7, 9, 13, 16, 19, 20, 21, 22, 23, 25, 31n2, 33–34, 44, 47, 57, 66–67,

69, 80, 106, 107, 109, 122–26, 130–31, 133, 135, 136–37, 140–41, 143, 153 fig. 5.1, 155–56, 160, 180, 185, 186, 187; *Unnatural Voices: Extreme Narration in Modern and Contemporary Fiction*, 123. *See also* unnatural construction

Rimmon-Kenan, Shlomith, 124

role-playing games (RPGs), 79, 109, 111, 163, 165–67, 169–170, 176, 181, 182–83, 184, 185, 187, 188. *See also* videogames

Rosenberg, John R., 143

Ryan, Marie-Laure, 2, 4, 13, 22–24, 26, 28–29, 32–33, 34–35, 39, 40, 45, 51, 52, 53, 55, 56, 70–71, 73, 75–76, 80, 84, 85–86, 89, 105–6, 111, 130, 144, 163, 165, 186

Same Day Test (Inglis), 39

Scream, The (Munch), 99

"Sea and Spar Between" (Strickland and Montfort), 144

Second Life (Linden Lab), 79

Self Help (Moore), 155

Short, Emily, 26, 133

Sorcery! (Jackson), 59

souffrances de l'inventeur, Les (Balzac), 51

spatiality, 3n3, 14, 15–16, 20, 32–33, 45–46, 85–88; impossible spatiality, 4–5, 5n4, 15–16, 83–85, 88–105

Spec Ops: The Line (Yager Development), 169–70, 176, 185

speech act theory (J. L. Austin), 156

Spot (Wiesner), 16, 101–2

Stanley Parable, The (Wreden), 116, 119–20, 122, 146–49, 148 fig. 4.2, 159, 184

Stimler, Neil, 78

Stir Fry Texts (Andrews), 144

story (fabula), 5, 10, 16, 19, 21, 25, 38, 39, 40, 45, 46, 105, 106–7, 109, 112, 114, 119, 160

Story City, 76

Storyland (Wylde), 144

Super Mario, 91, 93

temporality, 3n3, 11, 14, 16, 37, 45–46, 104, 183–84; impossible temporality, 4, 5, 5n4, 15, 16, 45, 46, 83, 85, 104, 105–17, 119

These Waves of Girls (Fisher), 30

Third Policeman, The (O'Brien), 88

Thomas Was Alone (Bithell), 121–22

Thon, Jan-Noël, 2, 20, 24, 28, 42, 43, 58, 61

Thoss, Jeff, 5n4, 53–55

Time Bandits (Gilliam), 108

Time's Arrow (Amis) 11, 107, 109

To the Moon (Freebird Games), 109–10

transmedial narratology, 2, 4–5, 9, 14, 53–54, 63, 67, 117, 119, 179, 180–81, 185, 187–89

Treachery of Sanctuary, The (Milk), 81–82

Trinity (Moriarty), 91–93, 111, 119

Tristano (Balestrini), 4

Tristram Shandy (Sterne), 6

Turing Test, the, 133

Turning Forest, The, 80

Ulysses (Joyce), 130–31, 134, 140

unconventionalization, 4, 6–8, 9–10, 68, 87, 94. *See also* conventionalization

Unfortunates, The (Johnson), 6, 21, 34, 66

Unnamable, The (Beckett), 136–37, 140–41

unnatural construction, 6–7, 12, 13–15, 19–20, 25, 33–34, 39, 41, 47, 66–67, 69, 80, 101, 105–6, 129, 134, 138, 140, 142, 144, 149, 175, 186

unnatural narrative and realism, 2, 3–10, 11–13, 14, 15–16, 20, 22, 24, 45, 46, 71, 72, 91, 107, 142, 179–80, 185–86, 187–89. *See also* natural narrative

unnatural narratology, 3, 4, 5–10, 11–13, 14, 15–16, 19, 20, 21, 22, 31n2, 56, 83, 89, 95, 107, 123, 126, 135–36, 142, 144–45, 179, 185–86, 187–89; cognitive turn in, 4; extrinsic, 6, 13–14, 16, 89, 180, 187; intrinsic, 6, 14, 46, 90, 92, 180, 185, 187; unnatural acts of narration, 83; unnatural minds, 83; unnatural storyworlds, 83–84. *See also* cognitive narratology

Vial, Stéphane, 78–79

videogames, 1, 2, 5n4, 9, 14, 15–16, 19–20, 21–22, 23, 24, 25, 42–48, 50, 52, 58, 79, 81, 84, 85, 86, 87, 89–91, 94–95, 99–101, 104–6, 109–13, 115–16, 117–18, 119–20, 121–22, 124–25, 127, 132, 139, 146–49, 148 fig. 4.2, 162, 163–64, 164n4, 165–67. *See also* role playing games

Virginie: Her Two Lives (Hawkes), 124
Virtual Reality (VR), 3, 15, 79–80

Walker, Jill, 34, 153 fig. 5.1, 156–57, 172, 177
WALLPAPER (Campbell and Alston), 49, 61, 62–63, 64, 80, 104, 134, 149, 184
Wardrip-Fruin, Noah, 163
We Are Angry (Prickitt), 69n4
What Remains of Edith Finch (Giant Sparrow), 93
White Hotel, The (Thomas), 108

Wilks, Christine, 96, 99, 103. See also *Inkubus* (Campbell and Wilks)
Wolf, Werner, 14, 51, 53–54, 56, 63, 160–61
Woodbury, Robert F., 63

Yacobi, Tamar, 108, 109, 126

Zombies, Run! (Alderman and Levene), 76–77, 78
Zork (Infocom), 26, 27 fig. 1, 182

THEORY AND INTERPRETATION OF NARRATIVE
JAMES PHELAN, KATRA BYRAM, AND FAYE HALPERN, SERIES EDITORS
ROBYN WARHOL AND PETER RABINOWITZ, FOUNDING EDITORS EMERITI

Because the series editors believe that the most significant work in narrative studies today contributes both to our knowledge of specific narratives and to our understanding of narrative in general, studies in the series typically offer interpretations of individual narratives and address significant theoretical issues underlying those interpretations. The series does not privilege one critical perspective but is open to work from any strong theoretical position.

Digital Fiction and the Unnatural: Transmedial Narrative Theory, Method, and Analysis by Astrid Ensslin and Alice Bell

Narrative Bonds: Multiple Narrators in the Victorian Novel by Alexandra Valint

Contemporary French and Francophone Narratology edited by John Pier

We-Narratives: Collective Storytelling in Contemporary Fiction by Natalya Bekhta

Debating Rhetorical Narratology: On the Synthetic, Mimetic, and Thematic Aspects of Narrative by Matthew Clark and James Phelan

Environment and Narrative: New Directions in Econarratology edited by Erin James and Eric Morel

Unnatural Narratology: Extensions, Revisions, and Challenges edited by Jan Alber and Brian Richardson

A Poetics of Plot for the Twenty-First Century: Theorizing Unruly Narratives by Brian Richardson

Playing at Narratology: Digital Media as Narrative Theory by Daniel Punday

Making Conversation in Modernist Fiction by Elizabeth Alsop

Narratology and Ideology: Negotiating Context, Form, and Theory in Postcolonial Narratives edited by Divya Dwivedi, Henrik Skov Nielsen, and Richard Walsh

Novelization: From Film to Novel by Jan Baetens

Reading Conrad by J. Hillis Miller, Edited by John G. Peters and Jakob Lothe

Narrative, Race, and Ethnicity in the United States edited by James J. Donahue, Jennifer Ann Ho, and Shaun Morgan

Somebody Telling Somebody Else: A Rhetorical Poetics of Narrative by James Phelan

Media of Serial Narrative edited by Frank Kelleter

Suture and Narrative: Deep Intersubjectivity in Fiction and Film by George Butte

The Writer in the Well: On Misreading and Rewriting Literature by Gary Weissman

Narrating Space / Spatializing Narrative: Where Narrative Theory and Geography Meet by Marie-Laure Ryan, Kenneth Foote, and Maoz Azaryahu

Narrative Sequence in Contemporary Narratology edited by Raphaël Baroni and Françoise Revaz

The Submerged Plot and the Mother's Pleasure from Jane Austen to Arundhati Roy by Kelly A. Marsh

Narrative Theory Unbound: Queer and Feminist Interventions edited by Robyn Warhol and Susan S. Lanser

Unnatural Narrative: Theory, History, and Practice by Brian Richardson

Ethics and the Dynamic Observer Narrator: Reckoning with Past and Present in German Literature by Katra A. Byram

Narrative Paths: African Travel in Modern Fiction and Nonfiction by Kai Mikkonen

The Reader as Peeping Tom: Nonreciprocal Gazing in Narrative Fiction and Film by Jeremy Hawthorn

Thomas Hardy's Brains: Psychology, Neurology, and Hardy's Imagination by Suzanne Keen

The Return of the Omniscient Narrator: Authorship and Authority in Twenty-First Century Fiction by Paul Dawson

Feminist Narrative Ethics: Tacit Persuasion in Modernist Form by Katherine Saunders Nash

Real Mysteries: Narrative and the Unknowable by H. Porter Abbott

A Poetics of Unnatural Narrative edited by Jan Alber, Henrik Skov Nielsen, and Brian Richardson

Narrative Discourse: Authors and Narrators in Literature, Film, and Art by Patrick Colm Hogan

An Aesthetics of Narrative Performance: Transnational Theater, Literature, and Film in Contemporary Germany by Claudia Breger

Literary Identification from Charlotte Brontë to Tsitsi Dangarembga by Laura Green

Narrative Theory: Core Concepts and Critical Debates by David Herman, James Phelan and Peter J. Rabinowitz, Brian Richardson, and Robyn Warhol

After Testimony: The Ethics and Aesthetics of Holocaust Narrative for the Future edited by Jakob Lothe, Susan Rubin Suleiman, and James Phelan

The Vitality of Allegory: Figural Narrative in Modern and Contemporary Fiction by Gary Johnson

Narrative Middles: Navigating the Nineteenth-Century British Novel edited by Caroline Levine and Mario Ortiz-Robles

Fact, Fiction, and Form: Selected Essays by Ralph W. Rader edited by James Phelan and David H. Richter

The Real, the True, and the Told: Postmodern Historical Narrative and the Ethics of Representation by Eric L. Berlatsky

Franz Kafka: Narration, Rhetoric, and Reading edited by Jakob Lothe, Beatrice Sandberg, and Ronald Speirs

Social Minds in the Novel by Alan Palmer

Narrative Structures and the Language of the Self by Matthew Clark

Imagining Minds: The Neuro-Aesthetics of Austen, Eliot, and Hardy by Kay Young

Postclassical Narratology: Approaches and Analyses edited by Jan Alber and Monika Fludernik

Techniques for Living: Fiction and Theory in the Work of Christine Brooke-Rose by Karen R. Lawrence

Towards the Ethics of Form in Fiction: Narratives of Cultural Remission by Leona Toker

Tabloid, Inc.: Crimes, Newspapers, Narratives by V. Penelope Pelizzon and Nancy M. West

Narrative Means, Lyric Ends: Temporality in the Nineteenth-Century British Long Poem by Monique R. Morgan

Understanding Nationalism: On Narrative, Cognitive Science, and Identity by Patrick Colm Hogan

Joseph Conrad: Voice, Sequence, History, Genre edited by Jakob Lothe, Jeremy Hawthorn, James Phelan

The Rhetoric of Fictionality: Narrative Theory and the Idea of Fiction by Richard Walsh

Experiencing Fiction: Judgments, Progressions, and the Rhetorical Theory of Narrative by James Phelan

Unnatural Voices: Extreme Narration in Modern and Contemporary Fiction by Brian Richardson

Narrative Causalities by Emma Kafalenos

Why We Read Fiction: Theory of Mind and the Novel by Lisa Zunshine

I Know That You Know That I Know: Narrating Subjects from Moll Flanders *to* Marnie by George Butte

Bloodscripts: Writing the Violent Subject by Elana Gomel

Surprised by Shame: Dostoevsky's Liars and Narrative Exposure by Deborah A. Martinsen

Having a Good Cry: Effeminate Feelings and Pop-Culture Forms by Robyn R. Warhol

Politics, Persuasion, and Pragmatism: A Rhetoric of Feminist Utopian Fiction by Ellen Peel

Telling Tales: Gender and Narrative Form in Victorian Literature and Culture by Elizabeth Langland

Narrative Dynamics: Essays on Time, Plot, Closure, and Frames edited by Brian Richardson

Breaking the Frame: Metalepsis and the Construction of the Subject by Debra Malina

Invisible Author: Last Essays by Christine Brooke-Rose

Ordinary Pleasures: Couples, Conversation, and Comedy by Kay Young

Narratologies: New Perspectives on Narrative Analysis edited by David Herman

Before Reading: Narrative Conventions and the Politics of Interpretation by Peter J. Rabinowitz

Matters of Fact: Reading Nonfiction over the Edge by Daniel W. Lehman

The Progress of Romance: Literary Historiography and the Gothic Novel by David H. Richter

A Glance Beyond Doubt: Narration, Representation, Subjectivity by Shlomith Rimmon-Kenan

Narrative as Rhetoric: Technique, Audiences, Ethics, Ideology by James Phelan

Misreading Jane Eyre: *A Postformalist Paradigm* by Jerome Beaty

Psychological Politics of the American Dream: The Commodification of Subjectivity in Twentieth-Century American Literature by Lois Tyson

Understanding Narrative edited by James Phelan and Peter J. Rabinowitz

Framing Anna Karenina: Tolstoy, the Woman Question, and the Victorian Novel by Amy Mandelker

Gendered Interventions: Narrative Discourse in the Victorian Novel by Robyn R. Warhol

Reading People, Reading Plots: Character, Progression, and the Interpretation of Narrative by James Phelan

www.ingramcontent.com/pod-product-compliance
Lightning Source LLC
Chambersburg PA
CBHW020653230426
43665CB00008B/428